Child Contact

Related titles available from Law Society Publishing:

Child Law Handbook: Guide to Good Practice
Liz Goldthorpe with Pat Monro (published with ALC)

Civil Partnership: Law and Practice
Andrea Woelke

Elderly Client Handbook (3rd Edition)
General Editors: Caroline Bielanska and Martin Terrell
Consultant Editor: Gordon R Ashton
(Published with Solicitors for the Elderly)

Family Law Protocol (2nd Edition)
The Law Society

Good Practice in Child Care Cases: A Guide for Solicitors Acting in Public Law Children Act Proceedings Including Cases Involving Adoption
The Law Society (in association with ALC, CCJLG and SFLA)

Health and Social Care Handbook
Caroline Bielanska with Fiona Scolding

Mental Capacity Act 2005: A Guide to the New Law
Nicola Greaney, Fenella Morris and Beverley Taylor

Pensions and Marriage Breakdown
David Davidson

Resolution Family Law Handbook
General Editor: Andrew Greensmith

Titles from Law Society Publishing can be ordered from all good legal bookshops. For further information or a catalogue, email our editorial and marketing office at **publishing@lawsociety.org.uk**.

CHILD CONTACT

Law and Practice

Miranda Fisher and Sarah Whitten

with Noel Arnold

23, 45 69, fact finding hearing

1, 2, 5, 7, 44, 57, 67, 75, 77 78/9, 63 (3 points), 142, 143/44.
153.

The Law Society

ISBN-10: 1-85328-548-X
ISBN-13: 978-1-85328-548-6

Published in 2006 by the Law Society
113 Chancery Lane, London WC2A 1PL

Typeset by J&L Composition, Filey, North Yorkshire
Printed by Antony Rowe Ltd, Chippenham, Wiltshire

Contents

Foreword

The role of the family courts, and in particular the question of their approach to child contact cases have come under increasing public scrutiny in recent years. In this publication, the Law Society and the authors have taken the opportunity to discuss the history and background factors culminating in the recent passage of the Children and Adoption Act 2006.

Child contact cases are coming before the courts in growing numbers, raising issues of increasing complexity. The book deals with the changes in the law brought about by the Act and anticipates that courts will become more closely involved in ensuring that orders for contact are complied with and by enforcing those orders which have been flouted, by the variety of new means made available.

The book provides a guide to the legislation and case law in this developing area of the law. The authors are alive to the growing recognition of the need to listen to the voice of the child in contact cases, and have included a chapter in which they discuss the practicalities of extending the separate representation of children, on which the government is presently consulting.

Practitioners are helpfully directed to published guidance and website resources for their conduct of proceedings on behalf of their clients. In Chapter 13, the authors rightly draw attention to the Law Society's *Family Law Protocol* (2nd edn) and appropriately remind advisers that 'court proceedings should normally only be commenced if all reasonable avenues have been considered and found to be inappropriate or unworkable or if this is the only way to offer the parties the opportunity of a mediated settlement'.

I welcome the publication of this invaluable guide to the legal profession.

Rt. Hon. Sir Mark Potter
President of the Family Division
Head of Family Justice
August 2006

Preface

This book is designed to summarise current law, practice and procedure in private law applications for contact with children, as at August 2006 (unless otherwise stated), and to guide the reader to sources of further reference. It includes points of practical assistance wherever possible, in recognition of the often difficult nature of child contact proceedings. It also covers areas of law and practice which the reader may need to consider such as immigration and jurisdiction aspects of contact applications.

The book focuses on the new enforcement provisions introduced by the Children and Adoption Act 2006, which are examined in detail together with the background to and reasoning behind the introduction of these new measures.

It should always be remembered that children and young people are at the centre of any contact application and the right of the child to be heard will hopefully become one of the most important features of such proceedings in the future. An important section of the book concentrates on the representation of children, including the present provisions and the government's proposals to extend separate representation in private law proceedings. However, this is not intended as definitive guide on separate representation and practitioners intending to act for children should also refer to specialist works on this area of practice.

Miranda Fisher and Sarah Whitten
August 2006

Acknowledgments

We would like to thank our departmental colleagues at Charles Russell LLP and Fisher Meredith for supporting this work and the secretarial staff and those in information services at Charles Russell LLP for their invaluable assistance. Miranda Fisher and Sarah Whitten are especially grateful to Sarah Anticoni at Charles Russell LLP for all her encouragement.

We also owe a debt of gratitude to the following:

- The President of the Family Division, Sir Mark Potter for kindly contributing the foreword.
- District Judge Nicholas Crichton, Inner London Family Proceedings Court for his helpful comments and assistance.
- Professor Jane Fortin, King's College London for being a source of information and inspiration.

Miranda Fisher would like to thank her parents, her sisters Justine and Lucy, and Jonathan Walsh for their unfailing encouragement and support.

Sarah Whitten would like to thank her family and in particular her husband Richard for his invaluable support.

Noel Arnold would like to thank his mother, Annaledchumy Arnold and his brother Joel Suriyakumar Arnold.

Miranda Fisher, Sarah Whitten and Noel Arnold
August 2006

Table of cases

Table of statutes

Table of statutory instruments

Table of international legislation

Abbreviations

ACA 2002	Adoption and Children Act 2002
ADR	alternative dispute resolution
AJA 1960	Administration of Justice Act 1960
CA 1989	Children Act 1989
CA 2004	Children Act 2004
CAA 2006	Children and Adoption Act 2006
CAFCASS	Children and Family Court Advisory and Support Service
C(AP)O 1991	Children (Allocation of Proceedings) Order 1991, SI 1991/1677
CFR	Children and Family Reporter
CJCSA 2000	Criminal Justice and Court Services Act 2000
CRC	United Nations Convention on the Rights of the Child
ECHR	European Convention on Human Rights
FAInS	Family Advice and Information Networks
FAO	family assistance order
FHDRA	first hearing dispute resolution appointment
FLA 1986	Family Law Act 1986
FPC	Family Proceedings Court
FPC(CA 1989)R 1991	Family Proceedings Courts (Children Act 1989) Rules 1991, SI 1991/1395
FPR 1991	Family Proceedings Rules 1991
FRPP	Family Resolution Pilot Project
GAL	guardian ad litem
HRA 1998	Human Rights Act 1998
IR	Immigration Rules
LASSA 1970	Local Authority Social Services Act 1970
NYAS	National Youth Advisory Service
PRFD	Principal Registry of the Family Division of the High Court
SGO	special guardianship order

Introduction

In a vast number of cases of relationship breakdown, whether this is in the context of divorce, dissolution of civil partnership or the separation of unmarried couples, arrangements have to be made for the children. Such arrangements include where they will live and how often they will see the other parent. The majority of families make their arrangements independently or with the help of mediation and without any need for the court's intervention. However, for an estimated 10 per cent of families there is such a need. Over recent years there has been a great deal of publicity about the inadequacy of existing provisions to ensure that where couples cannot agree on contact arrangements between children and the parent with whom they do not live, the court can impose satisfactory arrangements in the best interests of the children. In particular, various lobbying groups for fathers have been vocal in criticising the stance of the judiciary (accusing it of bias towards mothers) and the lack of a robust approach to using existing remedies. Since 2003, payments made by absent parents to the parent with care as assessed by the Child Support Agency have been reduced to take into account situations where children spend more than 52 nights a year with the absent parent. Arguably this has not assisted in facilitating contact arrangements between parents whose relationship has broken down.

Society is changing; increasingly, fathers play a hands-on role in the care of their children. Following a separation from their children's mother the other parent may expect to continue to be fully involved in their children's care. In recent years the number of contact applications has increased. There has also been an increasing number of applications for shared residence orders. The courts have shown an increased willingness to make such orders even where time between parents is not shared equally and parents do not live very near each other.

The Children and Adoption Act 2006 is intended to assist in the implementation of the Green Paper, *Parental Separation: Children's Needs and Parents' Responsibilities* published in July 2004 (www.dfes.gov.uk/childrensneeds). This paper makes interesting reading for any family law practitioner. The Green Paper was, in part, a response to the Children Act Sub-Committee's report to the Lord Chancellor *Making Contact Work* published in February 2002. The

Green Paper and its follow up report entitled *Next Steps* set out the perceived problems and inadequacies in the current system for encouraging the agreement of contact arrangements and the courts' ability to enforce contact arrangements in the face of opposition by one parent. Its authors made various recommendations for the promotion of contact following relationship breakdown (for instance, the use of parenting plans). They also made recommendations for changes in legislation to facilitate the enforcement of contact orders in the minority of cases of relationship breakdown where the court becomes involved.

This book provides an analysis of the provisions of the Children and Adoption Act 2006 (CAA 2006) which will bring a new approach to the issue of enforcing contact in those cases where the courts' assistance is sought and particularly where there is an implacably hostile parent who refuses to accept that any contact beyond the most limited form of contact is in the interests of a child. The CAA 2006 also makes a number of provisions about inter-country adoption which are outside the scope of this book.

The CAA 2006 applies to England and Wales but not Northern Ireland. It extends the current powers of the court to enforce contact orders. These extended powers enable a court to impose an unpaid work requirement on the parent who has breached a contact order or the payment of compensation for a parent who has suffered financial loss (such as the loss of a holiday which has been paid for) as the result of the breach of the order by the other parent.

In addition, the court has the power to make positive orders requiring a party to take part in an activity that will promote contact (such as counselling sessions, information sessions on contact arrangements or mediation). The court can require a parent to attend such activities as a condition of contact.

The CAA 2006 imposes a greater obligation on the officers of the Children and Family Court Advisory and Support Service (CAFCASS) and Welsh family proceedings officers to become more involved at an early stage of contact proceedings where there is a conflict between parents. These officers are required to carry out a risk assessment where they suspect that a child may be at risk of harm. The courts also have the power to direct that they should monitor a contact order.

The court will also have the power to use family assistance orders with greater frequency than currently as they will no longer be restricted to exceptional cases and the maximum duration will be extended from six to 12 months.

Whilst enforcement of contact orders relates to those orders successfully obtained, not every application for contact is successful where the person resisting contact can persuade the court that contact is not in the best interests of a child. This book also covers:

- the background to contact applications and who can make them (including where relevant the changes to the Children Act 1989 (CA 1989) following the implementation of the Civil Partnership Act 2004);
- shared residence orders: these orders are now more common than they used to be since the Court of Appeal decisions in *A* v. *A (Minors) Shared Residence Order* [1994] 1 FLR 669 and *D* v. *D (Shared Residence Order)* [2001] 1 FLR 495 and the more recent authorities of *Re G (Residence: Same-sex Partner)* [2005] 2 FLR 957 and *Re R (Residence: Shared Care: Children's Views)* [2006] 1 FLR 491;
- situations which arise where there are allegations of domestic abuse;
- the procedure involved (including practical tips for practitioners) and how the court tends to deal with such applications;
- the use of expert evidence and the role of CAFCASS and local authorities;
- provisions for the separate representation of children and the amendments to the CA 1989, inserted by the Adoption and Children Act 2002, which will permit the appointment of children's guardians in private law children cases. Practitioners will have to become familiar with the procedures applying to the representation of children which are dealt with in some detail in this book. It seems likely that the separate representation of children in private law proceedings will increase as a result of the increasing recognition of the courts that the voices of children should be heard. In the difficult and intractable contact cases, at which the provisions of the CAA 2006 are partly aimed, the courts have recommended the separate representation of the children concerned on a number of occasions;
- relevant aspects of human rights law which now have to be considered in all cases;
- relevant aspects of public funding and professional conduct.

It is not clear whether the increased powers of the court conferred by the CAA 2006 will lead to a sea-change in the way that contact applications are dealt with. The courts retain their existing powers, such as committal to prison for contempt of a parent who persistently flouts a contact order. They also retain their ability to alter residence arrangements for a child. These sanctions are used only infrequently as a result of the need to reconcile any such action with the best interests of a child. However, the CAA 2006, although watered down from its initial form (when a penalty such as the confiscation of driving licences was contemplated for persistent non-compliance with a contact order) demonstrates the intention of the legislature to empower the courts to deal robustly with parents who breach orders for contact. A number of judges have also made their views clear on this subject.

Some of these are set out in the cases referred to in this book. Practitioners will find that following the implementation of the CAA 2006, and as a result of the introduction of measures such as the Private Law Programme, the courts will become involved in a much more directional way in ensuring orders for contact are complied with or enforcing those orders that have been flouted.

CHAPTER 1

The Children and Adoption Act 2006

1.1 BACKGROUND

The Children (Contact) and Adoption Bill was published in draft on 2 February 2005 for pre-legislative scrutiny by an ad hoc joint committee of both Houses of Parliament. The scrutiny committee published its report on 12 April 2005 and the government's reply to the report was published on 8 June 2005. The Bill was formally confirmed in the Queen's Speech 2005 as part of the 2005–06 legislative agenda. It received Royal Assent on 21 June 2006.

The Children and Adoption Act 2006 (CAA 2006) provides the courts with new powers to promote and enforce contact orders made under section 8 of the Children Act 1989 (CA 1989).

The following documents are helpful in understanding the background to the CAA 2006 and the reasoning behind its measures:

- *Making Contact Work: The Advisory Board on Family Law, Children Act Sub-Committee's Report to the Lord Chancellor* on the facilitation of contact between children and their non-residential parents and the enforcement of contact orders (February 2002) (www.dca.gov.uk/family/abfla/mcwrep.pdf);
- *Parental Separation: Children's Needs and Parents' Responsibilities* (Cm 6273, July 2005) (www.dfes.gov.uk/childrensneeds);
- *Parental Separation: Children's Needs and Parents' Responsibilities: Next Steps* (Cm 6452, January 2005) (www.dfes.gov.uk/childrensneeds);
- *Report from the Joint Committee on the Draft Children (Contact) and Adoption Bill Session 2004–05* (HL Papers 100–I/HC 400–1) (www.parliment.the-stationery-office.co.uk/pa/jt/jtchilcon.htm);
- *Government Reply to the Report from the Joint Committee on the Draft Children (Contact) and Adoption Bill* (Cm 6583, 8 June 2005) (www.parliament.uk/documents(draftchildrencontact)govtresponse.pdf).

Making Contact Work

In February 2002, the Children Act Sub-committee (CASC) published its report to the Lord Chancellor: *Making Contact Work*.

The CASC reported on the consultation process relating to the enforcement of contact orders. It considered the court system to be seriously deficient and made recommendations for improvements including:

- Powers for the courts that allow for two stages:
  - non-punitive in which the resident parent would, for example, be directed to attend a parenting programme designed to address intractable contact disputes and in the event that such measures are ineffective;
  - the retention of the courts' power in contempt proceedings for fine or committal as a last resort.
- Wider powers for the courts to make a whole range of orders designed to give practitioners time to work with parents and children within a framework of services.
- Specific powers for the courts to:
  - refer the parties to mediation;
  - refer a defaulting parent to information meetings, meetings with a counsellor, parenting programmes/classes designed to deal with contact disputes;
  - refer the case to a psychiatrist or psychologist;
  - refer a non-resident parent who is violent or in breach of an order to an education/perpetrator programme;
  - place a party on probation with a condition of treatment or attendance at a class or programme;
  - impose a community service order on a party with programmes specifically designed to address the default in contact; and
  - award financial compensation from one parent to another (for example, where the cost of a holiday has been lost).
- Changes to family assistance orders so that:
  - they cease to be directed at a local authority and are directed to the Children and Family Court Advisory and Support Service (CAFCASS);
  - they should not be operational only in 'exceptional circumstances';
  - the ability to refuse to consent to the making of an order is removed;
  - the time limit of six months is removed.

In addition to the requirement of legislation, *Making Contact Work* also recommended government to allocate additional funding for the following:

- CAFCASS to enable it to address the roles identified for it in the report including to:
  - provide an in-court conciliation system at the first appointment in contact cases to be operated throughout the country at every level of the court;
  - facilitate the wider use of the representation of children by officers of CAFCASS in family proceedings;
  - make use of the changes in the Family Proceedings Rules in order for CAFCASS officers to be more closely involved with the children on whom they are reporting.
- Contact centres to develop additional facilities and more specialist contact centres.
- Additional facilities for resolving contact disputes by negotiation, conciliation and mediation.

Case law

The background to the CAA 2006 can also be seen in the frustrations of the judiciary in a number of difficult/intractable contact cases.The following cases are also addressed in detail in relation to current enforcement remedies in Chapter 7.

In *Re O (A Child) (Contact: Withdrawal of Application)* [2004] 1 FLR 1258, in giving permission to a father to withdraw his application for contact with his 12-year-old son, Wall J noted that the father had to accept his share of the blame for his son's reluctance to have contact with him, but set out the failings in the court system in such cases and, in particular, the conclusions contained in paragraphs 10.37 and 10.39 of *Making Contact Work*:

> 10.37 The court procedures are too slow. There is insufficient court time and a lack of resources: cases take too long to come to court. There are substantial delays which are detrimental to children and their parents.
>
> 10.39 The litigation process is adversarial and counter-productive. It entrenches attitudes rather than encouraging them to modify. It tends to focus on the arguments of the parents, not the needs of the child. It puts particular pressure on the divided loyalties of the children.

In *Re S (A Child) (Contact: Promoting Relationship with Absent Parent)* [2004] 1 FLR 1279, the Court of Appeal allowed a father's appeal against the dismissal of his application for direct contact with his six-year-old daughter, to the extent of directing a joint instruction of a child and adolescent psychiatrist to assess the family and report to the court below on the prospects for contact. At a previous court hearing, the recorder had rejected an application for a psychological assessment of the child despite expressing the view that the mother was primarily responsible for the failure of contact and had no intention of making it work. The (then) President expressed the view that a broad psychological assessment of the family, and not just the child alone, was the possible key to a reconsideration of future contact. She also highlighted the inadequacies of the current methods of enforcement of contact (committal to prison for contempt or fine):

> Most mothers do not have enough money to pay a significant fine and this sanction is seldom used, particular since she is the primary carer of the child. Equally the sanction of prison for mothers who refuse to allow contact is a heavy one and may well be a self-defeating one. It will hardly endear the father to the child who is already reluctant to see him to be told that the father is responsible for the mother going to prison. Prison is a sanction of last resort and there is little else the court can do.

In *Re D (A Child) (Intractable Contact Dispute: Publicity)* [2004] 1 FLR 1226, a wholly deserving father abandoned his five-year battle for contact with his seven-year-old daughter which had been obstructed by the child's mother from the outset. The mother continually sabotaged contact arrangements by means of threadbare excuses and groundless assertions and allegations, resulting in court orders, penal notices, suspended prison sentences and finally a period of imprisonment for her. There were 43 hearings conducted by 16 different judges after numerous adjournments. The parents' and experts' evidence totalled 950 pages. Munby J's analysis of the problems in the court system included:

(a) the length of the proceedings;
(b) the large number of hearings and lack of judicial continuity;
(c) the vast bulk of evidence which is constantly outdated;
(d) the constant adjournments, particularly of the final hearing;
(e) the delay in the court making findings of fact about what turned out to be groundless or gravely exaggerated allegations;
(f) the delay in seeking assistance from any expert other than the CAFCASS officer, for example, an independent social worker;
(g) the even longer delay in the appointment of a children's guardian;
(h) the characteristic judicial response when difficulties in contact emerge of reducing the amount of contact and replacing unsupervised with supervised contact.

One of the most concerning features of the case was the courts' failure to get to grips with the mother's defiance of its orders and the courts' failure to enforce those orders. Munby J noted that the fact that a contact case is intractable should be recognised at an earlier stage in order for the court to intervene effectively. He considered delay to be the 'scourge of the family justice system' and took the view that the principles of the Protocol for

Judicial Case Management in Public Law Children Act Cases could be applied to all but the simplest or most straightforward private law cases. Effective case management in private law cases should include:

(a) judicial continuity: cases to be allocated to a single judge or at most two judges;
(b) timetabling: to be set at the earliest practicable stage and for simpler cases to be timetabled to last weeks rather than months and even serious and complex cases to be timetabled within a period measured in months rather than years;
(c) strategy: proper judicial control and case management.

Munby J's recommendations included the following:

1. There should be a move away from the idea that experts are there simply to provide the court with reports. Experts should be used more to facilitate contact rather than writing reports including 'preparing the mother and child for contact, actually being there at hand on a Saturday morning to make sure that handover takes place, or even acting as the go-between if the mother cannot bring herself to meet the father and there is no independent friend or relative who can help'.
2. Courts should grasp the nettle in relation to false allegations of misconduct by a party by listing finding of fact hearings without delay. In particular, allegations which could have been made at an earlier stage should be viewed with appropriate scepticism.
3. Swift, efficient enforcement of existing court orders is required at the first sign of trouble as 'the flabby judicial response sends a very damaging message to the defaulting parent, who is encouraged to believe that court orders can be ignored with impunity, and potentially also to the child'.
4. Committal should be the remedy of last resort but there should be a proper use of imprisonment even for very short sentences, for example, one, two or three days, which could suffice to achieve the necessary deterrent or coercive effect without significantly impairing a mother's ability to look after her children.

In *V v. V (Children) (Contact: Implacable Hostility)* [2004] 2 FLR 851, Bracewell J transferred residence of two girls aged eight and six years to their father having found that the implacable hostility of the mother to contact was incompatible with them enjoying a normal relationship with him. Bracewell J commented that effective legislation was necessary to enable judges to do better for parents who were being denied contact, as currently there were only four options:

(a) to commit the defaulting parent to prison or make a suspended order for imprisonment, which may well not achieve the object of reinstating contact;

(b) to impose a fine on the defaulting parent, which is rarely possible because it is not consistent with the welfare of the child to deprive a parent on a limited budget;
(c) to transfer residence, which is not necessarily available to the court because the other parent may not have the facilities or capacity to care for the child full time or may not even know the child;
(d) to give up, which is the worst option and gives rise to the public blaming the judges for refusing to deal with recalcitrant parents.

Green Paper, *Parental Separation: Children's Needs and Parents' Responsibilities*

The CAA 2006 is intended to assist in the implementation of the Green Paper, *Parental Separation: Children's Needs and Parents' Responsibilities*, published in July 2005. It records some important statistics demonstrating social change in England and Wales over the past 30 years:

- each year between 150,000–200,000 (married and unmarried) parental couples separate;
- some 3 million of the 12 million children in England and Wales have experienced the separation of their parents;
- fathers are now more actively involved in caring for and helping to raise children, for example, fathers of children under five years old were spending less than 15 minutes a day on child-related activities in the mid-1970s, compared with an average of two hours a day in the late 1990s;
- fathers' time spent with children accounts, on average, for one-third of total parental childcare time and one-third of working mothers cite fathers as the main child carer whilst they are at work;
- more fathers wish to have active and close relationships with their children although some mothers would like their former partners to be more actively involved with their children;
- most children continue to live with their mothers after the separation of their parents;
- the non-resident parent initiates most contact cases and consequently most court applications for contact are initiated by fathers (60 per cent);
- only 10 per cent of separating couples with children have their contact arrangements ordered by the courts, although an increasing number of disputes are ending up in court;
- between 1992 and 2002 there was a rising trend in applications for contact orders, 99 per cent of which led to the making of an order, and in 2003 courts in England and Wales made 67,000 contact orders;
- satisfaction for both parents with arrangements based on informal agreements is significantly higher than court ordered arrangements:

- resident parents (usually mothers) are satisfied or very satisfied with informal agreements in 82 per cent of cases and with court orders in only 61 per cent of cases;
- non-resident parents (usually fathers) are satisfied or very satisfied with informal agreements in 88 per cent of cases and with court orders in only 35 per cent of cases.

The premise of the Green Paper is that a child's welfare must be the paramount concern and that this will usually be best secured through a continuing meaningful relationship with both parents, as long as it is safe. The government considered it unnecessary to introduce new legislation, or to amend the CA 1989, to clarify this as it is already the current, and correct, legal position.

The Green Paper states that the document uses the familiar language of the current system referring to 'resident' and 'non-resident' parents, 'private law cases' and issues about 'contact' or 'residence' and that these terms reflect the language of the CA 1989. It goes on to state that 'contact' means 'parenting time' and 'residence' means 'who the child lives with most of the time'.

Section 8(1) of the CA 1989 in fact states that:

- 'a contact order' means an order requiring the person with whom a child lives, or is to live, to allow the child to visit or stay with the person named in the order, or for that person and the child otherwise to have contact with each other; and
- 'a residence order' means an order settling the arrangements to be made as to the person with whom a child is to live.

'Parenting time' and 'who the child lives with most of the time' are more useful definitions which reinforce the equal status of both parents following separation. Amendments to the CA 1989 to prescribe such definitions could well be helpful.

The Green Paper recognised that parental separation often has a traumatic effect on children and, where there is deep conflict between parents, the effect will usually be very damaging. The main aim of the proposals is therefore to:

- help parents to resolve the issues associated with parental separation; and
- improve outcomes for those children whose parents' relationships are ending by ensuring a continuing relationship with both parents is secured for them.

Government's Response: *Parental Separation: Children's Needs and Parents' Responsibilities: Next Steps*

The Green Paper was followed by the government's response to the consultation and its proposals for further work in *Parental Separation: Children's Needs and Parents' Responsibilities: Next Steps*, published in January 2005.

The government refused to accept the view of some fathers' groups that the courts and the law are biased against them, but did accept that major changes are required to ensure that, where it is necessary for the state and the courts to intervene, they are much more effective in helping to secure resolutions which are in the interests of the child and this means ensuring that the child has a meaningful ongoing relationship with both parents.The system therefore needs to be better at securing this outcome by:

- minimising conflict and supporting good outcomes both for children and their parents, preferably without recourse to the courts;
- improving parents' access to those services which will enable them to reach agreements; and
- improving legal processes and service delivery for the 10 per cent of parents who do go to court.

The headline proposals set out in *Parental Separation: Children's Needs and Parents' Responsibilities: Next Steps* are for:

- access to quality information and advice: the government has developed new Parenting Plans (available at www.dfes.gov.uk/childrenandfamilies) in addition to information currently available through organisations such as Parentline Plus, Sure Start, Relate, NCH, CAFCASS and the Legal Services Commission;
- access to specialist legal advice: a pilot telephone helpline operated through the Legal Services Commission to help people avoid resorting to court in the first instance by directing them to other services which might help them to resolve their problems out of court;
- in-court conciliation, for example, the scheme in operation at the Principal Registry of the Family Division of the High Court (PRFD) in London (see section 8.6);
- the Family Resolutions pilot project: the scheme launched in September 2004 at three Family Proceedings Courts (FPCs): the Inner London and City FPC, Brighton and Sunderland (see section 8.11);
- a changing role for CAFCASS and the courts: CAFCASS will work with the courts at a local level to reduce report requests which will help to increase the role of CAFCASS in conciliation work; the focus of CAFCASS will be on reducing conflict, seeking agreements and what is in the child's best interests, and CAFCASS reports which are ordered will be focused and targeted to address specific areas;
- improving case management by the courts, for example, through the President of the Family Division's Private Law Programme (see section 8.12);
- contact centres: not to be seen solely as where contact takes place but also used more widely as a base for outreach services, which can support children and parents beyond any formal period of court-mandated contact,

and additional funding for new services to support contact will be provided;

- helping to ensure that contact arrangements work: targeting CAFCASS resources to include post-order work and new powers for the courts in the CAA 2006;
- better enforcement: new powers for the courts in the CAA 2006.

1.2 SUMMARY OF THE PROVISIONS RELATING TO CONTACT ORDERS

The powers of the courts when dealing with cases involving contact with children are added to by Part 1 of and Schedule 1 to the CAA 2006. In summary:

1. The court may, even if it does not make a contact order:
   (a) direct a party to take part in an activity that would promote contact with a child; or
   (b) make a similar provision by means of a condition in a contact order.
2. The powers of the court in cases involving a breach of a contact order (to include a condition attached to a contact order) are increased by adding to the current powers as to contempt or to alter residence and contact arrangements for a child:
   (a) a power to make an enforcement order imposing an unpaid work requirement;
   (b) a power to order one person to pay compensation to another for financial loss caused by a breach.
3. The existing powers of the court to make family assistance orders are reformed and a duty is imposed on CAFCASS officers to carry out risk assessments where they suspect a child is at risk of harm. (All references in the CAA 2006 to CAFCASS officers refer equally to Welsh family proceedings officers.)

The CAA 2006 inserts new sections in or amends existing sections of the CA 1989. The majority of the new sections are inserted after CA 1989, s.11, which contains the current provisions for a section 8 order to contain directions (CA 1989, s.11(7)(a)) or conditions (CA 1989, s.11(7)(b)). There is also a new Schedule A1 to the CA 1989.

Children and Adoption Act 2006	Children Act 1989	Provisions
Part 1 s.1	new ss.11A to 11G	contact activity directions and conditions
Part 1 s.2	new s.11H	monitoring contact
Part 1 s.3	new s.11I	warning notices on contact orders
Part 1 s.4	new ss.11J to 11N	enforcement orders/unpaid work requirements
Part 1 s.5	new ss.11O to 11P	financial compensation orders
Part 1 s.6	amendment to s.16	family assistance orders
Part 1 s.7	new s.16A	risk assessments
Sched. 1	new Sched. A1, Part 1	further provisions on unpaid work requirements
Sched. 1	new Sched. A1, Part 2	further provisions on the evocation or amendment of enforcement orders and the failure to comply with such orders

1.3 CONTACT ACTIVITY DIRECTIONS

Section 11A of the CA 1989 provides for the court to make orders for 'contact activity directions' which require a party to the proceedings to take part in an activity that promotes contact with the child concerned (s.11A(3)).

Contact activity directions can be made at any stage in the proceedings prior to a final order being made (s.11A(7)) where a court is considering whether:

- to make a contact order (s.11A(1)(a)); or
- to vary or discharge a contact order (s.11A(1)(b)).

In considering whether to make a contact activity direction, the welfare of the child concerned is to be the courts' paramount consideration (s.11A(9)).

Type of activities

The direction must specify the activity and the person providing the activity (s.11A(4)).

Section 11A(5) sets out the type of activities that may be required including in particular:

- programmes, classes and counselling or guidance sessions of a kind that may:

- assist a person in establishing, maintaining or improving contact with a child; or
- address a person's violent behaviour in order to enable or facilitate contact;

- sessions in which information or advice is given about making or operating arrangements for contact, including information sessions about mediation.

A contact activity direction cannot be used to require a party to undergo a medical or psychiatric examination, assessment or treatment or to actually take part in mediation sessions (s.11A(6)). Despite remaining committed to parties being offered the strongest possible encouragement to agree to mediation or other forms of dispute resolution, the government rejected the introduction of compulsory mediation sessions which would be undesirable and counter-productive.

Restrictions on contact activity directions

The power of the court to make a contact activity direction under section 11A is subject to the restrictions in sections 11B and 11E.

Under section 11B:

- a contact activity direction may only be made where there is a dispute about the provision for contact which the court is considering (i.e. whether to make a contact order at all, or what its detailed provision for contact should be) (s.11B(1));
- the court cannot order a child to take part in an activity unless that child is the parent of the child concerned, thereby preventing a child joined as a party to the proceedings from being capable of subjection to a contact activity direction (s.11B(2));
- the court cannot order an individual to take part in an activity unless that individual is habitually resident in England and Wales and, if an individual who is subject to a contact activity direction ceases to be habitually resident in England and Wales, the contact activity direction will cease to have effect (s.11B(7));
- contact activity directions cannot be used in proceedings where an application for an excepted order is being considered, which means where (s.11B(4)):
  - an adoption order is being considered at the same time as a contact order; or
  - post adoption, a court is considering making, varying or discharging a contact order in relation to someone who, but for the adoption, would have been a relative of the child; unless

– the adoption is, or was, by a partner of one of the child's parents or by a couple, one member of which is a parent of the child.

1.4 CONTACT ACTIVITY CONDITIONS

Section 11C provides for a court to make a 'contact activity condition':

- when making or varying a contact order under CA 1989, s.8 (s.11C(1));
- to require an individual to take part in an activity that promotes contact with a child (s.11C(2)).

Section 11C(5) provides that the activities that may be required by a contact activity condition are the same as those that may be required by a contact activity direction under sections 11A(5) and 11A(6).

The following may be subject to a contact activity condition (s.11C(3)):

(a) the person with whom the child concerned lives or is to live;
(b) the person whose contact with the child is provided for by the contact order;
(c) the person upon whom the contact order imposes a condition under CA 1989, s.11(7)(b) as follows:
  – the person in whose favour the order is made; or
  – who is a parent of the child concerned; or
  – who is not a parent of the child concerned but who has parental responsibility for the child; or
  – with whom the child is living;

The condition must specify the activity and the persons providing the activity (s.11C(4)).

Restrictions on contact activity conditions

As with contact activity directions:

- the court cannot order a child to undertake a contact activity condition, unless that child is the parent of the child concerned, thereby preventing a child joined as a party to the proceedings from being capable of subjection to a contact activity condition (s.11D(1));
- the court cannot order an individual to be subject to a contact activity condition unless that individual is habitually resident in England and Wales and, if an individual who is subject to a contact activity condition ceases to be habitually resident in England and Wales, the contact activity condition will cease to have effect (s.11D(3));
- under section 11D(2), contact activity conditions cannot be used in respect of a contact order which is an excepted order within the meaning of section 11B(4), which is where:

- an adoption order is being considered at the same time as a contact order; or
- post adoption, a court is considering making, varying or discharging a contact order in relation to someone who, but for the adoption, would have been a relative of the child; unless
- the adoption is, or was, by a partner of one of the child's parents or by a couple, one member of which is a parent of the child.

Making contact activity directions and conditions

Section 11E sets out the steps the court must take before it makes a contact activity direction or condition.

The court can only make directions or conditions if it is satisfied that (s.11E(1)):

- first, the activity proposed is appropriate in the circumstances of the case (s.11E(2));
- second, the person proposed as the provider of the activity is suitable to provide it (s.11E(3));
- third, the activity is available in a place to which it is reasonable to expect the person who would be subject to the direction or condition to travel (s.11E(4)).

The court must obtain and consider information about the individual and consider the likely effect of the contact activity on the person who would be required to undertake it (s.11E(5)). Such information about the likely effect of the activity may include (s.11E(6)):

(a) any conflict with the individual's religious beliefs;
(b) any interference with the times (if any) at which the individual normally works or attends an educational establishment.

The court may ask a CAFCASS officer to provide information about the individual who will be subject to the activity (s.11E(7)).

Safety implications of an order for parents and children

At committee stage, concern was expressed that prior to ordering a contact activity, or making an enforcement order, the court should be specifically directed to consider the safety implications of doing so, both for the individual parents and for the child. The government's response was that, certainly as far as contact activities are concerned, the CAA 2006 does not need specifically to address this point because:

- the child's welfare is paramount and must not be compromised when the court is making a contact activity direction or condition;

- decisions to make contact activity directions or conditions would be covered by the welfare checklist in CA 1989, s.1(3), which states explicitly that a court, when considering whether to make any contact order, must have regard to 'any harm which [the child] has suffered or is at risk of suffering', and that the definition of 'harm' includes the child witnessing others being harmed (as clarified by the Adoption and Children Act 2002 (ACA 2002));
- the new gateway forms will allow courts to hear about allegations of domestic abuse at the outset and to be aware of any domestic abuse issues when making contact activity directions or conditions;
- an enforcement order can only be made if an order has been breached without reasonable excuse and such an excuse could include genuine concerns about safety.

Using contact activity conditions to require a parent to have contact with a child

The Joint Committee on the Draft Children (Contact) and Adoption Bill invited the government to consider permitting either parent to apply to the court where contact has broken down which would enable resident parents to take action where, in their view, the non-resident parent was failing to discharge his or her responsibilities to the children. The court could then impose a contact activity upon that parent.

The government's reply was that it would be concerned about the implications if contact orders were used to force a parent to have contact, against their wishes, with a child. The child's welfare must be the paramount consideration in making decisions about their upbringing and there are serious issues raised about the potential distress, or even harm, such contact could cause to the child.

However, the government's view was that it is open to the court, under the existing provisions of CA 1989, s.11(7), to impose conditions on contact orders which must be complied with, including by any person in whose favour the order is made. That could include, for example, making it a condition of the order that the non-resident parent attends the ordered contact at a specified time and place. If a court does this, then a breach of that condition would constitute a breach of the contact order and the court could make an enforcement order as a result.

The government also commented that if a resident parent believes the non-resident parent is not fulfilling his or her responsibilities, for instance, by failing to attend contact provided for by the order, he or she can seek a variation or discharge of the contact order. The court should then have the power to make a contact activity condition whether or not the application is opposed.

Financial assistance for contact activity directions and conditions

Section 11F enables the Secretary of State, or the National Assembly for Wales, as appropriate, to make provision by regulations for payments to assist those required to undertake contact activities in paying for charges or fees of activity providers. Such regulations may provide:

- that the activity provider must have been approved by the Secretary of State (or the National Assembly for Wales depending on the ordinary residence of the child);
- a maximum amount of financial assistance that will be paid per contact activity;
- a sliding scale to determine how much assistance individuals receive depending on their financial circumstances;
- for payments to be made direct to activity providers rather than to individuals.

Monitoring contact activity directions and conditions

Section 11G provides that:

- a court may ask a CAFCASS officer to monitor compliance with contact activity directions or conditions (s.11G(2)(a));
- a court may further ask a CAFCASS officer to report to the court on any failure to comply with the direction or condition (s.11G(2)(b)); and
- it is the duty of the CAFCASS officer to comply with any such request (s.11G(3)).

1.5 WARNING NOTICES ON CONTACT ORDERS

Section 11(I) provides that whenever a court makes or varies a contact order, it must attach a notice warning of the consequences of failing to comply with it. Such consequences may be:

- an enforcement order;
- a financial compensation order; or
- use of the courts' existing sanctions for contempt.

Transitional provisions for warning notices

Section 8 of the CAA 2006 makes transitional provisions as regards contact orders made before the Act comes into force. The section provides two ways in which warning notices can be attached to such orders:

(a) a specific application can be made for a warning notice to be attached to the contact order; or

(b) if an existing contact order is in issue in any family proceedings, a warning notice can be attached.

Attaching a warning notice to an existing order makes it possible to apply for an enforcement order or an order for financial compensation provided the respondent has been effectively served with the notice.

1.6 ENFORCEMENT ORDERS

Sections 11J to 11N of the CA 1989 provide for the making of enforcement orders. A court can make an enforcement order if a contact order with respect to a child has been made (s.11J(1)). The breach of a contact activity condition, or other condition attached to a contact order under CA 1989, s.11(7), constitutes a breach of a contact order.

An enforcement order imposes an unpaid work requirement on a person who has breached a contact order but before making such an order the court must be satisfied beyond reasonable doubt that the person was in breach (s.11J(2)).

The government accepted the recommendation of the Joint Committee that enforcement orders should not include the imposition of electronic monitoring ('tagging') or curfews purely as punishment. The 'time and place requirement' to facilitate contact, which the Joint Committee did recommend, can be set out in a condition to a contact order under CA 1989, s.11(7). The consequences of breach of such a condition will be made plain to the parties by the warning notice attached to all contact orders whenever they are made or varied.

It is intended that unpaid work requirements will form part of the scheme operated by the National Offender Management Service (NOMS) which is set up to ensure that community service activities are appropriate to the individuals carrying them out. At local level probation officers have discretion to determine the type of work which should be undertaken, taking into account details of the breach of the order, the individual concerned and their circumstances.

Community orders

Part 1 of Schedule A1 to the CA 1989 provides that an enforcement order will have effect in the same way as a community order under Part 12 of the Criminal Justice Act 2003, subject to certain modifications. Specific modifications in paragraph 3 include:

- the ability of a CAFCASS officer appointed under section 11M to oblige the responsible officer who is conducting and supervising the enforcement order to report on:

   - any matters required by the CAFCASS officer for the purposes of making a report under section 11M(1)(c) (on any matters specified by the court) or section 11M(1)(d) (on the person's unsuitability to perform the work requirement);
   - the person's compliance with the enforcement order;

- a reduction in the maximum number of hours of unpaid work that may be required to 200 hours, rather than 300 hours which is the maximum that may be required by a criminal court;
- the work required to be performed during a 12-month period (although the 12-month period does not run during any suspension of the order under section 11J(9)).

Reasonable excuse

The court may not make an enforcement order if it is satisfied that the person concerned had a reasonable excuse for the breach of the contact order (s.11J(3)). In proving that there was a reasonable excuse:

- the burden of proof will fall upon the person claiming to have had a reasonable excuse; and
- the standard of proof is the balance of probabilities (s.11J(4)).

Who can apply for enforcement orders

Enforcement orders may only be made in response to an application by the following (s.11J(5)):

(a) the person who is, for the purposes of the contact order, the person with whom the child concerned lives or is to live;
(b) the person whose contact with the child concerned is provided for in the contact order;
(c) any individual subject to a CA 1989, s.11(7)(b) condition or a contact activity condition imposed by the contact order;
(d) the child concerned (with the leave of the court, which may only be granted if the court is satisfied that the child has sufficient understanding to make the application) (s.11J(6) and (7)).

Suspension of enforcement orders

The court may suspend an enforcement order for such a period as it thinks fit (s.11J(9)).

Multiple enforcement orders

The court can make more than one enforcement order in relation to the same person on the same occasion (s.11J(10)).

Restrictions on enforcement orders

The ability of the court to make an enforcement order is subject to certain restrictions under section 11K.

The court may not make an enforcement order against the person unless he or she has received a copy of a warning notice under section 11I or has been otherwise informed of the terms of the notice (s.11K(1)). It is therefore vitally important to ensure that the contact order including the warning notice is properly and effectively served at the time it is made or an application for enforcement may fail.

An enforcement order cannot be made:

- against a person who is aged under 18 at the time of the breach in question (s.11K(2)); or
- in relation to a breach of an excepted order within the meaning given by section 11B(4) (s.11K(3)); or
- against a person who is not habitually resident in England and Wales and any such order will cease to have effect if the person subject to it ceases to be habitually resident in England and Wales (s.11K(4)).

Making enforcement orders

Under section 11L, in deciding whether to make an enforcement order, the court must be satisfied that:

- the making of the order is necessary to secure compliance (s.11L(1)(a)); and
- the likely effect of the enforcement order is proportionate to the seriousness of the breach (s.11L(1)(b)).

Section 11L also requires the court, before making an enforcement order, to:

- satisfy itself that the enforcement measure is available within the local justice area in which the person subject to the enforcement order resides (s.11L(2)); and
- obtain and consider information about the person on whom the order would be imposed (s.11L(3)) to include:
  - any conflict with the person's religious beliefs; or
  - any interference with the times at which the person is at work or attending an educational establishment (s.11L(4)(a) and (b)); and

  - such information can be requested to be provided by a CAFCASS officer and it shall be the duty of the CAFCASS officer to comply with the request (s.11L(5) and (6));
- take into account the welfare of the child who is the subject of the enforcement order (s.11L(7)). As with existing enforcement remedies, the child's welfare is a material consideration but not paramount. In making the original contact order, the court will have decided that what it was ordering was best for the child, with welfare as the paramount consideration.

Monitoring enforcement orders

Under section 11M(1) the court is to ask a CAFCASS officer to:

(a) monitor or arrange for the monitoring of a person's compliance with any unpaid work requirement which is imposed;
(b) report to the court on any failure to comply if a report under paragraph 8 of Schedule A1 is received (such a report would be received from the supervisor of the unpaid work requirement if a person fails twice or more in a 12-month period to comply with it without reasonable excuse: a warning is given on the first occasion and a report made if failure to comply occurs more than once);
(c) report to the court on such other matters relating to the person's compliance as the court may specify in its request;
(d) report to the court if the person is, or becomes, unsuitable to perform work under the requirement.

It is the duty of the CAFCASS officer to comply with any request under section 11M(1) (s.11M(2)).

Warning notices on enforcement orders

Section 11N provides that where an enforcement order is made, the court must attach a notice warning of the consequences of breaching that order. The possible consequences are:

- the imposition of a new enforcement order; or
- making the existing order more onerous (under paragraph 9 of Schedule A1); or
- the making of a financial compensation order; or
- the use of existing sanctions for contempt.

The court must be satisfied that when any failure to comply with an enforcement order occurred, the person had been given a copy of the notice or had otherwise been informed of its terms, so effective service of the notice is important.

Power to amend or revoke enforcement orders

Part 2 of Schedule A1 gives powers to the court to amend or revoke an enforcement order. The enforcement order may be revoked by the court of its own motion or on an application by the person subject to the enforcement order (Sched. A1 para. 4(3)).

Under paragraph 4(2) the court may revoke the enforcement order if it appears that:

(a) no enforcement order should have been made;
(b) having regard to circumstances which have arisen since the enforcement order was made, it would be appropriate for it to be revoked; or
(c) having regard to the person's satisfactory compliance with any contact order, it would be appropriate for the enforcement order to be revoked.

Change in circumstances

In deciding whether to revoke the enforcement order on paragraph 4(2)(b) grounds (circumstances which have arisen since the order was made) the court is to take into account:

(a) the extent to which the person subject to the enforcement order has complied with it; and
(b) the likelihood that the person will comply with any contact order in the absence of an enforcement order.

Satisfactory compliance

In deciding whether to revoke the enforcement order on paragraph 4(2)(c) grounds (satisfactory compliance with any contact order) the court is to take into account the likelihood that the person will comply with any contact order in the absence of an enforcement order.

Amendment by reason of change of residence

Where the court is satisfied that the person subject to the enforcement order has changed, or proposes to change residence from the local justice area specified in the order to another local justice area, the court may amend the order by substituting the new local justice area.

The enforcement order may be amended in such circumstances:

- by the court of its own motion; or
- on an application by the person subject to the enforcement order.

Amendment of hours specified under unpaid work requirement

Under paragraph 6(2) of Schedule A1, if it appears to the court that, having regard to circumstances that have arisen since the enforcement order was made, it would be appropriate to do so, the court may reduce the number of hours specified in the order (but not below the minimum specified in Criminal Justice Act 2003, s.199(2)(a), being not less than 40 hours).

The court must be satisfied that the effect on the person of the amendment is no more than is required to secure his compliance with any contact order.

The enforcement order may be amended in such circumstances:

- by the court of its own motion; or
- on an application by the person subject to the enforcement order.

Amendment to extend unpaid work requirement

Under paragraph 7 of Schedule A1, if it appears to the court that, having regard to circumstances that have arisen since the enforcement order was made, it would be appropriate to do so, the court may extend the period of 12 months.

The period may be extended:

- by the court of its own motion; or
- on an application by the person subject to the enforcement order.

Warning and report following breach

Under paragraph 8(2) of Schedule A1, if the responsible officer who is conducting and supervising the enforcement order is of the opinion that the person subject to the order has, without reasonable excuse, failed to comply with the unpaid work requirement, the officer must give the person a warning which:

(a) describes the circumstances of the failure;
(b) states that the failure is unacceptable; and
(c) informs the person that, if within the next 12 months he again fails to comply with the unpaid work requirement, the warning and the subsequent failure will be reported to the appropriate person.

Where a warning has already been given once and the person again fails, without reasonable excuse, to comply with the unpaid work requirement in a 12-month period, beginning with the date on which the first warning was given, the officer must report the failure to the appropriate person.

The appropriate person in relation to an enforcement order is the CAFCASS officer who is required to report to the court on matters relating to the enforcement order under section 11M (Sched. A1 para. 8(7)).

Action to be taken on breach of an order

Under paragraph 9(2) of Schedule A1, if the court is satisfied beyond reasonable doubt that the person has failed to comply with the unpaid work requirement imposed by the first order, the court may:

(a) amend the first order so as to make the requirement more onerous; or
(b) make an enforcement order ('the second order') in relation to the person and (if the first order is still in force) provide for the second order to have effect either in addition to or in substitution for the first order.

Reasonable excuse

The court may not exercise its powers:

- if it is satisfied that the person had a reasonable excuse for failing to comply with the unpaid work requirements imposed by the first order; and
- the burden of proof lies on the person claiming to have had a reasonable excuse, and the standard of proof is the balance of probabilities.

Who can apply on breach of an order

If the failure to comply with the first order is a failure to comply with the contact order to which the first order relates, the court can only exercise its powers in relation to the first order on the application of a person who would be able to apply under section 11J for an enforcement order being:

(a) the person who is, for the purposes of the contact order, the person with whom the child concerned lives or is to live;
(b) the person whose contact with the child concerned is provided for in the contact order;
(c) any individual subject to a CA 1989, s.11(7)(b) condition or a contact activity condition imposed by the contact order;
(d) the child concerned (with the leave of the court, which may only be granted if the court is satisfied that the child has sufficient understanding to make the application) (s.11J(6) and (7)).

When can an application for amendment be made

An application for an amendment to the first order to make it more onerous or to impose another enforcement order may only be made whilst the first order is in force (Sched. A1 para. 9(7)).

Powers of the court on breach of an order

The court may, under paragraph 9(9):

(a) increase the number of hours specified in the first order (but not above the maximum 200 hours);
(b) extend the period of 12 months which the order is specified to run.

The court must be satisfied that, taking into account the extent to which the person has complied with the unpaid work requirement imposed by the first order, the effect on the person of the proposed exercise of those powers:

(a) is no more than is required to secure his compliance with any order; and
(b) is no more than is proportionate to the seriousness of his failures to comply with the contact order and the first enforcement order.

Restrictions on the powers of the court on breach of an order

Under paragraph 9(11), the court:

- may not exercise its powers where any failure to comply occurs before the person attains the age of 18 years;
- must satisfy itself that the enforcement measure is available within the local justice area in which the person subject to the enforcement order resides or is to reside (s.11L(2));
- must obtain and consider information about the person on whom the order would be imposed (s.11L(3)) to include:
  - any conflict with the person's religious beliefs; or
  - any interference with the times at which he is at work or attending an educational establishment (s.11L(4)(a) and (b)); and
  - such information can be requested to be provided by a CAFCASS officer and it shall be the duty of the CAFCASS officer to comply with the request (s.11L(5) and (6));
- must take into account the welfare of the child who is the subject of the enforcement order (s.11L(7));
- must ask a CAFCASS officer to monitor, or arrange for monitoring of, the person's compliance and report to the court (s.11M);
- must attach a warning notice of the consequences of failing to comply with the order (s.11N).

Requirements of the court when amending enforcement orders

Sections 11L(2) to (7), 11M and 11N also have effect where the court amends an enforcement order under the following provisions:

- paragraph 6(2) of Schedule 1: to reduce the number of hours specified in the order;
- paragraph 7(2) of Schedule 1: to extend the 12-month period of the order;
- paragraph 9(2)(a) of Schedule 1: to make the requirement more onerous.

Sections 11L(2) to (7), 11M and 11N require the court to:

- satisfy itself that the enforcement measure is available within the local justice area in which the person subject to the enforcement order resides (s.11L(2)); and
- obtain and consider information about the person on whom the order would be imposed (s.11L(3)) to include:
  - any conflict with the person's religious beliefs; or
  - any interference with the times at which the person is at work or attending an educational establishment (s.11L(4)(a) and (b)); and
  - such information can be requested to be provided by a CAFCASS officer and it shall be the duty of the CAFCASS officer to comply with the request (s.11L(5) and (6));
- take into account the welfare of the child who is the subject of the enforcement order (s.11L(7)). As with existing enforcement remedies, the child's welfare is a material consideration but not paramount. In making the original contact order, the court will have decided that what it was ordering was best for the child, with welfare as the paramount consideration;
- ask a CAFCASS officer (s.11M(1)) and it is the duty of the CAFCASS officer to comply (s.11M(2)) to:
  - monitor or arrange for the monitoring of a person's compliance with any unpaid work requirement which is imposed;
  - report to the court on any failure to comply if a report under paragraph 8 of Schedule A1 is received (such a report would be received from the supervisor of the unpaid work requirement if a person fails twice or more in a 12-month period to comply with it without reasonable excuse – a warning is given on the first occasion and a report made if failure to comply occurs more than once);
  - report to the court on such other matters relating to the person's compliance as the court may specify in its request;
  - report to the court if the person is, or becomes, unsuitable to perform work under the requirement;
- attach a notice warning of the consequences of breaching that order (s.11N), such consequences including:

- the imposition of a new enforcement order; or
- making the existing order more onerous (under paragraph 9 of Schedule A1); or
- the making of a financial compensation order; or
- the use of existing sanctions for contempt.

1.7 COMPENSATION FOR FINANCIAL LOSS

Section 11O allows the court to require a person who has caused financial loss to another as a result of breaching a contact order (which includes breaching a condition attached to a contact order) to pay compensation up to the amount of the loss. Prime examples of potential applications for compensation for financial loss, familiar to many practitioners, are the cost of a holiday where one parent refuses to allow the children to travel or of a pre-arranged event or outing for the children where one parent subsequently refuses to make them available without reasonable excuse.

Before making an order for compensation for financial loss, the court must:

- be satisfied that an individual has failed to comply with the contact order; and
- an entitled applicant has suffered financial loss by reason of the breach (s.11O(2)); and
- take into account the welfare of the child concerned (s.11O(14)) which, as with the imposition of a fine, may result in the court refusing to make an order if the welfare of the child would be detrimentally affected by depriving a parent on a limited budget.

Reasonable excuse

The court may not make an order for compensation for financial loss if it is satisfied that the individual in breach had a reasonable excuse for failing to comply with the contact order (s.11O(3)).

The burden of proof lies on the individual claiming to have had a reasonable excuse (s.11O(4)).

Who can apply for compensation for financial loss

Either the resident or non-resident parent may apply for a financial compensation order. An order may only be made on the application of a person who claims to have suffered financial loss (s.11O(5)) who must fall within one of the following categories (s.11O(6)):

(a) a person who is, for the purposes of the contact order, the person with whom the child concerned lives or is to live;
(b) the person whose contact with the child concerned is provided for in the contact order;
(c) an individual subject to a condition under CA 1989, s.11(7)(b) or a contact activity condition imposed by the contact order; or
(d) the child concerned with the leave of the court and leave may only be granted where the court is satisfied that the child has sufficient understanding to make the proposed application (s.11O(7) and (8)).

Recovery of compensation for financial loss

Any amount ordered to be paid as compensation may be recovered by the applicant as a civil debt due to him (s.11O(11)).

Restrictions on making financial compensation orders

The court may not make an order for financial compensation against a person unless it is satisfied that he or she has received a copy of a warning notice under section 11I or has been otherwise informed of the terms of the notice (s.11P(1)). It is therefore vitally important to ensure that the contact order including the warning notice is properly and effectively served at the time it is made or an application for enforcement may fail.

A court may not make a financial compensation order where:

- the failure to comply with a contact order occurred before an individual attained the age of 18 years (s.11P(2));
- the failure to comply is in relation to an excepted order within the meaning of section 11B(4) (s.11P(3)).

1.8 EFFECT ON ENFORCEMENT WHERE PROCEEDINGS ARE STAYED

Schedule 2 to the CAA 2006 provides for minor and consequential amendments including:

- provision that where proceedings are stayed under the Domicile and Matrimonial Proceedings Act 1973 the court may not make an enforcement order, or exercise its powers in relation to an enforcement order already in force, where at the time when the stay is imposed a contact order made in connection with the stayed proceedings is in force;
- provision that where proceedings are stayed under the Family Law Act 1986, and a contact activity direction or enforcement order has been made in those proceedings, the court may, when granting the stay, suspend the

contact activity direction or enforcement order and, if the stay is removed, bring the suspension to an end.

1.9 MONITORING CONTACT

Under section 11H, a court may ask a CAFCASS officer for a period of up to a year (s.11H(6)) to:

- monitor compliance with a contact order; and
- report to the court on such matters relating to compliance as the court may specify (s.11H(2)).

Those who can be subject to monitoring are the following (s.11H(3)):

(a) a person who is required to allow contact with the child;
(b) a person whose contact with the child is provided for; or
(c) a person who is subject to a condition under CA 1989, s.11(7)(b) as follows:
   - the person in whose favour the order is made; or
   - who is a parent of the child concerned; or
   - who is not a parent of the child concerned but who has parental responsibility for the child; or
   - with whom the child is living.

The court can prevent a recalcitrant parent from blocking the ability of a CAFCASS officer to monitor and report by ordering any individual falling within section 11H(3) to take specified steps to enable the CAFCASS officer to comply with the court's request for monitoring and reporting.

The court cannot make such an order with respect to a child unless he is the parent of the child concerned (s.11H(9)).

The court can make such a request to a CAFCASS officer on making or varying a contact order, or at any time during the subsequent course of the proceedings (s.11H(5)). It is the duty of the CAFCASS officer to comply with any such request (s.11H(7)).

Restrictions on monitoring contact

The court cannot request monitoring of an order which is an excepted order within the meaning of section 11B(4) which means where:

- an adoption order is being considered at the same time as a contact order; or
- post adoption, a court is considering making, varying or discharging a contact order in relation to someone who, but for the adoption, would have been a relative of the child; unless

- the adoption is, or was, by a partner of one of the child's parents or by a couple, one member of which is a parent of the child.

1.10 FAMILY ASSISTANCE ORDERS

Section 16 of the CA 1989 is amended so as to enable family assistance orders (FAOs) to be used more often and for a longer duration. The provisions are as follows:

- the requirement that FAOs be made only in exceptional circumstances is removed (CA 1989, s.16(3));
- the maximum duration of FAOs is extended from six to 12 months (s.16(5));
- where a FAO is to be enforced at the same time as a contact order with respect to a particular child, the FAO may direct the CAFCASS officer carrying out the FAO to give advice and assistance about improving and maintaining contact (s.16(4A));
- FAOs may direct the CAFCASS officer concerned to report to the court on matters regarding any section 8 order which is in force at the same time, including whether the order ought to be varied or discharged (s.16(6)).

The requirement for all adult parties named in the FAO to give consent remains as the government did not believe it would be constructive to make an order to 'advise, assist and befriend' an unwilling or hostile party. It is only those adult parties named in the FAO who need give consent, however, not all parties to the case, so a FAO cannot be blocked by an unnamed parent.

The CAA 2006 covers two distinct concepts:

- reformed FAOs which will remain facilitative measures only to be used with the consent of the parties;
- provision for the courts to require CAFCASS to monitor compliance with contact orders, contact activities and enforcement orders which do not require the parties' consent.

In determining what is most appropriate it is anticipated that the courts will consult CAFCASS prior to making the order, and will take into account the availability of local CAFCASS resources.The government's aim is for there to be a reduction in the number and length of CAFCASS reports commissioned by the courts to enable CAFCASS officers to focus more on their new problem-solving roles.

1.11 RISK ASSESSMENTS

A new section 16A of the CA 1989 requires CAFCASS officers to carry out a risk assessment and to provide this to the court if, in the course of carrying out any function in private family law proceedings under the CA 1989, the officer is given cause to suspect that the child concerned is at risk of harm.

Private family law proceedings are defined as including applications for residence and contact orders and applications for enforcement of contact orders. The duty applies:

- whenever an officer is involved in any function connected with such proceedings including for instance:
  - preparing a report for the court under CA 1989, s.7; or
  - monitoring contact orders under CA 1989, s.11H; or
  - working on alternative dispute resolution;
- where an officer is carrying out functions under a FAO.

1.12 PUBLIC SECTOR FINANCIAL IMPLICATIONS OF THE CAA 2006

CAFCASS

Concern and disappointment has been expressed in some quarters at the government's failure to increase the allocation of funding for CAFCASS, which was one of the recommendations in *Making Contact Work*. It is to be hoped that the lack of additional funding will not inhibit the ability of CAFCASS officers to assist practically in ensuring contact works.

The government anticipates that no net additional resources will be needed for CAFCASS in providing information on the availability of contact activities and the same applies as far as notifying courts of a breach of a contact activity or an enforcement order is concerned, since the actual monitoring of such orders will be carried out by those directly involved in their administration, who will in turn notify CAFCASS.

The government recognises that there may be some resource implications for CAFCASS in continuing their present role in administering, though this may be offset by a reduction in work associated with ongoing court proceedings, and the time taken by CAFCASS officers in compiling reports for the court, where FAOs are used to facilitate and support contact arrangements.

The courts

The government's expectation is that the new measures will help to reduce the number of repeat applications to the court for contact and applications for enforcement, and it is anticipated that savings for the court system will result as a consequence of the reduction in the number and duration of contested court cases.

The government's assumption is that the measures on contact orders in the CAA 2006 will reduce applications for enforcement of contact orders to the court by up to 80 per cent, reducing the annual caseload for enforcement applications from around 7,000 per year to around 1,400.

Contact activities

The government expects contact activities to be used in a proportion of all contact cases, not just those which require enforcement. If one or both parents are referred to contact activities in 20 per cent of cases, there will be a cost to the government of between around £71,000 and £406,000 a year for the contact activity depending on the level of the future reduction in applications. If parents were referred to contact activities in 50 per cent of the cases, this would mean a cost of between around £177,000 and £1,000,014 for the contact activities.

There will be costs to parents and families as a result of being expected to pay for courses and programmes which the courts direct them to participate in unless they are eligible for financial assistance under CA 1989, s.11F.

Enforcement orders

The cost of unpaid work requirements imposed by enforcement orders is estimated to be £2,000 for an order for 80 hours of unpaid work (based on five to six hours per day for 16 days including fixed costs and daily supervision fee).

If it is assumed that in one per cent of cases where an application for enforcement is made, an unpaid work requirement will be ordered, this would result in a public sector cost of between around £28,000 and £140,000 per year. If an unpaid work requirement is ordered in three per cent of cases, a cost of around £84,000 to £420,000 a year would result.

1.13 IMPLICATIONS OF THE CAA 2006

The implications of the CAA 2006 and how it will work in practice will depend largely on the extent to which the courts are prepared to embrace and use its measures, particularly in relation to the enforcement of contact orders.

The courts have struggled with the difficulties of using the existing penalties of committal, fine or transfer of residence to enforce contact, in circumstances where such measures may well be incompatible with the welfare of the children concerned. The courts may still struggle to make financial compensation orders, which are likely to cause similar problems, but the remedy of unpaid work requirements is designed to be a penalty which can be imposed on the defaulting parent without detrimentally affecting the welfare of the children. How effective the new enforcement provisions will be will depend on the readiness of the courts to impose unpaid work requirements, provided they are satisfied that such measures are necessary and proportionate to secure compliance with contact orders or conditions attached to contact orders.

It is to be hoped that the contact activities, including information and advice or counselling and guidance sessions, will improve the ability of parents to work together in agreeing future arrangements for contact and also the quality of contact for children.

The new role for CAFCASS in monitoring contact and providing advice and assistance on maintaining contact through FAOs will hopefully be a great leap forward in ensuring contact orders are complied with. The emphasis on CAFCASS officers facilitating contact on the ground rather than simply reporting on the problems surrounding contact when things have gone wrong, and making recommendations for the future, is likely to have a real impact for both parents in improving and maintaining contact arrangements.

CHAPTER 2

The current law

2.1 OVERVIEW

This chapter will deal with the principles which govern the determination of a child's welfare, largely as set out in the Children Act 1989 (CA 1989) with amendments in recent legislation. The chapter will also deal with parental responsibility, including who has it and who has the right to apply for it, in particular dealing with the recent changes to the law which have allowed step-parents and civil partners to acquire parental responsibility. The chapter will also deal with section 8 orders which are the main orders available in private law and summarise these briefly.

2.2 BACKGROUND

Welfare of the child and the welfare checklist

When the court considers any question in relation to the upbringing of a child, the child's welfare is the court's paramount consideration. This is set out in section 1(1) of the CA 1989. The court must have regard in particular to the welfare checklist when considering whether to make, vary or discharge a section 8 order (which includes orders for contact and residence). The 'welfare checklist' is set out in section 1(3) of the CA 1989. It comprises:

(a) the ascertainable wishes and feelings of the child concerned (considered in the light of his age and understanding);
(b) his physical, emotional and educational needs;
(c) the likely effect on him of any change in his circumstances;
(d) the age, sex, background and any particular characteristics of the child which the court considers relevant;
(e) any harm suffered by the child or which the child is at risk of suffering;
(f) how capable each of his parents, and any other person in relation to whom the court considers the question to be relevant, is of meeting the child's needs;
(g) the range of powers available to the court under the CA 1989.

No order principle

This is an important principle which underlies the court's involvement in any decisions relating to children. The court must not make a section 8 order unless 'it considers that doing so would be better for the child than making no order at all' (see CA 1989, s.1(5)).

The no order principle means that if parents can agree arrangements for their children there should in theory be no need for the court to be involved at all. However, practitioners should take note of the Court of Appeal's decision in *Re G* [2006] 1 FLR 771, where it was held that CA 1989, s.1(5) does not create a presumption one way or the other; it merely obliges the court to ask the question 'will it be better for the child to make an order than making no order at all?' Each case depends upon its own facts. In this particular case there was a justification for making a residence order. The unmarried parents had agreed finally that the father would have parental responsibility and contact and the mother would have residence. The mother wanted a residence order as this would give her security as she would know that she could rely on the order in the future. The Court of Appeal said that the court should have paid respect to the decision of the parents whose 'views were that an order would be beneficial to the management of their children's lives and that that management would be more beneficial with the order than without it'. The Court of Appeal granted the mother's appeal (supported by the father) and made a residence order in her favour.

In addition to the no order principle, the court must also have regard to the general principle that any delay in determining a question in relation to a child's welfare is likely to prejudice the welfare of that child (see CA 1989, s.1(2)). This is even more likely to be an issue given the rulings by the European Court of Human Rights on the prejudice that can be caused by delay (see Chapter 12).

2.3 PARENTAL RESPONSIBILITY

This is defined as all the 'rights, duties, powers, responsibilities and authority which by law a parent of a child has in relation to the child and his property' (see CA 1989, s.3). Amongst other responsibilities, this includes the power to choose the child's education, religion, name or medical treatment, to appoint a guardian for the child, to represent the child in legal proceedings, to have contact with the child and to agree to a child going on holiday or spending time out of the jurisdiction. Parental responsibility can be curtailed by a court order such as a specific issue order (for instance, determining the child's name or the school which they are to attend) or a residence or contact order setting out with whom a child should live and with whom they should have contact. A useful summary of those items which relate to the exercise of parental responsibility is set out in schedule form at the end of the judgment of Wall J in *A* v. *A (Shared Residence)* [2004] EWHC 142 (Fam), [2004] 1 FLR 1195.

Who has parental responsibility?

The mother has parental responsibility automatically. Where a child's father and mother are married to each other at the time of the birth, each has parental responsibility from the date of birth of the child. See section below on non-biological parents for what happens if it is established by DNA testing that the man married to the mother at the time of the birth of the child is not the child's biological father.

Unmarried biological father

Where a child's father and mother are not married at the time of the birth, the mother has parental responsibility. The father will not have it automatically unless he has registered his details on the child's birth certificate (in the case of children born after 1 December 2003), in which case he too will automatically acquire parental responsibility (see Adoption and Children Act 2002 (ACA 2002), s.111). This provision does not have retrospective effect.

If a father does not automatically have parental responsibility as a result of being registered on the birth certificate (after 1 December 2003), he can acquire parental responsibility in the following ways:

- by agreement with the mother (called a parental responsibility agreement). Such agreement must be on Form C in accordance with the Parental Responsibility Agreement Regulations 1991, SI 1991/1478 and must be registered at court;
- by way of a residence order or a parental responsibility order;
- by subsequent marriage to the mother, provided that he is domiciled in England and Wales at the time of marriage, or, if not, provided that the law of the country of origin of the father legitimises the child by virtue of the marriage;
- if a child was born prior to 1 December 2003 and the register does not have any entry for the father's details, the registrar can register the father's details and the father can acquire parental responsibility in this way even if the re-registration was after 1 December 2003. This will require the mother's cooperation unless the father already has parental responsibility or there is an order under Schedule 1 to the CA 1989 for financial relief. See Births and Deaths Registration Act 1953, s.10A;
- by being appointed as the child's guardian;
- by adopting his child.

The child's welfare will be the paramount consideration in the court deciding whether it is appropriate to make a parental responsibility order. In *Re H*

(Minors) (Local Authority: Parental Rights) (No. 3) [1991] 2 All ER 185, the court took a number of factors into account:

(a) degree of commitment demonstrated by applicant towards the child;
(b) degree of attachment between the child and the applicant;
(c) reasons why the application was being made.

Following on from this are a number of authorities outside the scope of this book but these should be referred to in the event of making an application for parental responsibility. See also *Re G (A Minor) (Parental Responsibility Order)* [1994] 1 FLR 504.

For a recent case on parental responsibility see the case of *Re D (Contact and Parental Responsibility: Lesbian Mothers and Known Father)* [2006] 1 FLR 556, where Mr B, the biological father of D, was granted parental responsibility over a child in the care of a lesbian couple. He was not in a relationship with either of the couple (A and C) but had responded to their advertisement to father A's child. He was granted parental responsibility on the basis of his offering to be bound by conditions preventing him from being intrusive in the 'obvious situations which might be anticipated as problem areas, [such as the child's] schooling and health care'. The order set out that parental responsibility was granted in reliance on the father's undertakings.The judge stated that if he broke these undertakings the court could reconsider the question of parental responsibility (as opposed to considering the committal of the father). Granting parental responsibility would entitle the father, who had contact with the child, to consent to adoption and would recognise his status in the child's life. However, the restrictions upon his parental responsibility reflected the fact that the child's day-to-day parents were the lesbian couple. Practitioners can compare this approach with the decision in *Re G (A Child)* [2006] EWCA Civ 348 when a suspended parental responsibility order was set aside by the Court of Appeal. The trial judge had made a parental responsibility order, but suspended it on condition that the mother provided the father with information about the education and health of the child. In this case the child had been conceived during a 'one night stand' and the child had been brought up by the mother and with another person acting as his father. The father had made determined efforts to have contact in the face of the mother's opposition to this and an order for direct contact on a twice yearly basis was made. The Court of Appeal held that the judge was not permitted to make a suspended parental responsibility order and that the application for parental responsibility would be adjourned with liberty to restore if the undertakings of the mother were not complied with.

Step-parent (married to the mother or in civil partnership with parent)

Step-parents are those who are married to or in a civil partnership with the child's parent but are not the child's biological parent themselves.

Step-parents used to have to apply for a residence order (often shared with the mother) in order to acquire parental responsibility. Recent changes in legislation (the bringing into force of section 112 of the ACA 2002 on 30 December 2005) allow a step–parent to acquire parental responsibility if both parents with parental responsibility (or one if there is only one) agree to make an agreement to that effect. Alternatively, the step-parent can apply to the court for an order that he or she acquires parental responsibility. These new provisions may well prove to be popular as, to date, step-parents, even though they can be acting effectively as parents the majority of the time, legally have not had the right to consent to medical treatment for a child or be involved in decisions about their education or other important issues in relation to their wellbeing.

A step-parent who is (or was) married to the child's parent and treated the child as a child of the family can also apply for a residence order with respect to that child. If a residence order is made in favour of a step-parent, this will confer upon him parental responsibility for the duration of the order with certain limitations (for example, he will not be able to appoint a guardian for the child). He will also be subject to the same restrictions as any residence order holder in that he will not be able change the child's surname or take him out of the United Kingdom for one month or longer without the written consent of all those with parental responsibility or a court order (see CA 1989, s.13(1)).

A step-parent can also acquire parental responsibility by adopting the child.

Unmarried partner who is also not a civil partner

The unmarried partner of a mother (who is also not a civil partner) who is not the biological parent of a child will not be able to benefit from the provisions of the ACA 2002 and will remain reliant on obtaining a residence order in order to obtain parental responsibility. This parental responsibility will not survive the removal of the residence order. In a landmark decision in April 2005, *Re G (Children) (Residence: Same Sex Partner)* [2005] 2 FLR 957, the Court of Appeal granted a lesbian partner a shared residence order, and therefore parental responsibility, in respect of her former partner's biological children. This case is referred to in greater detail at section 5.4. After various further proceedings the shared residence order with the biological mother providing the primary home was restored by the House of Lords in *Re G (Residence: Same Sex Partner)* [2006] 1 WLR 2305.

Cases concerning unmarried non-biological fathers in mixed sex relationships are analogous to the use of shared residence orders for same sex partners, as a method of providing non-biological parents with parental responsibility. An application for leave to apply will be necessary where the non-biological father has not lived with the child 'for a period of at least 3 years' (CA 1989, s.10(5)(b)).

In deciding whether or not to make an order for shared residence, the court must treat the child's welfare as its paramount consideration and take into account the section 1(3) checklist of factors set out in the CA 1989. It is also incumbent on the court to have regard to the no order principle enshrined in section 1(5) of the CA 1989.

There are several situations where the court is likely to consider it better for the child to make an order than not. If the court has had to resolve a dispute between the parents, it is likely to be better for the child to make an order about it. Even if there is no dispute (and it is possible there would not be in a case where the mother wished to afford parental responsibility to a non-biological father by the method of a shared residence order by consent), the child's need for stability and security may be better served by making an order.

There may also be specific legal advantages in acquiring parental responsibility by virtue of an order for shared residence. One example is where abduction of the child is a possibility, since a court order is necessary for enforcement proceedings in other parts of the United Kingdom under the Family Law Act 1986 (FLA 1986), and under the European Convention on the Recognition and Enforcement of Decisions Concerning Custody of Children and on Restoration of Custody of Children 1980. Also, under the Hague Convention on the Civil Aspects of International Child Abduction 1980, an order will be necessary if the aggrieved party is, for example, an unmarried father or a relative or a non-biological parent who would not otherwise have rights of custody. Another advantage of having a residence order is that the child may be taken out of the country for periods of less than a month without the permission of other persons with parental responsibility, or the court, whereas without an order this could amount to an offence under the Child Abduction Act 1984. Depending on the circumstances of the case, the court might therefore be persuaded that an order would be in the child's interest.

If the non-biological father and the mother are married or were to marry, the non-biological father could apply for parental responsibility as the child's step-father, or enter into a parental responsibility agreement with the mother, under ACA 2002, s.4A. There are obviously significant financial consequences of a decision to marry which both the non-biological father and the mother would have to take into consideration.

The mother can delegate the exercise of parental powers to the non-biological father if she chooses under CA 1989, s.2(9), which provides that a person with parental responsibility can delegate parental responsibility to another person, but such arrangements are not legally binding and can be revoked at will. The mother could therefore delegate parental responsibility powers to the non-biological father by saying that she does so, or by putting this in writing, but could revoke this at any time and this offers neither the non-biological father nor the child any real security for the future.

At common law, the genetic father of a child is regarded as the legal father. There is a presumption (rebuttable by DNA evidence to the contrary) that a man who is married to a woman at the time of the child's birth is the child's father. A married father automatically has parental responsibility.

Also under common law, the entry of a man's name as that of the father on the birth certificate is prima facie evidence of paternity (*Brierley* v. *Brierley* [1918] P 257). This is also rebuttable by DNA evidence to the contrary. In 2005, Divorce-Online reported that 10,000 DNA tests are carried out each year and one in four men who demand those tests establish that they are not the biological father of the child concerned. On the face of it, therefore, a non-biological father may be a child's legal father but, if he obtains DNA evidence to the contrary, he is aware that this presumption could be rebutted. To acquire parental responsibility, in the event that the presumption of paternity is rebutted and his parental responsibility acquired by virtue of registration as the father on the child's birth certificate is removed, the non-biological father could make an application for a shared residence order.

Special guardian

Whilst the purpose of this book is not to deal with care proceedings, it is of note that the ACA 2002 has brought in the concept of special guardianship which is likely to be used with children who are in long-term care. A special guardian will exercise parental responsibility to the exclusion of all others with parental responsibility even though there is no adoption order. Provisions in relation to special guardians are set out in section 115 of the ACA 2002 which inserts sections 14A–14G into the CA 1989. The new provisions came into force on 30 December 2005.

Special guardianship orders (SGOs) could be described as innovative in the law relating to children as they cross the boundaries of both private and public law. A SGO bridges a gap for the child for whom adoption is not suitable, yet still affording him or her certainty and constancy.

Under the previous law, permanency for a child arising from family proceedings was only obtainable through a residence or adoption order (noting the private/public arenas respectively). For various reasons adoption might not be thought suitable for particular children. Adoption orders also operate to extinguish parental responsibility of the child's birth parents which could be flawed in certain circumstances where formal severance of that relationship may not be desirable. However, generally, research has shown that children have a preference for the security that adoption provides as opposed to long-term foster care (see *Adoption: Prime Minister's Review. A Performance and Innovation Report*, Cabinet Office (2000)).

An order for special guardianship meets these concerns as it does not eradicate the parental rights of the birth parents. By giving the special guardian a right to exercise his or her parental responsibility over and above any non-special guardian, the special guardian's exercise of parental responsibility is elevated. An example of where this may be appropriate is the situation where the natural parents suffer from a mental illness or are not to be found and a family member is caring for a child. The limitation is that no person (including the special guardian) can cause the child to be known by a new surname or remove him from the United Kingdom without either leave of the court or the written consent of every person with parental responsibility of the child (CA 1989, s.14C(3)). The special guardian is permitted to remove the child from the United Kingdom for a period of less than three months without obtaining leave or consent (CA 1989, s.14C(4)). These limitations, however, do not apply if a placement order is in force (CA 1989, s.14C(6); ACA 2002, s.29(7)).

Applicants for a SGO cannot be under 18 years and cannot be the parent of the child in respect of whom a SGO is sought. Besides these exemptions, those who are entitled to apply are (CA 1989, s.14A(5)):

- any guardian of the child;
- any person with a residence order in respect of the child;
- a local authority foster carer with whom the child has lived for at least one year prior to the date of application;
- any person with whom the child has lived for at least three years (corresponding with CA 1989, s.10(5)(b), so that the three years need not be continuous but the period should not have begun more than five years before nor ended three months before the date of application);
- any person who (where a residence order is in force with respect to the child) has the consent of each person who has the favour of that order;
- any person (where the child is in the care of a local authority) who has the consent of that authority; and
- in any other case, a person who has the consent of each person with parental responsibility for the child.

The latter three categories correspond to CA 1989, s.10(5)(c). Any other person seeking a SGO must have obtained leave of the court to make an application. The court can make a SGO of its own motion with respect to any child in any family proceedings in which a question as to the welfare of that child arises.

Prior to making an application, three months' written notice should be given to the local authority stating the intention to apply for a SGO. This will be the local authority which has 'looked after' responsibility of the child and where the child is not looked after, the local authority in whose area the child is resident. An exemption to this notice period exists for an applicant who has leave of the court to bring an application for a SGO where adoption proceedings are underway so that those proceedings are not unduly prejudiced. The local authority must then investigate and report to the court. When this is complete and the court makes a decision on the application, it has a duty to consider whether it should make a contact order at the same time and whether it should vary or discharge any section 8 order already in existence (CA 1989, s.14B(1)). As SGOs concern the upbringing of a child, the no order and delay principles will apply (see above) and a specific amendment to section 1(4) of the CA 1989 means that on any application to make, vary or discharge a SGO, the court must consider the welfare checklist.

Practitioners should be aware that local authority support (financial or otherwise) for persons seeking residence orders is limited. In the past this has led to some non-parent carers of children not applying for residence orders.These considerations appear to have been borne in mind by the framers of special guardianship. Special guardianship support services are dealt with in section 14F of the CA 1989 and in the Special Guardianship Regulations 2005, SI 2005/1109.

As SGOs were only introduced relatively recently, it will be some time before any real evaluation can be made as to how popular they are and whether their use will lead to a decline in adoption orders. Their relationship with contact orders will be interesting. Contact orders between child and birth family are generally rare in adoption proceedings if the prospective adopters are opposed to the making of such an order. However, special guardianship, by its nature, is intended not to exclude preservation of the connection. The court must give consideration to making a contact order before it makes a SGO. A birth parent also remains able to make an application for contact in the form of an application for a section 8 order. Leave of the court will be required (unless otherwise stated not to be required) before he or she can make an application for a residence order in respect of a child who is the subject of a SGO (CA 1989, s.10(7A)).

Civil partner

The Civil Partnership Act 2004 is now in force and a civil partner may acquire parental responsibility over their civil partner's child by either of the following methods:

- agreement between the parent (and any other parent with parental responsibility) and the civil partner; or
- by court order on the application of the civil partner.

A civil partner's parental responsibility is not affected by any subsequent dissolution of the civil partnership.

2.4 SECTION 8 ORDERS

In private law proceedings, orders under section 8 of the CA 1989 are frequently used to resolve issues between parents about matters relating to a child's welfare. The court cannot make an order which is intended to last beyond a child's 16th birthday unless it is satisfied that the circumstances of the case are exceptional (CA 1989, s.9(6)) in which case the order can be made until the child's 18th birthday (CA 1989, s.91(11)). The different Section 8 orders are set out below.

Residence order

This is an order settling the arrangements as to who the child is to live with. A residence order gives parental responsibility automatically to any person in whose favour the order is made, for the duration of the order. This includes a family member or step-parent (see section 2.3 above). It does not prevent any other person retaining parental responsibility unless the previous residence order holder was not a parent. Given the increasing number of cases where shared residence is being ordered (or agreed between parents), a separate chapter has been devoted to this topic (see Chapter 5). The making of a residence order will generally be accompanied by a contact order setting out arrangements for contact between a child and the parent with whom they do not live for the majority of their time.

Where a residence order is in force no person shall cause the child to be known by a different surname or remove him from the United Kingdom for a period of one month or more without either the written consent of every person who has parental responsibility over the child or the leave of the court (CA 1989, s.13).

Contact order

This is an order requiring the person with whom a child lives, or is to live, to allow the child to visit or have such other contact with a named person as may be specified in the order. The wording of a contact order will generally be that 'X parent makes the child available for contact with Y'. In most cases contact is direct (i.e. the child visits or stays overnight with a particular person). In some instances it can be indirect only (i.e. by letters, e-mails, presents, telephone calls or a combination of these). In most cases, courts do not place restrictions upon indirect contact unless it is being used in a way that unreasonably interferes with the child's family life at the home in which he lives for the majority of the time. Indirect contact orders may oblige the parent with whom a child lives to read letters to the child or to ensure that the child calls the other parent at a particular time or that he is available to speak to that parent at the agreed time.

Contact orders can be for staying contact (i.e. overnight) or for a number of hours. In acrimonious cases, it is recommended that the order specify the detail of the proposed contact including, if need be, the time and dates for such contact, so as to avoid further dispute. Provision should be made for significant dates such as the children's birthdays and religious holidays. In cases where contact has been agreed prior to the order being made (although in such cases there may be no need for an order at all bearing in mind the no order principle) or where it is anticipated that contact can be agreed, the words 'such contact as is reasonable or agreed between the parties' can be used in the order. Practitioners may wish to suggest to parents that they draw up a schedule of contact on a half yearly or yearly basis or that they annotate a calendar setting out when contact is to take place in order to provide certainty for all involved, in particular the children. They should consult school calendars so that they can take into account special events in a child's life, in addition to birthdays and religious holidays.

Contact is the right of the child not the parent. There is a presumption that it is in a child's interests to continue the relationship with the parent with whom the child does not live, although there are exceptions to this. The fact that there may have been a considerable period of time since contact last took place will not of itself be sufficient to prevent an order being made, although there may need to be a period of re-introduction, particularly if the child does not remember the parent who is seeking contact. Cases where one parent is implacably hostile to contact between the child and the other parent are dealt with in Chapter 7. The way the court deals with contact in cases where there are allegations of domestic abuse is considered in Chapter 6. The court has to make findings of fact about the allegations in such cases before deciding if contact should be ordered.

In certain circumstances, where there is sufficient evidence to recommend this, the court may decide that in the first instance contact should be supervised by a third party. This may be agreed (for instance, supervision could be by a neutral family member or friend). However, the court is not entitled to impose such an obligation on anyone not a parent or having parental responsibility or in whose favour a section 8 order is made or with whom the child lives (CA 1989, s.11(7)). If the court wishes to order contact to be supervised by a local authority or a CAFCASS officer, a family assistance order should be made (see CA 1989, s.16).

The European Court of Human Rights has emphasised that the preservation of contact between a parent and a child is an important aspect of the right to family life (see in particular Article 8 of the European Convention on Human Rights which is reproduced and considered in detail in Chapter 12). Parents have the right to expect their national authority to take steps to reunite them with their children and oblige their national authority to take action. See Chapter 12 for examples of this in decided cases.

Who can apply for contact is dealt with in Chapter 4. The current remedies available to the court in the enforcement of contact orders are dealt with in Chapter 7. The additional remedies available following the implementation of the CAA 2006 are discussed in Chapter 1.

The increasing number of shared residence orders being made means that in those cases there will be no contact order. In the past these cases might have concluded with residence being given to one parent and staying contact to the other. As set out in Chapter 5, the distinction is really one of labelling in some cases rather than there being a distinct difference in the type of arrangement which is being sanctioned by the court.

The no order principle is very important to consider when deciding whether to make an application for contact. Where there is no dispute about the arrangements for a child, the expectation will be that there is no need for an order. An order may be justified as a means of enabling a child to feel a greater sense of security about arrangements. In rare cases the court may make an order of its own motion rather than by application to the court. The court has the power to make an order of its own motion where it considers that the order should be made even though no such application has been made (CA 1989, s.10(1)(b)).

Length of contact orders

A contact order requiring a parent with whom a child resides to allow contact with the other parent ceases to have effect:

- if the parents live together continuously for a period of over six months (CA 1989, s.10(6));
- by order of the court;
- on the making of a care order in favour of a child (CA 1989, s.91(2));
- when a child reaches 16 years unless the court has stated that the contact order should have effect beyond that date; to do this the court must be satisfied that there are exceptional circumstances (CA 1989, s.9(6));
- if the court makes an order that the contact order should have effect beyond the child's 16th birthday then it will cease to have effect when the child reaches 18 years (CA 1989, s.91(11)).

Variation of contact orders

The court can vary an order in any family proceedings in which the welfare of the child is considered (see CA 1989, s.10) or on a variation application. See Chapter 4 for details as to who can apply for such variation without leave of the court and who will need leave.

A helpful list of the principles which the courts in England and Wales should consider when dealing with an application for contact is provided in a case decided by Wall J (see *Re P (Contact: Supervision)* [1996] 2 FLR 314). Those principles are as follows:

1. Overriding all else, as provided by section 1(1) of the CA 1989, the welfare of the child is the paramount consideration, and the court is concerned with the interests of the mother and the father only in so far as they bear on the welfare of the child.
2. It is almost always in the interest of a child whose parents are separated that he or she should have contact with the parent with whom the child is not living.
3. The court has the power to enforce orders for contact, which it should not hesitate to exercise where it judges that it will overall promote the welfare of the child to do so.
4. Cases do, unhappily and infrequently, but occasionally, arise in which a court is compelled to conclude that in existing circumstances an order for immediate direct contact should not be ordered, because so to order would injure the welfare of the child.
5. In cases in which, for whatever reason, direct contact cannot for the time being be ordered, it is ordinarily highly desirable that there should be indirect contact so that the child grows up knowing of the love and interest of the absent parent with whom, in due course, direct contact should be established.

In dealing with applications for contact the court frequently has to determine allegations made by the person who is disputing the merit of there being contact or the level of contact requested. The court will often seek the guidance of CAFCASS or other professional or outside agencies in order to advise the court as to whether and, if so, what contact accords with the welfare of the child. It is not the role of these experts to determine issues of fact in dispute, which are matters for the court alone to decide. Such experts will often meet the children and may attend contact sessions or contact centres to enable them to form a picture of how any contact is progressing. Experts are dealt with in more detail in Chapter 9.

Experts may also be asked to assess the validity and independence of children's objections to the contact proposed. Children's views will be taken into account from a relatively young age but the views of a younger child will carry much less weight than those of an older child. The weight to be given to the views of a child is a matter for the discretion of the judge and very much depends on how well reasoned these views are. A well reasoned view of a 14-year-old may well prove to be determinative. The extent to which the court takes the views of children into account will depend in part on the judge's assessment as to whether the child is sufficiently mature to understand the issues involved.

The procedure for applications for contact is set out in Chapter 8 but applicants should be aware that they may well have to attend some form of dispute resolution hearing at an early stage. In particular, at the Principal Registry in London, applicants should be aware that children over nine years are required to attend court for conciliation appointments (unless the court has specifically directed otherwise) (see *District Judge's Direction (Children: Conciliation)* [2004] 1 FLR 974). The children will not enter the courtroom but will be seen by a CAFCASS officer to ascertain their views. See Chapter 8 for a fuller discussion of what is to be expected at conciliation appointments and Chapter 12 concerning the representation of children and their views generally.

In exceptional cases, the applicant may consider applying to the court for a direction that conciliation should be by-passed but generally the court will be keen for the correct process to be followed even if one parent's hostility to the contact makes resolution unlikely without a determination by the court.

The court aims to be constructive in difficult cases and will explore options such as contact taking place in contact centres or in the presence of a third party. It can impose conditions on the parents if need be, but not local authorities or CAFCASS officers unless a FAO is made (see Chapter 7) or where a local authority has applied for the order itself.

The court can make an interim contact order if it is in the interest of the child. Practitioners should consider carefully whether to make such an application. (If no contact has been taking place for some considerable time then the court may direct that the status quo of no contact should be continued pending a final hearing.) Unsuccessful interim contact may prove to be very damaging. See *Re D Contact: Interim Order* [1995] 1 FLR 495 for the analysis by Wall J of the approach to interim contact orders. Interim orders can be made as part of the adjudication process, particularly where they will enable an expert to assess the quality of the contact and its effect on the children. They will only be made if there is sufficient information to make an order for contact and may be made even where there is a possibility that the court will not make a contact order at the final hearing. Usually a CAFCASS officer will need to report before this decision can be made. Interim orders may also be made where contact itself is not in dispute but rather the type or amount. Where there are allegations of domestic violence it is difficult to make such an order.

Specific issue order

This is an order giving directions for the purpose of determining a specific question which has arisen, or which may arise, in connection with any aspect of parental responsibility for a child.

Examples include determining issues in relation to the name, religion, medical treatment (including immunisation, circumcision or HIV testing) or the choice of education of a child. This book does not deal with such applications in detail.

Prohibited steps order

This is an order that no step which could be taken by a parent in meeting his parental responsibility for a child, and which is of a kind specified in the order, shall be taken by any person without the leave of the court.

Examples may be orders preventing the removal of a child from a jurisdiction of England and Wales, or preventing a change of name of the child or undertaking specific medical treatment.

Again, this book will not deal with such orders in detail. However, it is worth noting that a prohibited steps order can be used to prohibit a named person from having contact with a child or to prevent contact taking place abroad if there are good reasons for this.

2.5 SUMMARY

The CA 1989 remains the statute which dominates the law relating to children, although it has been amended by recent legislation. The concept of the family has evolved, reflecting changes in society and the way in which children are brought up. New categories of individuals have been created who can acquire parental responsibility without having to make an application to the court. This may result in more applications being made to the court to deal with issues in dispute such as education, medical treatment, residence or contact. If the CAA 2006 brings a greater confidence in the court using its new powers to enforce contact we may also see an increase in the number of applications.

The most important underlying principles are the welfare of the child, the no order principle, the principle that prejudice may be caused by delay and the fact that the preservation of a relationship between a parent and a child is recognised as a fundamental aspect of the right to family life under Article 8 of the European Convention on Human Rights. These principles govern the court's consideration of an application for any section 8 order.

CHAPTER 3

Jurisdiction

3.1 INTRODUCTION

Before issuing an application for an order under section 8 of the Children Act 1989 (CA 1989) (a 'section 8 order'), practitioners should ensure that the courts have jurisdiction to entertain the application. They should also ensure that the background to the matter does not give rise to a suspicion that their client has been responsible for a wrongful removal or a wrongful retention of a child within the meaning of Article 3 of the Child Abduction and Custody Act 1985. If an application is issued in such circumstances, the court will be under a specific duty to take steps, including notifying the Child Abduction and Contact Unit at the Department of Constitutional Affairs, that the matter raises potential issues of child abduction. (See *R* v. *R (Residence Order: Child Abduction)* [1995] 2 FLR 625.) This is likely to lead to the client facing an application for the summary return of the child to a foreign jurisdiction.

This chapter deals with the relevant law on jurisdiction which every practitioner needs to consider in cases with an international angle. It also deals with the relevant jurisdictional issues relating to cross-border enforcement of contact orders.

3.2 FAMILY LAW ACT 1986

The court's jurisdiction to hear applications for a section 8 order is governed primarily by Parts I and II of the Family Law Act 1986 (FLA 1986). Part I (and section 1) of the 1986 Act sets out a list of orders to which that Part applies. These include:

- an order made by a court in England and Wales under section 8 of the CA 1989, other than an order varying or discharging such an order (FLA 1986, s.1(1)(a)); and
- an order made by a court in England and Wales in the exercise of the inherent jurisdiction of the High Court with respect to children so far as it gives care of a child to any person or provides for contact with, or the

education of, a child, but excluding an order varying or revoking such an order (FLA 1986 s.1(1)(d)).

From the summary set out above, practitioners will note that there is no restriction on the court's ability to vary or discharge its own orders although their ability to do so might be circumscribed on an application for a stay of proceedings (see below). Practitioners should also note that there is a slight difference in the jurisdictional basis for making orders under section 8 of the CA 1989 and orders under the inherent jurisdiction of the High Court. Save where specified below, references to contact orders include all such private law orders (whether made under CA 1989, s.8 or the inherent jurisdiction) and excludes orders varying or discharging such orders.

3.3 BRUSSELS II REVISED

If the proceedings are ones to which Council Regulation (EC) 2001/2003 (the 'Council Regulation') applies, the courts of England and Wales only have jurisdiction to make an order for contact if they have jurisdiction to do so under the Council Regulation (see FLA 1986, s.2(1)(a) and (3)(a)). This Council Regulation, known informally as 'Brussels II Revised', replaces the earlier Council Regulation (EC) 1947/2000 ('Brussels II'). It came into force on 1 March 2005. Its transitional provisions are not dealt with here. At the time of writing all the European Union members apart from Denmark are signatories to the Council Regulation.

The Council Regulation contains a detailed set of rules for determining whether the courts have jurisdiction to deal with 'matters of parental responsibility over a child', which include contact. The basic rule, contained in Article 8 of the Regulation, is that the courts of the Member State in which a child is habitually resident will have jurisdiction over him. Habitual residence is not defined and is to be determined by the judge in each case. The basic rule is subject to the exceptions set out in Articles 9, 10, 12, 13 and 15 of the Regulation. The following is a summary of the exceptions:

1. Article 9 deals with the situation where a child has moved lawfully from one Member State to another. In such cases, the courts of the Member State of the child's former habitual residence will retain jurisdiction for a limited period of three months following the move for the purposes of modifying a judgment on access rights given before the move took place. Note this only applies where there is a decision in the original Member State where the child was habitually resident and only where the move is lawful.
2. Article 10 relates to cases involving child abduction. In such cases, unless the exceptions specified in Article 10 apply, the courts of the Member

State in which the child was habitually resident before he became the subject of a wrongful removal or retention will retain jurisdiction.

3. Article 12 concerns cases where either (i) the courts of a Member State in which the child is not habitually resident are exercising jurisdiction in relation to proceedings for divorce, nullity or judicial separation, or (ii) the child has a 'substantial connection' with a Member State in which he is not habitually resident. In such cases, those courts can acquire jurisdiction to deal with matters of parental responsibility in limited circumstances which include an acceptance by both parents of their jurisdiction.
4. Article 13 allows jurisdiction to be founded on the basis of the child's presence within a Member State where his habitual residence cannot be established and jurisdiction cannot be determined on the basis of article 12.
5. Article 15 enables the court to transfer the case to another Member State if it considers that a court of another Member State with which the child has a particular connection would be better placed to hear the case and where this is in the best interests of the child. The five situations described where there is a particular connection with another Member State are:

   (a) habitual residence there after the court of origin was seized;
   (b) the other Member State is the former habitual residence of the child;
   (c) it is the place of the child's nationality;
   (d) it is the habitual residence of a holder of parental responsibility;
   (e) the child owns property in the other Member State and the case concerns measures for the protection of the child relating to the administration, conservation or disposal of this property.

The requirement to find that transferring the case would be in the best interests of the child contrasts with the approach adopted by the English courts when dealing with applications under section 5 of the FLA 1986 for a dismissal or stay of proceedings falling outside the scope of the Council Regulation (see below).

Article 14 of the Council Regulation provides that where no court of a Member State has jurisdiction pursuant to articles 8 to 13, jurisdiction shall be determined, in each Member State, by the laws of that state. Only a small minority of cases will fall outside the scope of the Council Regulation. An obvious example would be a case involving a child who is habitually resident in a country that is not a signatory to the Council Regulation, but is physically present within the jurisdiction of England and Wales.

If the proceedings fall outside the scope of the Council Regulation, unless the case is a 'matrimonial' one, in summary the court only has jurisdiction to make an order for contact if on the relevant date (as defined in FLA 1986, s.7(c), the date of the application, or, if no application has been made, the date upon which the court is considering whether to make an order) either:

(a) the child is habitually resident in England and Wales (see FLA 1986, s.3, which, subject to exception, excludes the jurisdiction of the courts where at the relevant date matrimonial proceedings are continuing in the courts of Scotland, Northern Ireland or a specified dependent territory: such cases will arise only very rarely in practice); or
(b) the child is physically present in England and Wales and is not habitually resident in any other part of the United Kingdom or specified dependent territory (see also FLA 1986, s.3); or
(c) the child concerned is present in England and Wales on the relevant date and the court considers that the immediate exercise of its powers is necessary for his protection (see FLA 1986, s.2(3)(b)(ii)). In such circumstances the court has the power to make orders under the inherent jurisdiction, but not under section 8 of the CA 1989. It follows that an application which relied upon this ground as a basis for jurisdiction would need to be made in the High Court.

3.4 MATRIMONIAL PROCEEDINGS

There is a further basis for jurisdiction where the question of making a contact (or other section 8) order arises in or in connection with matrimonial proceedings. In such cases the courts will have jurisdiction if:

(a) the matrimonial proceedings are for divorce or nullity and are continuing (the same test applies to judicial separation proceedings, although jurisdiction is excluded in certain circumstances where after the grant of a decree of judicial separation, proceedings for divorce or nullity have been commenced in Scotland, Northern Ireland or a specified dependent territory; see FLA 1986, s.2A(1)(b), (2) and (3));
(b) the matrimonial proceedings have been dismissed after the beginning of the trial but either (i) the contact order is being made forthwith, or (ii) the application for the order was made on or before the dismissal of the matrimonial proceedings.

Article 3 of the Council Regulation sets out what happens when there are competing jurisdictions for proceedings for divorce, judicial separation or annulment and is relevant for all European Union countries except Denmark. Where there are proceedings relating to parental responsibility relating to the same child and involving the same cause of action in two different Member States, the court second seized will of its own motion stay its proceedings until jurisdiction of the court first seized is established. Where jurisdiction of the court first seized is established, the court second seized will decline jurisdiction in favour of the court first seized.

3.5 DISCRETION OF THE COURT

Where the courts of England and Wales have jurisdiction to deal with contact applications, they may in certain circumstances refuse to do so or grant a stay of proceedings:

- section 5(1) of the FLA 1986 gives the court discretion to refuse to make a contact order where the matter in question has already been determined in proceedings outside England and Wales;
- section 5(2) of the FLA 1986 gives the court discretion to stay proceedings where it appears to the court:
  - that proceedings with respect to the matters to which the application relates are continuing outside England and Wales; or
  - that it would be more appropriate for those matters to be determined in proceedings to be taken outside England and Wales; or
  - that it should exercise its powers under Article 15 of the Council Regulation (transfer to a court better placed to hear the case).

Practitioners should note that a number of first instance judges in those decisions that have been reported to have held that an application under section 5 of the FLA 1986 is not a matter concerning the 'upbringing' of a child and that, therefore, the welfare of the child is not the court's paramount consideration, although it is a very important consideration. See *Re S (Residence Order: Forum Conveniens)* [1995] 1 FLR 314 per Thorpe J, *Re D (Stay of Children Act Proceedings)* [2003] 2 FLR 1159 per Bracewell J and *Re V (Forum Conveniens)* [2005] 1 FLR 718 per Munby J. By contrast, in *H* v. *H (Minors) (Forum Conveniens) (Nos 1 and 2)* [1993] 1 FLR 958, Waite J came to the opposite conclusion.

In such cases, the courts have held that the principles to be applied were those set out in *Spiliada Maritime Corporation* v. *Cansulex Ltd* [1987] AC 460. Although important, the child's habitual residence is not determinative of the issue.

By contrast with this approach, a court considering whether to transfer a case to another Member State under Article 15 of the Council Regulation cannot do so unless satisfied that this would be in the best interests of the child concerned. The wording of the article, however, does not oblige a court to transfer the matter if it reaches such a conclusion: it has a discretion over whether to do so or not. The article makes it clear that such transfers are to be made 'by way of exception'.

3.6 ENFORCEMENT OF CROSS-BORDER CONTACT

Articles 40 and 41 of the Council Regulation (Brussels II Revised) ensure that a judgment in a contact (access) case in one Member State is automatically recognised and enforceable in another Member State, provided that it is accompanied by a certificate in proper form. (See Annex 111 to the Regulation for the certificate.) It must set out the practical arrangements and confirm that the child had the right to be heard at the hearing at which the judgment was given unless it was decided that this was inappropriate due to the age or maturity of the child.

CHAPTER 4

Who can apply for contact?

4.1 INTRODUCTION

This chapter sets out who can apply for contact, including parents, step-parents, grandparents, siblings and civil partners.

4.2 WHO CAN APPLY?

The following are entitled to apply for any section 8 order including a residence or contact order in respect of a child without needing leave from the court:

(a) any parent, guardian or special guardian of the child (CA 1989, s.10(4)(a));
(b) any person in whose favour a residence order is in force with respect to the child (s.10(4)(b));
(c) any person who by virtue of CA 1989, s.4A has parental responsibility for the child; this will include step-parents or civil partners.

The following are entitled to apply for a residence or contact order without needing leave from the court:

(a) any party to a marriage (whether or not subsisting) in relation to whom the child is a child of the family (CA 1989, s.10(5)(a));
(b) any civil partner in a civil partnership (whether or not subsisting) in relation to whom the child is a child of the family;
(c) any person with whom the child has lived for a period of at least three years (s.10(5)(b));
(d) any person who:
   - in any case where a residence order is in force with respect to the child, has the consent of each of the persons in whose favour the order was made; or
   - in any case where the child is in the care of the local authority, has the consent of that authority; or

   – in any other case has the consent of each of those (if any) who have parental responsibility for the child (s.10(5)(c));

(e) any person in whose favour an existing order for contact has already been made.

Practitioners should note that in certain circumstances a person who would not otherwise be entitled to apply for the variation or discharge of an order can make an application if the original order was made on his application or he is named in the order (if it is one for contact). This includes a child's application for indirect contact to be varied to direct contact. However, a child who is named in a contact order for contact with a parent will still need permission under CA 1989, s.10(8). See Chapter 11 for a detailed analysis of applications by a child.

Step-parent

A step-parent is defined as a party to a marriage or civil partnership (whether or not subsisting) where there is a child who is not their biological child. As set out in Chapter 2, step-parents will increasingly obtain and exercise parental responsibility without having to apply for a residence order. Whether they have parental responsibility or not, they can apply for a residence order or contact order in respect of a child who was treated as a child of a family in a civil partnership or a marriage.

Step-parents are allowed to apply to the court for a contact order as of right. A child of the family includes a child of either parties to the marriage or civil partnership, or any other child who was placed with the couple as foster parents by a local authority or voluntary organisation who has been treated by both the parties as a child of their family.

Carer for three years

Any person with whom the child has lived for a period of at least three years is entitled as of right to apply for a residence or contact order. The three years does not necessarily have to be continuous but must have begun in the last five years before the application and not ended more than three months before the date on which the application is made. If more than three months are allowed to elapse, the applicant has to obtain the leave of the court before making such an application.

Applicant with consent

The applicant can apply for a residence or contact order without needing the leave of the court if:

- he has the consent of all those with parental responsibility; or
- if the child is in care, he has the consent of the local authority; or
- if there is a residence order in force, he has the consent of all those in whose favour a residence order is made.

Applicant for a contact order with leave from the court

If an applicant does not fall into any of the categories above and cannot automatically apply for a section 8 order, he can apply to the court for leave to make the application. Leave will be required in the following circumstances:

(a) where an applicant is not automatically entitled to apply for an order;
(b) where a child is subject to a care order;
(c) where an applicant has been prevented from making an application without prior leave under CA 1989, s.91(14) or where leave is required under s.91(15);
(d) where the applicant is a local authority.

Applicants who require leave can include the grandparents and siblings of a child (if they do not fall within the specific categories of people who do not require leave). The fact that the court grants leave for an application to be made does not mean that the application will necessarily succeed.

Where an application for leave to apply for a section 8 order is made, the court has to have particular regard to the following (see CA 1989, s.10(9)):

(a) the nature of the proposed application;
(b) the applicant's connection with the child;
(c) any risk of disruption to the child by the application to such an extent that he would be harmed by it;
(d) if the child is being looked after by a local authority, the authority's plans for the future;
(e) the wishes and feelings of the child's parents.

Child applicant

A child needs permission to apply for a contact order unless he is applying to vary or discharge an order and the order was made on his application (CA 1989, s.10(6)). This includes an application for direct contact where the previous order was for indirect contact only (see 'Application for a contact order with leave from the court' above). When the child needs the permission of the court, the court must be satisfied that he has sufficient understanding to make an application and that in all the circumstances it is appropriate to grant permission. Usually a child applicant should make such an application represented by a litigation friend but he may make the application himself in certain circumstances (see Chapter 11 for details of the requirements which must be met for a child to make an application himself, the judicial approach to such applications and the representation of children generally).

It is likely, particularly given the importance that the European Court of Human Rights has attached to representation for the child (see Chapter 12), that we will see increasing numbers of children being directly represented in applications for contact and residence orders as opposed to their views being conveyed to the court through a CAFCASS officer or other expert.

CHAPTER 5

Shared residence

5.1 BACKGROUND

Recent years have seen significant developments in the court's approach to the concept of shared residence. A shared residence order is one where the children reside for different periods of time with each parent. In some of the authorities shared residence orders have been described (confusingly) as 'joint residence orders'. However, the term 'joint residence order' conventionally refers to the situation in which a child resides with two parties all of the time (such as a parent and step-parent who remain in a relationship) as opposed to a shared residence order by which a child divides his time between two parties.

In 1993, in *Re H (A Minor) Shared Residence* [1994] 1 FLR 717 following the implementation of the Children Act 1989 (CA 1989), the Court of Appeal held that a shared residence order could be made but would rarely be made and would depend on there being exceptional circumstances. That decision was made very much against the background of there being a presumption that the children needed to have one main home whilst recognising that they should have regular contact with the parent with whom they did not live for the majority of the time.

In 1994, 18 months after the *Re H* decision referred to above, the Court of Appeal held that a shared residence order could be made if there were 'unusual' but not necessarily 'exceptional' circumstances and where it was shown that such an order would provide a positive benefit for the child (see *A* v. *A (Minors) Shared Residence Order)* [1994] 1 FLR 669). By 2001, when the Court of Appeal came to decide *D* v. *D (Shared Residence Order)* [2001] 1 FLR 495, it held that where the basic arrangements were settled, the fact that there was a continuing dispute about some of the details did not prevent there being a shared residence order. Butler Sloss P questioned whether it was still necessary to demonstrate a positive benefit to the children as long as the order could be shown to be in a child's interest. This represented a significant step and was followed up in 2003 by a Court of Appeal decision in the case of *Re F (Shared Residence Order)* [2003] 2 FLR 397. In that case the Court of Appeal said that the fact that parents lived some distance from each other did not mean that the children's time during the year could not be divided in such a way as to justify making a shared residence order. The child's time did not have to be shared equally in order to justify making a shared residence order.

This chapter deals with the developments that have taken place over recent years in the law relating to shared residence orders and the inter-relationship between these orders and contact orders.

5.2 WHAT IS SHARED RESIDENCE AND WHAT CAN IT BE?

A shared residence order sets out arrangements whereby children live with each parent for a period of time and treats both parents as having residence (as opposed to one having residence and the other staying contact). This can be sharing of weeks or any arrangement in which the children spend significant time living in the homes of both parents. It no longer has to be an equal sharing of time between parents. As stated above, there can be considerable distance between where each parent lives. It is plain that where parents live near to each other and the children are of school age, shared residence arrangements are more likely to be practical and work well but the judiciary has also recognised that they can be useful in confirming that the parents have an equal authority and competence with regard to arrangements for the children. The case of *A* v. *A (Shared Residence)* [2004] 1 FLR 1195, was particularly fraught and was heard by Wall J. In that case, the parents were not able to work in harmony but the judge decided that a shared residence order was appropriate as it reflected the reality of the children's lives and the fact that the parents were equal in the eyes of the law and had equal duties and responsibilities towards their children. In that instance the judge felt that a shared residence order was not only still appropriate but needed. He was concerned that there was a risk that a sole residence order could be misinterpreted as enabling control by one parent when what was required was cooperation between the parents.

Practitioners tend to approach the issue of shared residence as being most appropriate where couples are able to communicate and be flexible and prioritise the children above their own needs. However, the 2004 case of *A* v. *A* is useful in demonstrating that the judiciary is prepared to take a firm line where children are sharing their time with each parent (by the time the final order was made in this case the children were spending half their time with each parent) and that the ability of the parents to get on with each other is not necessarily going to be determinative. (This case is also useful for setting out, in a schedule at its end, items which relate to the exercise of parental responsibility (see Chapter 2).)

The Court of Appeal has gone further, in *Re R (Residence: Shared Care: Children's Views)* [2006] 1 FLR 491, in emphasising that parents do not need to show an ability to cooperate with each other for a shared residence order to be made. In that case, the children spent time equally with each parent under a shared residence agreement reached following court proceedings. Both parents subsequently sought sole residence orders, with the father seeking shared residence in the alternative. The children strongly favoured a continuation of the shared residence arrangements. The judge took the view that shared residence orders were not usually in the best interests of children and that such orders were not appropriate unless there was an extremely good relationship between the parents. He awarded sole residence to the mother. The Court of Appeal found the judge's approach to shared residence to be unsupportable and stated, in particular, that there was no basis for the conclusion that a harmonious relationship between parents was a prerequisite to a shared residence order. The judge had also paid insufficient regard to the views of the children, then aged 10 and eight years. However, due to the lapse of time of nearly a year prior to the appeal hearing, it was held not to be in the interests of the children for there to be further litigation by ordering a retrial and the father's appeal was dismissed.

Similarly, in *Re W (Children)* (2006) (Lawtel, 26 April 2006), the Court of Appeal held that in a case where there was substantial contact between the children and both parents and where a shared residence order was made, there were bound to be teething troubles, particularly where the parents could not communicate with each other. The Court of Appeal allowed the father's appeal against an order made under CA 1989, s.91(14) that neither he nor the mother were entitled to make any further applications without the court's permission. The Court of Appeal stated that as a matter of policy, a judge should adopt a hands-on approach so that if either party had difficulty with any aspect of the arrangements they could go to the judge for further guidance. This is further evidence of the court's increasing willingness to make and support shared residence orders even where there remains some conflict between the parents.

The increasing number of shared residence orders perhaps reflects the more frequent involvement of both parents in sharing time with and caring for children on a more equal basis.

In *Re P (Children) (Shared Residence Order)* [2006] 1 FCR 309 (also known as *Pengelly* v. *Enright-Redding*), the children's time was divided almost equally between the parents but the judge at first instance refused to make a shared residence order as it might empower the father in a way which would be contrary to the interests of the children. The Court of Appeal allowed the father's appeal and instituted a shared residence order which reflected the reality that the parents had established, to their credit and the advantage of the children.

In *Puxty* v. *Moore* [2006] 1 FCR 28, one of four children had resided primarily with the mother until she relapsed into alcoholism. The mother sought a sole residence order but the court made a joint residence order. The father appealed seeking sole residence. The Court of Appeal accepted that the mother was disruptive but found a shared residence order to be pragmatic to enable the child to enjoy quality time with both the parents and siblings.

5.3 INTERACTION WITH CONTACT ORDERS

Where a shared residence order is made there will be no order for contact but the court will set out the blocks of time that the children should spend with each parent. This will usually mean dividing the weeks and months and school holidays (not necessarily equally) between parents. If parents do not live locally then arrangements such as spending school time with one parent and holidays with the other parent may also come under the umbrella of a shared residence order.

It is important to remember that the no order principle still applies and there are many separated couples who have shared residence arrangements for the children without the court's specific sanction by way of a shared residence order being sought or necessary.

5.4 SAME SEX PARTNERS

Shared residence orders have been used to give a former same sex partner parental responsibility. Even in cases where the parties are not subject to a registered civil partnership the court can make a shared residence order to confer parental responsibility on one of the partners if it is in the interests of the child to do so.

In the case of *Re G (Residence: Same Sex Partner)* [2005] 2 FLR 957, the Court of Appeal granted a joint residence order to the female applicant, W (known as CW in subsequent proceedings) who was the former partner (but not in a civil partnership) of the biological mother, G (known as CG in subsequent proceedings) of two children who had been conceived during the relationship by anonymous donor insemination. The trial judge had not granted joint residence saying that sharing parental responsibility would result in 'endless disputes between the parties which may require the court's intervention to resolve issues of education, accommodation, elective medical procedures and so forth which could not be in the long term interests of these children'. She stated that the important role that the applicant would play in the children's lives would be adequately protected by a defined contact order. This was in contrast to the recommendation of the CAFCASS officer who had stated that without parental responsibility the applicant would be marginalised in the lives of the children. The Court of Appeal referred to the judgment in *A* v. *A* (see above) and said that the parties needed to cooperate and that making a shared residence order would make that clear. In the case of *Re G*, a shared residence order (the applicant not being a civil partner or step-parent) was the only way that the mother's former partner could obtain parental responsibility. The biological mother, G, still provided the primary home for the children within the shared residence agreement.

There is a postscript to this case relevant to enforcement. The biological mother, CG, moved overnight to Cornwall with her new partner, in breach of a specific order that she should not relocate and without informing her former partner, CW. CG applied to have the prohibition lifted and to reduce contact to CW. CW applied to become the children's primary carer with shared residence. The children's guardian, whilst on balance recommending that the children should stay with CG, also stated that the court needed to be confident that any further orders would be complied with. The trial judge preserved the shared residence order but granted primary care to CW giving consideration to the welfare checklist and this decision was upheld by the Court of Appeal (see *Re G (Children) (Residence: Same Sex Partner)* [2006] EWCA Civ 372). Thorpe, LJ stated that where the care of a child was shared in a same sex relationship, the child would not distinguish between one woman and another on the grounds of a biological relationship and neither should the court. The trial judge had felt no confidence in CG promoting the relationship between the children and CW if she remained in Cornwall and so to leave the children with CG would diminish their relationship with CW. Balancing the harm of moving the children now against the risk of future harm to the children in denying them the relationship with CW, she said that welfare dictated a change in the primary carer and the Court of Appeal agreed. However, the biological mother appealed to the House of Lords and their decision (*Re G (Children) (Residence: Same Sex Partner)* [2006] 1 WLR 2305) was to reverse the change in primary care. Lord Nicholls of Birkenhead stated that '. . . A child should not be removed from the primary care of his or her biological parents without compelling reasons.' Baroness Hale of Richmond, in the lead judgment, said that '. . . the fact that CG is the natural mother of these children in every sense of that term, while raising no presumption in her favour, is undoubtedly an important and significant factor in determining what will be best for them now and in the future.' See Chapter 7 for a fuller discussion of change of residence by way of enforcing contact.

5.5 STEP-PARENTS

In *Re H (Shared Residence: Parental Responsibility)* [1995] 2 FLR 883, it was held appropriate to give a step-parent shared residence to avoid a child being confused about the role of his respective parents. However, much will depend on the circumstances of the case. Where a step-parent does not play a particularly significant role, shared residence will not be deemed appropriate by the court, particularly given that now step-parents can obtain parental responsibility by agreement with the other parent (or parents), or by order of the court (see Chapter 2).

5.6 CONDITION ON RESIDENCE ORDERS

In exceptional cases, the court has the power to make orders specifying where a child should live geographically with one parent. In exceptional cases, the court may consider if this is necessary to avoid a parent moving to frustrate the intention of a shared residence order.

5.7 SUMMARY

The courts are now much more willing to consider an order for shared residence. It is not essential that the children should spend an equal amount of time with each parent before such an order can be made. However, what should also be remembered is that parents are often very concerned about the label which is given to the time that they spend with their children and that can be their reason for applying for shared residence. Whether the time a child spends with them is called contact or shared residence will not matter hugely to the child and, indeed, the association of specialist family solicitors, Resolution, has suggested that the description 'parenting time' should be used in place of the term 'contact' to avoid the concern parents often have about the label of the time their children spend with them. This point was also picked up in the Green Paper, *Parental Separation: Children's Needs and Parents' Responsibilities* (see Chapter 1).

Shared residence orders can be a way of enforcing contact and ensuring that the relationship with both parents is maintained.

CHAPTER 6

Domestic abuse

6.1 INTRODUCTION

Where the court makes a finding of fact that there has been abuse of the parent with whom a child lives by the other parent, it is of fundamental importance in the decision by a court whether to order contact.

The current state of the law is still summarised in the case of *Re L (Contact: Domestic Violence), Re V, Re M, Re H* [2000] 2 FLR 334. In that case, the Court of Appeal heard four appeals where applications for direct contact had been refused following findings of fact that there had been domestic abuse of the mothers with care of the various children involved. The Court of Appeal considered the report of the Children Act Sub-committee of the Advisory Board on Family Law on parental contact and domestic violence cases and a joint expert report prepared by two child psychiatrists instructed by the Official Solicitor, Dr J C Sturge and Dr D Glaser. Their report can be found at [2000] Fam Law 615 under the heading *Contact and Domestic Violence: The Expert's Court Report* and practitioners are advised to read both the Court of Appeal case and the report.

The case emphasised the following:

1. Courts need to have heightened awareness of the existence and consequences of children being exposed to domestic abuse.
2. The first stage will be for the court to decide whether the allegations of domestic abuse are really likely to affect the outcome of the case. If they are, then there must be adjudication on those allegations.
3. If, following the fact-finding exercise, the allegations are proved, then there is no automatic bar upon direct contact. However, the court will have to consider whether the person who has committed the domestic abuse can recognise their past conduct and acknowledge that their conduct represented a failure of parenting, both as a failure to protect the child's carer and a failure to protect the child emotionally. The perpetrator of the violence must recognise the need to change.
4. When making an interim order for contact before any findings of fact on the allegations made, the court must ensure the safety of the child and

f the residential parent and weigh up in the balance the seriousness domestic violence, the risks involved and the impact on the child of contact against the positive factors (if any) of contact between the parent alleged to have been violent and the child.

6.2 DEFINITION OF HARM

The court can make a care order or supervision order only if it is satisfied that a child concerned is suffering or likely to suffer significant harm and that the harm or likelihood of harm is attributable to the care being given to the child or likely to be given to them and this not being the care that it would be reasonable to expect a parent to give to him or the child being beyond parental control (see Children Act 1989 (CA 1989), s.31). The Adoption and Children Act 2002 (ACA 2002), s.120, as implemented on 30 December 2005, has expanded the definition of significant harm in CA 1989, s.31(9), to add the words 'including for example impairment suffered from seeing or hearing the ill-treatment of another'. Practitioners should be aware that this amendment may result in an increase in applications for CA 1989, s.37 reports for the local authority to investigate and potentially issue public law proceedings in cases where a child is witnessing domestic abuse.

6.3 APPLICATIONS FOR CONTACT

New forms for the application for contact (see Chapter 8) were introduced in 2005 and require all applicants for contact to mention any allegation of domestic violence to ensure that proper attention is given to any such allegation. It is possible that this will also lead to the courts ordering more reports to be prepared by the local authority (see also above regarding the expansion of the definition of significant harm following the ACA 2002).

6.4 FACT-FINDING HEARINGS

These are used to determine disputed allegations of conduct and are adversarial (see Black J's judgment in *Re A (Contact: Risk of Violence)* [2006] FLR 283). In this case, a fact-finding hearing was listed with directions to be complied with beforehand. These were not complied with and there was considerable delay. The judge summarised what was good practice in such cases and practitioners should bear her comments in mind. She stated the following:

1. Time estimates must be sufficient and include time for the judge's reading, judgment preparation and giving of judgment.
2. It was unacceptable for copious documentation to arrive last minute.
3. Allegations of domestic violence, particularly of the gravity of the allegations in this case (a long history of violence and threats to kill was alleged) had to be proved rigorously. The leading case on the standard of proof where serious allegations are made in cases involving children (amongst others) is *Re H and R (Child Sexual Abuse: Standard of Proof)* [1996] 1 FLR 80, to which practitioners should refer. The principles set out in this case are of general application to all cases in which serious allegations are made against one of the parties.
4. The court expected and required the best possible evidence to be able to make its decision.
5. It was impossible to provide a blueprint for preparation but the lawyers should do whatever was necessary, including reviewing at an early stage what they had to seek to establish or to cast doubt upon and by what means and what evidence they could best do so.
6. Case management by judges did not transfer the responsibility for preparing the case to the judge. It was still up to practitioners to seek specific directions when problems were encountered.
7. If directions were needed the judge should be presented with a precise draft of the order sought.
8. Full statements by the parties would identify what facts were in issue and therefore required proof and which facts were accepted.
9. Schedules of allegations and responses in tabular form (like a pleading) would assist.
10. Where first hand evidence was available in documentary or witness form it should be presented.
11. If a witness was unable to give a statement, hearsay evidence should be recorded in a statement from the applicant rather than drawn out in oral evidence.
12. Attention must be given to the issue of evidence that might be corroborative or alternatively give rise to doubt about important allegations.
13. It was a matter of good practice to consider whether there were police records of domestic violence incidents and whether there might be material police witnesses and also whether there might be medical evidence to corroborate the assertion that a particular assault had taken place and caused injuries.

6.5 DOMESTIC ABUSE AND THE CHILDREN AND ADOPTION ACT 2006

Wonderson chap 4

If the courts use the Children and Adoption Act 2006 to give teeth to current or future orders for contact, inevitably there are going to be some instances where parents who claim to have been victims of domestic abuse will not comply with the contact orders. Some of the remedies contemplated in the Act are unlikely to be effective in cases where domestic abuse has been alleged. However, it is hoped that the court's ability to direct the parties to attend information sessions or meetings with a counsellor or attend parenting programmes may be the remedies that can be used most appropriately in cases such as these. Also, the court has a duty to investigate allegations of domestic abuse so ought to make findings of fact and appropriate orders in cases where it finds that domestic violence has taken place.

CHAPTER 7

Enforcement: current remedies

7.1 INTRODUCTION

This chapter deals with the case law surrounding contact applications where one parent is resolutely against there being any contact with the other parent seeking contact as a result of what is often referred to as 'implacable hostility'. It also deals with the existing remedies for parents making such an application for contact and the extent of the overlap with the Children and Adoption Act 2006 (CAA 2006).

The case law in this area is particularly important in showing the extent to which the courts will currently go to enforce contact orders which have been flouted repeatedly and the views of various members of the judiciary on improvements which could be made to the existing law, some of which have been incorporated into the CAA 2006 and some of which have not. Practitioners and their clients who are making repeated applications to enforce contact orders can often be frustrated by the fact that a parent with whom the children live (conventionally but by no means exclusively the mother) can effectively prevent anything more than minimal contact. Often the court will not be able to use even the current remedies available as these may be incompatible with the overriding obligation to consider the child's welfare. In setting out the remedies in this chapter, we are dealing with the situation where the applicant for contact has demonstrated that the other parent is unreasonably obstructing contact as opposed to the cases where the other parent can demonstrate reasons which satisfy the court that their opposition to contact is justifiable and that in the circumstances of the case no contact order should be made in the interests of the child.

7.2 IMPLACABLE HOSTILITY: THE CASES

There have been five important decisions in the last three years dealing with contact disputes where the proceedings have become extremely protracted. Detailed judgments discussing the power of the court with respect to current remedies available and the appropriateness of these remedies have been handed down. Practitioners experiencing problems in enforcing existing contact orders or who anticipate that there will be such problems are recommended to read these five decisions but they are also summarised below.

Re O (Contact: Withdrawal of Application) [2003] EWHC 3031 (Fam), [2004] 1 FLR 1258

In this case the parents of a 12-year-old boy separated and divorced. Contact took place initially by agreement. When the father subsequently applied for more contact this was ordered by the court. The father then applied to enforce the order. The child was joined as a party to the proceedings. An independent social worker was appointed. At a full hearing, the judge found that the child had divided loyalties and that the mother was not deliberately thwarting contact as had been alleged by the father. Contact was reduced in accordance with the child's wishes and subsequently suspended. At a further hearing the trial judge rejected the father's case that the social worker was unprofessional and biased or that the mother was seeking to alienate the child from the father. The judge ordered indirect contact only. The father appealed this order. The appeal was allowed in part. A direction was made for an expert to assess the child. The expert reported in terms unfavourable to the father's application. The father sought a second opinion and also applied to be released from his undertakings not to go to the child's school or the mother's home. The judge refused this application. The father then applied for leave to withdraw his application for direct contact. He argued that the refusal to release him from his undertakings made it impossible for him to continue with his application. With reluctance, Wall J gave the father permission to withdraw the contact application. He said that each parent had to take their share of responsibility for the state of affairs that they had created. In this case, the father had not accepted in any way that the principal reason why contact had been terminated was because of his conduct towards the boy and the mother, and not because the mother was attempting to alienate the child from him.

The judge also referred to the report *Making Contact Work* produced by the Children Act Sub-Committee (see www.dca.gov.uk/majrepfr.htm) and government response (March 2004, available at www.dca.gov.uk/family/abfla.cascresponse.pdf) (see Chapter 1), but the father could not blame the system where the substantial share of the responsibility for the breakdown in contact lay with him.

The judge did not accept that this case was one of parental alienation by the mother against the father. It was the judge's view that the father was simply attempting to absolve himself of responsibility for the fact that his behaviour had alienated his child so that contact could not progress as originally anticipated.

Re D (Intractable Contact Dispute: Publicity) [2004] EWHC 727 (Fam), [2004] 1 FLR 1226

This was a case where the parents were involved in a contact dispute concerning their seven-year-old child. They had separated in 1998 and the child lived with the mother. Contact had always been difficult. The father had not seen his daughter since December 2001. The mother had continually sabotaged contact arrangements in spite of a number of court orders, penal notices, suspended prison sentences and finally a period of imprisonment. There had been 43 hearings conducted by 16 different judges.

Munby J took the unusual step of handing down part of his judgment in open court so that there could be open and public debate about the problems that had arisen in the case.

The judge found that the court had failed to get to grips with the mother's groundless allegations and her defiance of its orders.

He stated that the all too frequent judicial response to significant problems with contact had been to list the case for further directions, reduce contact in the meantime and obtain experts' reports and direct further evidence. This led to further delay which could rapidly lead to a situation becoming irretrievable.

The judge also stated that it should not be assumed that the conventional domestic approach to enforcement of contact orders met the requirements of the European Convention on Human Rights (see Chapter 12).

The judge also stated that the principles of the Protocol for Judicial Case Management in Public Law Children Act Cases could be applied to all but the simplest or most straightforward private law cases and in particular there should be a consistent judicial approach to case management and strategy. (See the Protocol for Judicial Case Management in Public Law Children Act Cases, June 2003.)

The judgment demonstrates the judge's frustration with the way contact disputes are dealt with and the need for tighter case management of those cases where one parent is being hostile to the other parent, in order to avoid protracted litigation where both parents are likely to become more entrenched and the welfare of the child least well served.

Re S (Contact: Promoting Relationship with Absent Parent) [2004] EWCA Civ 18, [2004] 1 FLR 1279

Parents who were not married separated in 1999 when the child was two years old. The mother and child went to live with the maternal grandparents. Initially, the parents remained on friendly terms. When the relationship deteriorated the mother was granted a without notice injunction. The father had no further contact with the child until attempts at supervised contact were made a year or so later. The father denied all the allegations of domestic violence made against him by the mother. CAFCASS reporters had found the father to be quite aggressive at supervised contact sessions and that it appeared that the child had witnessed an altercation between the father and maternal grandmother.

The father appealed a decision by the recorder hearing the case that there should be no psychological assessment of the child. The recorder found that although the mother was primarily responsible for the failure of contact, there should be indirect contact only. An order was made under CA 1989, s.91(14) preventing the father from making any further application for a year.

The appeal was allowed to the extent of directing the joint instruction of a child and adolescent psychiatrist to assess the family and report on the prospects of contact. The case should then be restored to a district judge for directions and ideally the same judge would then hear the case.

Butler-Sloss, then President of the Family Division, made it clear in her judgment that the mother and father had equal rights before the court and that the courts were not 'anti father and pro mother or vice versa'. She stated that the court should have the greatest flexibility in determining the type and quantity of contact in each case. Specifically she said:

> It has been suggested by parents that there should be a presumption of equality of time spent by the child with each parent. This approach to contact would not be in the best interest of many children whose welfare is the issue before the court. The court is not and should not be tied to a certain number of days which would be automatically ordered to be spent with the absent parent with the child. Children of all ages and circumstances may be the subject of contact orders and one blanket type of order may inhibit the court arriving at the decision which reflects the best interest of each individual child.

She also concluded that no parent was perfect but that 'good enough' parents should have a relationship with their children 'for their own benefit and even more in the best interests of children'. She stated that the court should not abandon its efforts to promote contact between a child and the non-resident parent until 'it is clear that the child will not benefit from continuing the attempt'.

A broad psychological assessment of the family and not just of the child alone was a possible key to reconsideration of future contact and should be explored.

There should only be a CA 1989, s.91(14) restriction on further applications being made by an applicant for contact when there was a serious risk that the child or mother would be subject to unacceptable strain if such an order were not made.

V v. *V* [2004] EWHC 1215 (Fam), [2004] 2 FLR 851

Bracewell J decided this case which concerned two children aged eight years and six years. The children had lived with their mother following the parents' separation. The father had been denied contact and applied for a contact order. The parties subsequently agreed contact, but the mother (with whom the children lived) unilaterally stopped contact on several occasions. She made a series of allegations of sexual, physical and emotional abuse of the children against the father and his relatives. Investigations by the police and social services repeatedly found that the mother's allegations were untrue. The courts continued to make orders for contact and to try to ensure that the contact orders were complied with.

The mother continued to make allegations of mistreatment of the children by their father and his family and repeatedly involved the police, doctors and social services. The father applied for a residence order. The judge found that this was an exceptional case where due to the mother's intransigent attitude, residence should be transferred to the father to enable the children to have a relationship with him.

This was a case where there had been numerous court orders and 16 different judges had been involved. Bracewell J commented on the problems which arose in enforcing contact orders. She referred to the comments made by Munby J in *Re D* (see above). She set out the improvements that needed to be made, which make interesting reading alongside the provisions of the CAA 2006:

1. There needed to be improvements in the court process, including:

   (a) case management from the date of application to the court;
   (b) judicial continuity;
   (c) timetabling to suit the needs of the case;
   (d) proactive orders such as Munby J had envisaged and the attaching of conditions to residence orders (i.e. that the parent with residence must permit contact).

   She commented that such improvements would be dependent upon a change in the role of CAFCASS officers so that in addition to writing reports, which must be timetabled to the needs of the case, the officer could also be present at the initial stages of contact and help with handover arrangements if necessary. There is provision in the CAA 2006 for CAFCASS officers to monitor compliance with contact directions or contact activity conditions and the contact order itself. (See Chapter 1.) The judge believed that such early monitoring in a case would prevent the frustration and animosity between parents that so often arises. She also commented that this approach needed to be combined with well resourced, supervised and specialist contact centres, which are currently too few in number.

2. Bracewell J referred to changes in legislation. At present she stated that there are only four options available to the court, which is unsatisfactory (see below).
3. The judge stated that there should be reforms (requiring legislation), including giving judges and magistrates the powers to refer parties to mediation at any stage of the proceedings. Family assistance orders should be directed to CAFCASS rather than local authorities to make these effective and the time limit of six months should be removed. They should not be limited to exceptional circumstances.This is one of the provisions of the CAA 2006. They must be properly funded.
4. There also needed to be legislation relating to enforcement with a clear commitment by the legislature that the court should have real powers to deal with a defaulting parent. These should include:
   (a) the power to refer such a parent to a variety of resources, including information meetings, meetings with a counsellor, parenting programmes and classes designed to deal with contact;
   (b) the power to refer a parent to a psychiatrist or psychologist;
   (c) the power to refer a non-resident parent who is violent or in breach of an order to an education-for-perpetrators programme;
   (d) the power to place a parent on probation with a condition of treatment or attendance at a given class or programme;
   (e) the power to impose a community service order with programmes specifically designed to address the default in contact;
   (f) the power to award financial compensation from one parent to another, for example, where the cost of a holiday has been lost.

These comments echo the views of many practitioners and professionals who are involved in dealing with contact disputes about the shortcomings in the current system. The extent to which these are addressed by the CAA 2006 is dealt with in Chapter 1 but see below for a summary of the current remedies.

Re M (Intractable Contact Dispute: Court's Positive Duty) [2006] 1 FLR 627

This was a complicated case where two children aged nearly 16 and 13 did not want any form of contact with their mother as a result of an incident 11 years earlier which had taken place when the mother was depressed. They had not seen her for eight years. The father had mispresented the circumstances of the incident to the children and was implacably hostile to contact. There had been previous proceedings. In the light of the welfare officer's report which concluded that the children did not wish to have contact and the father's negative attitude towards any such contact, only indirect contact was ordered. This did not work and the judge ordered no direct contact. The mother applied for a review in 2004, for further expert reports, for a transfer of the proceedings to the High Court and for a guardian to be appointed to act on behalf of the children. The CAFCASS report showed that the children were still very hostile to contact of any sort with their mother. The circuit judge ordered there to be quarterly indirect contact by letters or cards, the father to provide biannual reports to the mother on the children and then dismissed all other applications.

The Court of Appeal allowed the mother's appeal. It directed a transfer to the High Court, made provision for the appointment of an expert and indicated that the High Court should consider the appointment of a guardian to represent the children. The Court of Appeal said that although the children's views would ordinarily carry great weight given their ages, the court also had to look at their understanding and this had been 'corrupted' by the presentation of the position to the children by their father. The Court of Appeal stated that the court should not stand by and take no positive action. The court must do all it could to break the deadlock. Where problems were sufficiently serious in intractable disputes involving implacable hostility, a transfer to the High Court was appropriate. See also the importance of the duties acquired by the state in Articles 6 and 8 of the European Convention (see Chapter 12).

7.3 CURRENT REMEDIES

Send the parent obstructing contact to prison or make a suspended order for imprisonment on the basis of contempt of court

This has been used in a few cases in recent years. An example is *Re S (Contact Dispute: Committal)* [2004] EWCA Civ 1790, [2005] 1 FLR 812, when the Court of Appeal, faced with the complete defiance of a mother who refused to comply with a contact order or even attend the committal hearing, upheld the decision of the judge in the lower court to commit the mother to prison for seven days coupled with an interim residence order in favour of the father.

In the case of *Re A (A Child)* [2002] EWCA Civ 1313, a mother was sentenced to 10 months' imprisonment following her deliberate attempts to frustrate contact including removing the child from the reach of the court and the father to Nigeria and making no effort to comply with any orders for the child's return. The Court of Appeal upheld the sentence.

There are obvious limitations to the option of sentencing an implacably hostile parent to prison. The child may blame the applicant parent for committing his or her carer to prison and the order itself may disrupt the child's life to an unacceptable extent. If a child cannot reside during the prison sentence with the other parent or with another suitable carer, the child will be placed in foster care. This may well not be a satisfactory outcome given the fact that the parent who has been committed to prison may have no fault as a parent other than not complying with the contact order.

The precursor to committing a parent who is frustrating contact to prison is to apply for the attachment of a penal notice to an order for defined contact. In the absence of a penal notice, committal proceedings cannot be brought. A penal notice may work as a 'last warning' to the parent who is in breach of an order but will not necessarily work with the really intractably hostile parent.

Any application for committal must be compliant with the Human Rights Act 1998. See CPR Practice Direction: Committal Application (supplemental to RSC Order 52 (Sched. 1 to CPR) and CCR Order 29 (Sched. 2 to CPR).

It is also worth noting that the Court of Appeal also held in the case of *Re M (Contact Order)* [2005] EWCA Civ 615, [2005] 2 FLR 1006, that a custodial sentence should only be used where justified and it was contrary to principle to impose a custodial sentence where a fine would be appropriate. In this case a father was in breach of a contact order by returning his child to the mother late and had previously broken other orders. The trial judge found that he could not pay a fine so sentenced him to prison for seven days. The Court of Appeal held that the judge should not impose a custodial sentence merely because the father could not pay a fine.

Impose a fine on the parent obstructing contact

This option is rarely used because it is not consistent with the welfare of a child as it will mean depriving the parent with whom they live of funds in a situation where they may already live on a limited budget with which they support the child or children.

Transfer or change residence

This can be done where the implacably hostile parent is seen to be acting against the best interests of a child in frustrating the court orders for contact. An example of when this has been done is *V* v. *V (Contact: Implacable Hostility)* (see above). However, again such an option is not necessarily available to the court because the other parent may not have the facilities or the capacity to care for the child full time.

See Chapter 5 for a discussion of shared residence orders. These are being made in increasing numbers and can be a way of ensuring the relationship with both parents is maintained. In particular, see *Re G (Residence: Same Sex Partner)* [2005] 2 FLR 957. In this case the parents were a lesbian couple and CG was the biological mother. CW was her former partner. The original shared residence order was made by the Court of Appeal to confer parental responsibility on CW and to ensure that CG received a 'clear and strong message' that she could not marginalise CW from the children's lives.

Following CG's unilateral move from Leicester to Cornwall with the children in direct breach of a court order, Bracewell J (upheld by the Court of Appeal) transferred primary care within the shared residence order to CW. She said that she had no confidence that CG would promote the children's essential close relationship with CW and her family without the change in primary care. However, CG's appeal to the House of Lords was allowed *(Re G (Children) (Residence: Same Sex Partner)* [2006] 1 WLR 2305) and primary care was restored to the children's biological mother, CG. Baroness Hale of Richmond stated that the mother had 'behaved very badly' but once she had been located and contact arrangements reinstated she had abided by them. There was no justification for 'changing the children's primary home and schooling while contact was continuing in accordance with the court's order'. She added 'Of course, were the contact itself to be further frustrated, that would be a different matter.'

Discussing possible transfers of residence she confirmed that 'it may well be in the interests of the children to change their living arrangements if one of their parents is frustrating their relationship with the other parent who is able to offer them a good and loving home' but emphasised that such a change was 'unlikely to be in their best interests while that relationship is in fact being maintained in accordance with the court's order.'

Make an order for indirect contact

This may be done as a short-term solution with a view to rebuilding direct contact but as Bracewell J set out in *V* v. *V (Contact: Implacable Hostility)*, following this option gives the public the impression that judges will not deal with implacably hostile parents and may give the impression to implacably hostile parents that they need not fear the wrath of the court if they disobey court orders for contact. However, it may be appropriate in certain cases. Bracewell J referred to the only other option being that of 'giving up'.

Section 37 report

Under the CA 1989, s.37, the court can direct a section 37 report from the local authority to investigate whether a child is at risk of emotional harm due to the behaviour of the implacably hostile parent and to consider whether care proceedings are appropriate.

This was used by Wall J in the case of *Re M (Intractable Contact Dispute: Interim Care Order)* [2003] EWHC 1024 (Fam), [2003] 2 FLR 636. See Chapter 10 for details of this and the circumstances in which Wall J said such a direction could be made. Wall J stated that to use the section 37 procedure, the court must be satisfied that the criteria for invoking this procedure were met and that the action contemplated (which would be that the local authority would remove the children from the residential parent's care for assessment or a change of residence) must be in the children's best interests. There must be a coherent care plan.

Costs orders

Whilst not strictly part of enforcement, the making of a costs order against a parent being unreasonable in contact proceedings may well act as a deterrent.

In the case of *Gojkovic* v. *Gojkovic (No. 2)* [1991] 2 FLR 233, the Court of Appeal reiterated the point that it is 'unusual to order costs in children cases'. In 1994, in the case of *Sutton London Borough Council* v. *Davis (No. 2)* [1995] 1 All ER 65, Wilson J was asked to hear the appeal by a local authority against a costs order made against them as the order was made in proceedings relating to children. Wilson J held that it was not wrong in principle for a costs order to be made against the local authority as, although the proceedings were brought under the CA 1989, they concerned the applicant's fitness to be registered as a child-minder and were distinct from proceedings under the CA 1989 concerning the welfare of children where it would be unusual to order costs.

Wilson J referred to the case of *Gojkovic*. He stated that the proposition that costs orders were unusual in children cases arose from the fact that where there were proceedings regarding a child's future, the 'aspiration is that in their outcome the child is the winner and indeed the only winner. The court does not wish the spectre of an order for costs to discourage those with a proper interest in the child from participating in the debate. Nor does it wish to reduce the chance of their cooperation around the future life of the child by casting one as the successful party entitled to his costs and another as an unsuccessful party obliged to pay them'.

However, Wilson J also stated that this did not apply where 'the conduct of one party has been reprehensible or the party's stance has been beyond the band of what is reasonable'.

In the more recent case of *Re T (A Child)* [2005] 2 FLR 681, the mother had not complied with the contact schedule recommended by professionals and ordered by the court. The court then made a residence order in favour of the father. The case is reported because the Court of Appeal dismissed the mother's appeal against an order for costs made against her and upheld the order that she should pay the costs of the father for three hearings (and the costs hearing itself) where the father said that the mother had made unfounded allegations against him and the judge had made findings of fact in his favour. A costs order in this sort of case is still exceptional but it shows that the court is increasingly willing to penalise the unreasonable parent as long as the unreasonableness is related to the conduct of the litigation.

Wall LJ stated:

> We do not think that the orders for costs which we have upheld in the instant case are further likely to or should deter a resident parent from advancing a reasonable opposition to contact which is genuinely based on a proper perception of the child's interests. But those who unreasonably frustrate contact need to be aware that the court has the power to make costs orders in appropriate cases, and that the consequences of such unreasonable behaviour may well be an order for costs made against the resident parent who has behaved unreasonably.

Practitioners need to be wary of advising their clients that there is little prospect of an order for costs being made against them if they object to contact unless they can demonstrate the reasonableness of such objections.

In addition, practitioners should also be aware that, although rare, costs orders may be made against those in receipt of public funding where they have acted unreasonably in children proceedings: see *EC-L* v. *DM* [2005] [2005] 2 FLR 772.

Family assistance orders

The court can oblige CAFCASS or a local authority officer to advise, assist and (where appropriate) befriend a named person or persons (CA 1989, s.16). The persons named can be a parent or guardian of the child or a person with whom the child is living or in whose favour a contact order is made or the child himself. The court must be satisfied that the circumstances are exceptional and that it has the consent of every person named in the order other than the child. The order can only be made for six months although may be repeated. The CAA 2006 contemplates better use of these in that they will no longer be used in exceptional circumstances only (see Chapter 1). It extends the time limit for their use from six to 12 months. The CAA 2006 also provides that where a contact order is also in force there may be a direction to CAFCASS or a local authority officer to give advice and assistance on contact and to report to the court on whether a CA 1989, s.8 order ought to be varied or discharged.

7.4 SUMMARY

The hope is that the CAA 2006 will give teeth to the court's attempts to bring implacably hostile parents into line where the court finds that there is no justification for their hostility and that it is in the best interests of a child to have contact. However, although relatively tough remedies are now available (for instance, fines, change of residence, committal to prison), the fact that the court has to consider what will be best for the children may nevertheless undermine the tougher remedies envisaged under the CAA 2006.

CHAPTER 8

Procedure

8.1 INTRODUCTION

This chapter deals with the procedural considerations and process involved in contact proceedings. There is no particular focus on either advising or representing those who bring or respond to applications for a contact order. What is provided is an overview of the form that proceedings can generally be expected to take during their course.

The procedural rules are set out primarily in two key statutory instruments, which have been amended over the years:

- Family Proceedings Rules 1991, SI 1991/1247 (FPR 1991); and
- Family Proceedings Courts (Children Act 1989) Rules 1991, SI 1991/1395 (FPC(CA 1989)R 1991).

Unless mention is given to the contrary, the guidance set out in this chapter applies to procedure in both the county court and the Family Proceedings Court (FPC). Although the word 'court' refers to both the county court and the FPC, its reference here includes the proper administrative office in the county court or the justice's clerk in the FPC.

Alternative dispute resolution (ADR) is dealt with at section 8.10.

8.2 PRIOR TO ISSUING PROCEEDINGS

The Family Law Protocol recommends that 'court proceedings should normally only be commenced if all reasonable avenues have been considered and found to be inappropriate or unworkable or if this is the only way to offer the parties the opportunity of a mediated settlement' (para. 3.8.1). For those acting for publicly funded clients, they will have to comply with the relevant aspects of the Funding Code which require mediation to have been attempted before funding for the issue of proceedings will be granted (see Chapter 15).

If the view is taken that proceedings should be issued, some consideration will need to be given as to whether leave to apply is required and as to the most appropriate court in which to issue. Advice should be given to the client on this question.

Leave to apply

The solicitor will need to determine whether or not leave to make an application is necessary. This will depend on who seeks to bring the application. Leave to apply is covered in Chapter 4. As far as procedure and process is concerned, an application for leave to apply for a contact order (and any section 8 order) is as follows:

1. The applicant should make his application on prescribed Form C2 and set out reasons for making the application.
2. The application should be filed with a draft application C1 (the substantive application for a contact order).
3. A sufficient number of copies for service on all respondents will need to be filed.
4. A fee will be payable; the precise amount should be checked on Her Majesty's Court Service website (www.hmcs.gov.uk) as the fees are subject to change.
5. Thereafter, the court may either grant the application for leave or direct that a date for the hearing of that request be fixed.

8.3 THE APPLICATION

An application for a contact order can be made free-standing or within existing family proceedings. The power of the court to make a section 8 order, on the basis of an application for such or of its own volition, is dealt with in CA 1989, s.10(1).

Commencement

If an application is being made for a contact order within existing proceedings, that application will be filed at the court which is hearing the proceedings. So far as a free-standing application for a contact order is concerned, the application can be made in any court; that is a magistrates' court (FPC), county court, or the High Court. Where the application will then fall to be heard and determined will be subject to the principal governing statutory instrument: the Children (Allocation of Proceedings) Order 1991, SI 1991/1677 (C(AP)O 1991).

There are three forms of county court which have standing to hear different CA 1989 applications:

- designated county courts (previously known as divorce centres): subject to some exceptions, if a contact order application is made to a county court, it should be made to a designated county court (C(AP)O 1991, art. 14); however, where the court is notified that the application will be opposed, the application will be transferred for trial to a family hearing centre;
- family hearing centres;
- care centres: these can hear and dispose of all applications under the CA 1989, including public law applications.

The rules dealing with transfer both up and down the court hierarchy are provided in articles 5–13 of C(AP)O 1991 and where a district judge orders the transfer of proceedings down to the FPC an appeal can be made against that order pursuant to C(AP)O 1991. Practitioners should be familiar with the factors which indicate a transfer to a new level of court may be desirable and reference should be made to the relevant articles in C(AP)O 1991 as to these factors when seeking a direction for transfer.

Currently, there is a reported under-use of FPCs and projects are being introduced to seek more effective and appropriate management and allocation of cases between the county courts and FPCs. It is anticipated that there may be a shift in business allocation of cases, seeing further encouragement of use of FPCs. A pertinent factor will be the discrepancy in remuneration structures between the courts for practitioners representing publicly funded clients.

There are various instances when an application should be heard in the High Court. Article 12 of C(AP)O 1991 sets out when this should occur but the article is broad, stating that the county court may transfer proceedings to the High Court where, having regard to the delay principle, it takes the view that the proceedings 'are appropriate for determination in the High Court' and that such determination is in the best interests of the child (C(AP)O 1991, art. 12(1)). Naturally, case law has developed and established precedents for the various circumstances which will mean a case is appropriate to be heard in the High Court. A helpful summary can be found in *Hershman & McFarlane's Children Law and Practice*, Jordan Publishing (looseleaf), Divider B, para. 69.

The court in which a client may choose to issue an application should be considered against the following:

- distance for travel;
- facilities in the court;
- availability of conciliation schemes; and
- listing and waiting times.

In the case of publicly funded clients, the solicitor will need to check the client's certificate of public funding. The LSC may have entered a restriction that proceedings should only be commenced in the FPC. To issue in the county court in non-compliance with the condition would be a clear breach of the obligation to act within the scope of the certificate and is likely to result in some form of penalty.

Application forms

An application for a contact order is made on the prescribed Form C1 (see Appendix 3). It should be lodged at court with payment of the appropriate fee. The wording that is used on the forms and any other accompanying documents should consist of factual and non-emotive language (see Family Law Protocol, para. 3.9.1). The form should state the order that is sought and solicitors should consider whether a parenting plan or draft minute of order should be supplied to indicate clearly to the court what order the client is hoping to secure. In such circumstances, the solicitor should make the client aware that the court will make the order it deems appropriate notwithstanding any proposed wording that is submitted on the client's behalf.

Where a party has good reason for not wishing disclosure of his or her address or that of the child, FPR 1991, r.10.21 states that Form C8 should be supplied which requires the addresses to be provided to the court. The form indicates that save for an order by the court saying otherwise, the address will not be disclosed to any other person.

Form C1A (see Appendix 3) is a relatively new tool which has been introduced by HMCS and is known as a 'gateway form'. The objective is for the court to be able readily to identify issues of domestic abuse. It may be the case that the solicitor will have to spend some time with the client to ensure that he or she understands the 'harm' which is relevant to the question of domestic abuse since the word now includes the seeing or hearing of the ill-treatment of others. The new form was launched pursuant to FPR 1991, r.4.4(1A)(iii) and a corresponding question has been inserted into Form C1. The applicant must tick a 'yes/no' answer to question 7 on Form C1 and where that answer is 'yes', Form C1A must be completed and supplied as part of the issue stage. Form C1A is not intended to be an opportunity to adduce evidence; it should be completed succinctly and unemotively in order to appraise the court of issues of domestic abuse. The Department of Constitutional Affairs has commissioned an evaluation of the introduction of the C1A (Gateway) Form in child contact proceedings for two years. The research will be conducted by the Centre for the Study of Safety and Wellbeing (SWELL) based at the University of Warwick.

Where an application is being made within existing proceedings, the correct application form is Form C2 (application for an order within proceedings). The rules relating to Form C1 as to domestic abuse will apply to Form C2 and likewise the supplemental information Form C1A will need to be filed where question 4 is answered in the affirmative.

Without notice applications (ex parte)

It is rare that an application for a contact order will need to be made on a without notice basis but the rules do not discriminate between the different section 8 applications where without notice applications are concerned. Where such an application is made in the FPC, leave of the justices' clerk is required. The application should be filed at the time of making the application; the substantive nature of the application will be the same as described above. Where the application is made by telephone, the application must be filed in accordance with FPR 1991, r.4.4(4)(i)(a), that is within 24 hours after the making of the application. Service upon the respondents of the without notice application should be made within 48 hours after the making of any order.

Where a without notice application is made in the FPC, the FPC(CA 1989)R 1991 are, unlike the FPR, silent as to telephone applications. Given that leave from the justices' clerk is required and that he or she is able to direct when the application should be filed, practitioners can seek to make applications by telephone.

Service

The application should be served on all respondents and any other persons to whom notice should be given. Service is effected by serving each respondent (at least 14 days before the date of the hearing or directions date) with:

- a copy of the application, which will include Form C1A if filed as part of the application;
- notice of proceedings forms provided by the court in Form C6 (notice to parties);
- a blank Form C1A in the event that the respondent may wish to raise allegations of harm (provided by the court with the endorsed application); and
- blank Form C7 (Acknowledgement) (provided by the court with the endorsed application).

Service on other persons to whom notice should be given is effected by serving notice of proceedings (Form C6, notice to non-parties) at least 14 days before the date of the hearing or directions date.

The other persons who will require notice of the application are described in FPC(CA 1989)R 1991, Sched.2, col.(iv) and FPR 1991, App.3, col.(iv). These are:

- any local authority providing accommodation for the child;
- persons caring for the child at the time when proceedings commenced;
- the person providing refuge to the child (if it is alleged that the child is staying in a refuge which is certified under CA 1989, s.51(1) or (2));

- every person the applicant believes to be named in a court order with respect to the child which continues to have effect save for where the applicant believes the court order is not relevant to the present application;
- every person the applicant believes to be a party to pending proceedings in respect of the child save for where the applicant believes the pending proceedings are not relevant to the present application; and
- every person the applicant believes the child has lived with for at least three years prior to the application.

It is useful to note that both sets of procedural rules impose obligations for parties to comply with time limits in relation to any direction. Waiver of service or extension of time can be granted by the court as it sees fit and an application for the same must be made in the form of a request for directions under the rules. Once service is effected the serving solicitor is required to file at or before any first directions date or hearing Form C9 (Statement of Service) detailing the manner, date, time and place of service upon each respondent and notice of proceedings on persons to whom notice should be given. The rules of service, including method of service, are given in FPR 1991, r.4.8 and FPC(CA 1989)R 1991, r.8. Attention should also be given to the guidance published by Resolution (formerly the Solicitors Family Law Association) in September 1994 (see [1995] Fam. Law 206) and now consolidated in the organisation's *Guides to Good Practice* (Spring 2006). In summary, it states the following:

1. In general, service (whether personally or via solicitor) should be effected as soon after issue as possible. Tactical delay of service is considered bad practice.
2. Where serving personally on an unrepresented party, he or she should be written to (mindful of tone and balance of the letter) with:

   (a) advice as to entitlement to and benefit of seeking legal advice;
   (b) a list of the documents being served;
   (c) a statement of any urgency regarding the matter; and
   (d) reiterating any contempt warning from the court order if applicable.

3. The recipient's solicitor should be written to in order to advise of the intention to commence proceedings/that proceedings have commenced and to ascertain whether the solicitor can accept service.
4. Where the solicitor does not have instructions to accept service, enquiries should be made as to how best to serve their client as inoffensively and sensitively as possible, maybe with the assistance of the recipient's solicitor or by arranging a time and place for service (including the possibility of the recipient attending his or her solicitor's office for that purpose).
5. Once personal service is effected it is helpful to send to a solicitor known to be acting (but not accepting service) copies of the documents served or just the vital documents if bulky.

6. Caution should be exercised when using process servers or agents to serve papers in the family law context.
7. Unless otherwise impossible, service should not take place during contact or where children are present.

The suggestions in this guidance are not obligatory and will not be applicable in every instance, although practitioners should have these considerations in mind and follow the guidance where it is proper to do so.

8.4 RESPONDING TO AN APPLICATION

Those who are automatic respondents will need to respond to the application. Each must file and serve on the parties an acknowledgement (Form C7) and Form C1A where applicable within 14 days of service of the application.

Notwithstanding the requirement to acknowledge the application, there may be instances where the respondent wishes to cease being a party. A request will need to be made on Form C2. The court will order a hearing date to be fixed for consideration of the request or invite parties to make written representations as to whether the request should be granted.

In the case of joinder where a person who is not automatically a respondent wishes to be made a respondent, he or she will make an application similar to that stated above. Where such an application is made it will be considered in the same way as where a party requests to cease being a party, with the exception that the request may be granted without a hearing or representations being made where the court sees fit. The court must grant the request of any person with parental responsibility seeking to join the proceedings under the rules governing joinder (FPR 1991, r.4.7(2)(a) and FPC(CA 1989)R 1991, r.4.7(2)(a)).

8.5 DIRECTIONS

The directions date or notice of hearing will have been fixed as part of the court's processing of the application and the applicant will be notified of this on Form C6. The rules specify (non-exhaustive) directions which may be given. These will vary and will correspond to the local court scheme in operation. Service of this form and any Form C1A (where applicable) is discussed above. An application for directions (detailing the directions sought) can be made on Form C2 which must be filed and served on the other parties. Alternatively, directions can be sought following agreement and the consent of the other parties. The request should be made on Form C2 and be signed by the parties or their representatives before filing with the court. The court will then either grant the request or list the matter for a hearing giving not less than two days' notice to the parties of the date fixed. Where a matter is urgent, the request for directions can be made (with leave of the court) orally, or without notice to the parties, or both. Where an application for directions (not agreed between the parties) is sought and not made on an urgent basis, the court will fix a date for the hearing of the request and give not less than two days' notice to the parties of the date fixed. Notice is provided on Form C6.

The court has discretion to give directions of its own motion. Where this is being considered by the court, notice must be given to the parties of that intention in addition to the opportunity to attend and be heard or to supply written representations. All parties must attend any directions hearings unless the court has directed otherwise. The court can proceed, irrespective of non-attendance of the parties, if convinced that the parties had reasonable notice of the hearing or that the circumstances of the case justify proceeding in their absence. The no delay and welfare principles (see Chapter 2) will be of significant influence to the court when considering whether to continue in the absence of a party.

8.6 PRINCIPAL REGISTRY OF THE FAMILY DIVISION: CONCILIATION

District Judge Philip Waller's *District Judge's Direction: Children: Conciliation* [2004] 1 FLR 974 was made on 12 March 2004 and refers to the scheme in operation at the Principal Registry of the Family Division of the High Court (PRFD) in London (the original scheme under Practice Direction: Conciliation: Children (18 October 1991) [1992] 1 FLR 228 no longer applies). The direction applies to all applications for CA 1989, s.8 orders, as well as applications to vary or discharge these. The direction states that these applications will be listed in the conciliation list as soon as they are issued. The conciliation appointments operated at the PRFD are not strictly mediation sessions but have been described as 'mediation with boots on' ([2005] Fam Law 496).

The features of the scheme insofar as contact issues are concerned, are as follows:

1. The court seeks to operate five conciliation lists (two on Monday and Tuesday and one on Wednesday).
2. A district judge attends to matters on the list accompanied by a CAFCASS officer who sits alongside the district judge.
3. Both parties and their legal representatives should attend and sit alongside each other.
4. At the appointment:

    (a) the nature of the application will be set out;
    (b) matters in dispute will be outlined;

(c) the appointment will continue in an attempt for the parties to reach an agreement;
(d) discussion outside the courtroom will be facilitated if appropriate to secure an agreement;
(e) the child (to whom the proceedings relate) if aged nine or over must be brought to the appointment by the parent with whom the child resides and is to be seen by the CAFCASS officer; the child is seen outside the courtroom by the CAFCASS officer, who then reports back to the district judge and the parties; the exception to this is if a district judge has made a direction to excuse attendance of the child;
(f) where the above applies, any younger child to whom the application relates may also attend;
(g) if agreement is reached the judge will make orders as appropriate;
(h) where an agreement is reached in part, the aspects remaining in dispute could be dealt with, if thought appropriate, at a further conciliation appointment that the court would offer; and
(i) if agreement is not reached to dispose of the application, the judge will give directions accordingly, to include timetabling with a view to an early hearing and disposal of the application.

5. A matter can be excluded or removed from the conciliation list and listed in another way if a district judge directs this. Such applications should be made to the district judge of the day. An opposed application will be listed in the normal way. An application to by-pass conciliation might be made where one party lives abroad.
6. Conciliation is deemed legally privileged, therefore all discussions will be privileged and will not be disclosed at any subsequent hearing, save for any further conciliation appointment, neither will they be disclosed upon any later application. To ensure effectiveness, the district judge and CAFCASS officer will not be involved in any further application or proceedings between the parties, other than subsequent conciliation appointments or similarly privileged hearings.
7. Urgent applications made without notice are not affected by the conciliation scheme and will continue to be heard by the district judge of the day. At that hearing, it will consider whether or not any further hearing should be listed within the conciliation list.

8.7 EVIDENCE AND WITNESSES

Solicitors should note FPR 1991, r.4.17 and FPC(CA 1989)R 1991, r.17 which govern when evidence should be filed and state that no party should file or serve any document unless either done in compliance and pursuant to the rules or otherwise with leave of the court.

The rules also stipulate that no statement should be filed until the court directs. When statements are required to be filed, the solicitor should assist the client in the drafting to ensure that inflammatory and emotive language is avoided. Where a solicitor is acting it is commonplace for the statement to be drafted accurately from clients' instructions and as close to their own use of language as possible. This will then need to be read very carefully by the client and instructions taken as to amendments required. The statement of the client applicant or respondent will form the basis of their evidence in chief at the final hearing and they will be cross-examined on it.

Witness statements are required to be drafted in a certain way in family proceedings. These details are contained in the rules. The statements and any other evidence that is relied on should be filed (as directed) and served on all the other parties and the CAFCASS officer or children's guardian. In the absence of filing evidence as directed, a party can only rely on evidence (not filed) with leave of the court. A document which has been filed or served can only be amended with leave of the court. The rules deal with requests of this nature and also state that a supplementary statement can be filed and served. There is no requirement to obtain leave of the court to do this but it can only be done subject to any timetabling directions as to the filing of statements.

The Children Act Advisory Committee's *Handbook of Best Practice in Children Act Cases* (1997) states that 'to prevent unnecessary delay at the first directions appointment, prepare at least draft statements by: (a) the applicant, and (b) any witnesses who it is known will have to give evidence' (para. 41).

Aside from evidence that is filed by the parties, expert evidence can also be ordered in contact cases. Expert evidence is dealt with in Chapter 9. Where any order is made in proceedings which requires the evidence of an expert (joint or otherwise), that order should specify that once the expert has been identified, the letter of instruction to the expert should be filed at court. Evidence or information from the Home Office can be obtained within proceedings by following the guidance in the Protocol from the President's Office (Communicating with the Home Office). This relates to immigration queries which parties or the court require to be clarified and is more often needed in public law cases.

8.8 HEARINGS

Following the submission of evidence in accordance with any directions, the bundle of documents for the hearing should be agreed between the parties if possible and prepared in accordance with the *Practice Direction Family Proceedings: Court Bundles* [2000] 1 FLR 536 (Universal Practice to be applied in all courts other than the family proceedings court) 27 July 2006 (in force 2 October 2006). Reference should also be made to the Practice Note of Wall J provided in *B* v. *B (Court Bundles: Video Evidence) (Note)* [1994] 1 FLR 323.

Pre-hearing reviews are not usually necessary for private law cases in the FPC. They may be necessary where issues are complex or the case is listed for more than one day.

Usually a final hearing date will have been listed at the initial stage of timetabling. Some contact cases are listed to be heard as split hearings. In such cases, the hearing will consist of a finding of fact hearing at which the evidence will be tested so the judge can make findings. Thereafter, a further hearing will be listed for final disposal of the matter and consideration by the judge of the findings which will influence how the matter is disposed of, whether an order is made and in what form.

Finding of fact hearings are more common in contact cases which have allegations of domestic abuse that will impact on the substantive issues of contact.

8.9 APPEALS

When considering the matter of appeals, the solicitor will have to make a judgment as to whether the matter should be appealed (to be decided by a higher court) or should be reviewed by the court that made the decision complained of.

In the FPC, the magistrates do not have powers to order a rehearing and the proper course of action will be to lodge a notice of appeal to the High Court. The relevant procedural rule for appeals is FPR 1991, r.4.22. Where the order was made in the county court by a district judge, an appeal will lie to a judge of the same court but consideration will need to be given to permission for appeal and whether or not a review or rehearing will be the more appropriate action. An appeal from the High Court lies to the Court of Appeal. A practitioners' text should be consulted for more detail on appeals in family proceedings.

8.10 MEDIATION

Mediation in the context of family disputes has long been recognised and used. It is recommended as a method of dealing with the sensitive area of family law work. In relation to child contact proceedings, there is no compulsion on mediation to be explored either prior to or as part of the proceedings. There is much discussion and comment as to alterative dispute resolution (ADR), early resolution and the promotion of both within proceedings. The prominence given to ADR has fallen short of mandatory mediation and commentators have argued that a compulsory form of mediation is not desirable. Where a client is agreeable to mediation, on any referral to a mediator and especially where solicitors are providing mediation themselves, regard should be had to Principle 22.04 of the *Guide to the Professional Conduct of Solicitors* and Annex 22B to the Guide, the Law Society's Code of Practice for Family Mediation: Practice Information.

Where publicly funded cases are concerned, mediation must be considered by the solicitor and this is expanded upon in Chapter 15. Currently, the closest that the courts come in relation to mediation are the schemes detailed in the following sections which discuss conciliation and early resolution schemes.

8.11 FAMILY RESOLUTIONS PILOT PROJECT

In September 2004, the Department for Education and Skills (DfES) launched a pilot scheme: the Family Resolutions Pilot Project (FRPP). The scheme ran at three FPCs: the Inner London and City FPC, Brighton and Sunderland. The aim of the FRPP was 'to assist parties who have been referred by the court to which they have applied to reach agreement in resolving their differences about contact with children following separation or divorce' (*Information for Parents and Families* leaflet). Under the scheme, where an application was lodged, the first stage was to identify the presence of any domestic abuse or other issues making the application unsuitable for the project. Then the parties would be invited to participate in the FRPP and the usual expectation was that parents would take part although the scheme itself was not compulsory.

The FRPP worked in the following way:

1. Stage 1 would commence within two weeks of the application being lodged at court. The parents were invited to a parents session and to view a video about difficult contact situations. Part of the focus was to illustrate the harm and distress caused to children who are at the heart of contact disputes.
2. Parents then attended a facilitation session to discuss the video and understand some of the issues through role-play.
3. Stage 2 involved another group session where parents discussed what they learnt from the first facilitation session. Some guidance and teaching was offered on the skills of compromise, negotiation and responding in different ways than those which might otherwise come naturally in disputes. Guidance was also provided to assist in improving cooperation skills and help parents make arrangements for the children whilst keeping their own issues separate and at arm's length.
4. Parents were invited to participate in the above two sessions separately.
5. Stage 3: the parents would attend a joint meeting with a CAFCASS officer and hopefully agree a parenting plan.

At any point a parent had the choice to withdraw from the FRPP and would also do the same if they jointly wished to agree their own plan without any further participation in the project.

The DfES published its evaluation report (see www.dfes.gov.uk/research/data/uploadfiles/RR720.pdf) in March 2006. Prior to this it was reported ([2006] Fam. Law 65) that solicitors were somewhat dubious about the scheme. Publicly-funded clients would already have been referred to mediation in order to obtain funding for a court application, and as mediation had not worked or else had been deemed unsuitable, there was some confusion as to whether the FRPP was merely a different name for something that had previously not worked for their clients. The DfES evaluation itself reports on the project's problems, its low uptake and limited success. Certainly, as suggested by the report, if the project is to continue in some form, it may be as one of the contact activities available to parents involved in contact disputes (see Chapter 1 for 'contact activities' which were created by the CAA 2006).

8.12 PRIVATE LAW PROGRAMME

The then President of the Family Division, Butler-Sloss P, launched the Private Law Programme (PLP) on 9 November 2004. The intention was for the PLP to form the basis of best practice in such cases and provide a framework for local schemes to be created. Although the FRPP (see above) was being piloted in three FPCs in England, the PLP was intended to allow that scheme and others being run in different courts to be incorporated or developed in creating family dispute resolution mechanisms. The PLP operates on three main levels which are described here in brief. The full guidance is reproduced at www.dca.gov.uk/family/plpguide.pdf

First Hearing Dispute Resolution Appointment (FHDRA)

The FHDRA aims, by exercising effective court control and management, to identify:

- any immediate safety issues;
- the aims of the proceedings;
- timescales within which each aim will be realised;
- what the issues are;
- any opportunities for resolution of any of the issues by referrals for support and assistance; and
- any further steps that may be taken or required.

The FHDRA should be listed within four to six weeks and where possible should be attended by a CAFCASS practitioner, whose primary aim will be to facilitate early dispute resolution rather than necessarily produce a formal report. This aspect of reduced report writing has now been suggested by CAFCASS itself in its recent consultation document (see N Arnold, 'Everyday Matters at CAFCASS' [2005] Fam. Law 971). Unless an immediate agreement is likely to be reached which simply requires some facilitation or there are exceptional circumstances, there should be a direction that the family be referred for support or assistance to a FRPP or other locally available resolution services.

Effective court control

This involves active and continuous case management. Of specific mention is judicial availability and continuity, effective listing schemes in each court to ensure access for review and/or enforcement, avoidance of unnecessary delay, guidance for transfer of cases between different levels of family court to make productive use of court resources, identifying the aim of each hearing and achieving that aim, monitoring and reviewing outcomes, enforcing court orders and controlling the use and costs of court resources.

Flexible facilitation and referral

Best interests decisions and agreements will be facilitated by the use of:

- Parenting Plans (newly revised: available through the DfES at www.orderprocessor.co.uk);
- a CAFCASS practitioner to supervise or facilitate orders as well as arrangements that may be vital to make orders or agreements actually work;
- rehabilitative training, therapy and treatment;
- enforcement powers (see Chapter 7); and
- directions that require parties and others involved to report on progress; this will allow the court to respond where necessary by way of urgent review to safeguard the welfare of the child.

8.13 COLLABORATIVE LAW

The concept is relatively new in the United Kingdom and originates from the USA and Canada. There is some resemblance to mediation but whereas mediation does not usually involve lawyers, the collaborative law process seeks to involve both parties and their advisers working together to reach a settlement. Where meetings are held with a view to working though issues and towards settlement, the parties and their legal representatives attend and the parties can be advised constantly through the process.

The process usually commences with an agreement signed by the parties stating that they will not retain their respective collaborative lawyers if the process breaks down and the matter is taken to court. Those respective firms will not be allowed to be instructed if proceedings commence and the parties would need to instruct new solicitors. The idea is to reaffirm at the outset that the process is a collaborative one (four-ways) between the two parties and their lawyers. Mediation of itself is not excluded from the process as the parties and their lawyers could agree to introduce any professional into the process if it is agreed that this would be useful. However, the lawyers would also be involved in those meetings unless otherwise agreed.

8.14 DISCLOSURE

The concepts of confidentiality and privacy are ingrained in children proceedings (*Scott* v. *Scott* [1913] AC 417). The jurisprudence of this area, however, is difficult. The statutory basis is provided in CA 1989, s.97(2):

> No person shall publish to the public at large or any section of the public any material which is intended, or likely, to identify:
>
> (a) any child as being involved in any proceedings before the High Court, a County Court or a magistrates' court in which any power under this Act or the Adoption and Children Act 2002 may be exercised by the court with respect to that or any other child; or
> (b) an address or school as being that of a child involved in any such proceedings.

A person who acts contrary to the above will be guilty of an offence (CA 1989, s.97(6)) and liable on summary conviction to a fine which will not exceed level 4 on the standard scale. A defence can be argued under CA 1989, s.97(3) that the accused did not know and had no reason to suspect that the material published was intended or likely to identify the child. Where the rule becomes slightly opaque is consideration of the definition of 'publish'. The section only provides that 'publish' includes inclusion in a programme service (as per the Broadcasting Act 1990) or 'cause to be published'. The statute does not go very far to assist as to what else might constitute publish nor indeed actions which will not fall foul of the offence. A similar offence for contempt of court is provided by section 12(1)(a) of the Administration of Justice Act 1960 (AJA 1960), which relates to proceedings in the county court and High Court. The provision states that 'the publication of information relating to proceedings before any Court sitting in private shall not of itself be a contempt of court except in the following cases, that is to say . . . are brought under the Children Act 1989' (AJA 1960, s.12(1)(a)(ii)). A cursory glance at the two provisions outlined would give the impression that both provisions are similar.

Disclosure is also the subject of the FPR.These were amended and the previous rule 4.23 has now been omitted and a new rule 10.20A provided which includes a table setting out circumstances when information and documents can be disclosed, to whom and for what purpose.

In *Re B (A Child) (Disclosure)* [2004] EWHC 411 (Fam), [2004] 2 FLR 142, Munby J warns of the 'inherent difficulties' of attempting to summarise the law in this area. He does go on to provide a helpful whistle-stop guide. He states that the definition of publication will be the same as that of the law of defamation and thus most forms of communications will be caught as being publications. The exception will be a 'communication of information by someone to a professional, each acting in furtherance of the protection of children' (*Re B* at para. 82(iii) which affirmed an aspect of the judgment in *Re M (Disclosure: Children and Family Reporter)* [2002] EWCA Civ 1199 and [2002] 2 FLR 893). As far as disclosure of information from contact proceedings are concerned, AJA 1960, s.12 has been held not to prohibit publication of, amongst other aspects (*Re B (A Child) (Disclosure)* [2004] EWHC 411 (Fam), [2004] 2 FLR 142, at para. 82(v), per Munby J):

- the fact that a child is the subject of proceedings;
- the name, address or photograph of such a child or the parties;
- details of time, location and date of any hearing either in the past or future;
- the nature of the dispute in the proceedings; and
- the text or summary of the whole or part of any order made.

Despite this interpretation of the section, anything published which is intended to likely to identify a child as being involved in proceedings under the CA 1989 is prohibited by section 97(2). If the word 'publish' in this section is ascribed the same meaning as given to the word in AJA 1960, s.12, then virtually any dissemination of information which allows identification of the child in contact proceedings will be caught. It seems, then, that the CA 1989 provision will override that of the AJA 1960.

Practitioners must exercise caution in this regard, for example, where writing a letter on behalf of a client to his employers explaining that he will not be at work on a particular day as he is attending a hearing relating to an application for contact. This will potentially fall foul of the section if 'publish' is taken to have the same meaning as in AJA 1960, s.12. Nothing in such a letter should identify that the child has been involved in CA 1989 proceedings. Practitioners must also note that the definition of publication is a wide one and will include oral communications. It may be the case that these questions will be the subject of litigatation and case law will furnish greater clarification but until then assiduous consideration and scrutiny of any documents and communications is advised before disclosure of information relating to the child or the proceedings is made.

8.15 MCKENZIE FRIENDS

Rights of audience and to conduct litigation are governed by the Courts and Legal Services Act 1990, ss.27 and 28. The court has discretion to grant unqualified individuals such rights in exceptional circumstances only. In private law children proceedings, an unrepresented party may, with the leave of the court, rely on the assistance of a McKenzie friend (*McKenzie* v. *McKenzie* [1970] 3 All ER 1034).

Role of a McKenzie friend

A McKenzie friend may:

- provide moral support for the litigant;
- take notes;
- help with case papers;
- quietly give advice on:
  - points of law or procedure;
  - issues that the litigant may wish to raise in court;
  - questions the litigant may wish to ask witnesses.

A McKenzie friend may not:

- act on behalf of the litigant in person;
- address the court (the role of an advocate with rights of audience);
- examine any witness (the role of an advocate with rights of audience);
- attend a closed court unless the litigant has received permission from the court for the McKenzie friend to do so at the start of the hearing;
- act as the agent of the litigant in relation to the proceedings;
- manage the litigant's case outside court (e.g. by signing court documents).

Appointment of a McKenzie friend

Guidance from the President of the Family Division ([2005] Fam. Law 405) regarding the role of a McKenzie friend confirms that there is a strong presumption that an unrepresented litigant has the right to have reasonable assistance from a McKenzie friend. A litigant in person who intends to exercise this right should inform the court at the outset of the hearing and indicate who his McKenzie friend will be. Where the court forms the view that the assistance of the McKenzie friend has impeded or will impede the efficient administration of justice it should, before refusing to allow a McKenzie friend to act or continue to act, consider whether a firm and unequivocal warning to the litigant and/or the McKenzie friend might suffice instead of a refusal.

In the conjoined appeals to the Court of Appeal in *Re O (Children) (Representation: McKenzie Friend)*; *Re W-R (Child) (Representation: McKenzie Friend)*; *Re W (Children) (Representation: McKenzie Friend)* [2005] 2 FLR 967 the Court accepted that Article 6 of the European Convention on Human Rights (the right to a fair trial) is engaged in any application by a litigant in person for the assistance of the McKenzie friend and held that:

- the presumption in favour of the litigant being allowed the assistance of a McKenzie friend is a strong one;
- such a request should not be refused without good reason, even where the proceedings relate to a child and are being heard in private.

The Court of Appeal made the following points regarding the manner in which applications for the appointment of a McKenzie friend should be treated:

1. The purpose of allowing a litigant in person the assistance of a McKenzie friend is to further the interests of justice by achieving a level playing field and ensuring a fair hearing. The presumption in favour of allowing a litigant in person the assistance of a McKenzie friend is very strong, and such a request should only be refused for compelling reasons. In the event that a judge identifies such reasons, he must explain them carefully and fully to both the litigant in person and the would-be McKenzie friend.
2. Where a litigant in person wishes to have the assistance of a McKenzie friend in private law children proceedings, the sooner that intention is made known to the court and the sooner the court's agreement to the use of a particular McKenzie friend is obtained, the better. In the same way that judicial continuity is important, the McKenzie friend will be most useful to the litigant in person and to the court if he is in a position to advise the litigant throughout.
3. It is not good practice to exclude the proposed McKenzie friend from the courtroom or chambers whilst the application by the litigant in person for his assistance is being made. The litigant who needs the assistance of a McKenzie friend is likely to need that assistance to make the application for the appointment in the first place. It is also helpful for the proposed McKenzie friend to be present so that any concerns about him can be ventilated in his presence and so that the judge can be satisfied that the McKenzie friend fully understands his role (and in particular the fact that disclosure of confidential court documents is made to him for

the purpose of the proceedings only) and that the McKenzie friend will abide by the court's procedural rules.

4. It will always be helpful for the court if the proposed McKenzie friend can produce either a short curriculum vitae or a statement about himself, confirming that he has no personal interest in the case, and that he understands both the role of the McKenzie friend and the court's rules as to confidentiality.
5. The following do not constitute compelling reasons for the refusal of an application:
   (a) that the litigant in person appears to the judge to be of sufficient intelligence to be able to conduct the case on his own without the assistance of a McKenzie friend;
   (b) the fact that the litigant appears to the judge to have a sufficient mastery of the facts of the case and of the documentation to enable him to conduct the case on his own without the assistance of a McKenzie friend;
   (c) the fact that the hearing at which the litigant in person seeks the assistance of a McKenzie friend is a directions appointment, or a case management appointment;
   (d) the fact that the proceedings are confidential and that the court papers contain sensitive information relating to the family's affairs.

Disclosure to a McKenzie friend

A party may communicate any information relating to the proceedings to a lay adviser or McKenzie friend so as to enable the party to obtain advice or assistance in relation to the proceedings. In seeking advice prior to any application to the court for the appointment of a particular McKenzie friend, it is not contempt for the litigant in person to show court documents to the person from whom advice is sought. Documents and information disclosed must not be used by the (proposed) McKenzie friend for any other purpose and he must not publish them to any third party or outside body without the court's permission.

CHAPTER 9

Expert evidence

9.1 SOURCES OF GUIDANCE

The following are useful sources of guidance for the instruction of expert witnesses:

- Children Act Advisory Sub-committee *Handbook of Best Practice* (June 1997): section 5 relates to experts and the court;
- Part 35 of the Civil Procedure Rules 1998 (CPR): this is not directly applicable to children's cases as CPR r.2.1(2) states that it does not apply to 'family proceedings', other than ancillary relief cases by virtue of FPR 1991, r.2.61C, but in reality the courts will have regard to the provisions of Part 35 of the CPR;
- Law Society (2006) *Family Law Protocol* Law Society Publishing: section 3.11 relates to experts in private law children cases;
- Protocol for Judicial Case Management in Public Law Children Act Cases (June 2003): Appendix C is the Code of Guidance for Expert Witnesses in Family Proceedings.

9.2 CODE OF GUIDANCE FOR EXPERT WITNESSES IN FAMILY PROCEEDINGS

Although the Code of Guidance for Expert Witnesses in Family Proceedings ('the Code') is appended to the Protocol for Judicial Case Management in Public Law Children Act Cases (Public Law Protocol) and uses its terminology, it can be adapted and used for the instruction of experts in private children law proceedings, particularly as the title describes it as a code for 'family proceedings' and does not limit it to public proceedings only. A proposed adaptation of the Code is at Appendix 2.

The aim of the Code is to provide the court with early information to enable it to determine whether it is necessary and practicable to ask an expert to assist the court and to:

(a) identify, narrow and where possible agree the issues between the parties;
(b) provide an opinion about a question that is not within the skill and experience of the court;
(c) encourage the early identification of questions that need to be answered by an expert;
(d) encourage disclosure of full and frank information between the parties, the court and any expert instructed.

The accumulated wisdom of public children case law (including *Re CB and JB (Care Proceedings: Guidelines)* [1998] 2 FLR 2 11 and *Re R (Care: Disclosure: Nature of Proceedings)* [2002] 1 FLR 755) has largely been incorporated into the Code which sets out:

- the responsibilities of all legal advisers involved in a particular case;
- the responsibilities of the court itself in case management;
- the duties of appointed experts.

The following summarises points of particular importance for private children law practitioners:

1. The issues on which expert opinion is needed and the exact field of expertise required should be clearly identified.
2. The initial instruction should be for a single joint expert.
3. Practitioners should ensure that the proposed expert is able to deal with the case in the necessary timescale and can attend court on any appropriate hearing date to give oral evidence if necessary.
4. The expert should be assisted with clear instructions, orderly papers and a chronology.
5. Practitioners should ensure that the expert understands his role as an expert, including the importance of keeping a full and balanced note of relevant conversations or meetings.
6. Practitioners should keep a full note of any conversations with a jointly instructed expert, which should be disclosed to all parties, to ensure the expert's impartiality, and the perception of his impartiality, is protected.
7. The expert's report should be carefully checked to ensure that all questions raised with the expert have been dealt with. If matters have not been dealt with, or new matters have been raised, these should be resolved promptly by amendment to the report if necessary.
8. Where appropriate, experts should communicate with one another to identify issues of agreement and disagreement and to narrow and clarify the issues.
9. Experts should be updated throughout the proceedings by the provision of information and documentation, particularly prior to any hearing where an expert is expected to give oral evidence.
10. Arrangements for the giving of oral evidence should be coordinated by practitioners to minimise inconvenience to the expert.

11. Consideration should be given as to whether the expert needs to hear the evidence of anyone else involved in the case, particularly any other expert, to maximise the value of their evidence for the court.
12. To assist in the preparation of the report, consideration should be given as to whether the expert should be provided with:

    (a) the proposed adapted Code of Guidance for Expert Witnesses in Family Proceedings; and/or
    (b) a copy of Appendix C of the Public Law Protocol; and/or
    (c) Part 35 of the CPR.

The expert's attention should be drawn to the need to apply the latter two documents to the private children law context as Appendix C to the Protocol, and CPR Part 35, are not directly applicable to such proceedings.

9.3 APPLICATION FOR LEAVE TO INSTRUCT AN EXPERT

A psychiatrist or psychologist may be instructed to assess and advise upon the appropriate course to be taken with regard to a child, for example, in enforcing contact where there has been a break in contact and/or where the child is reportedly reluctant for contact to take place or is refusing contact altogether.

A child cannot be medically or psychiatrically examined, or otherwise assessed, for the purpose of the preparation of expert evidence for use in proceedings without the leave of the court (Family Proceedings Rules 1991 (FPR 1991), r.4.18(1)).

The following procedure should be followed:

1. Leave must be sought by all parties to the proceedings, including the parents of the child and also any other person, for example, children's guardians, social workers etc.
2. The application should be made using Form C2 clearly describing the order or directions sought with brief reasons why the application has been made.
3. The purpose of the report and the issue on which it will assist the court must be clearly identified.
4. The application shall be served on all parties to the proceedings and on the children's guardian, unless the court otherwise directs (FPR 1991, r.4.18(2)).

The court will base its decision as to whether to grant leave on the following:

- the circumstances of the case;
- the welfare of the child, although the court may take the view that CA 1989, s.1(1) does not strictly apply to the decision;

- the interests of the parties;
- the need for a fair hearing at which the issues can be properly determined.

Where the court refuses to grant leave to instruct the expert, no evidence arising out of an examination or assessment may be adduced without the leave of the court (FPR 1991, r.4.18(3)).

9.4 ANONYMOUS INSTRUCTIONS

An expert should not be provided with information about the case in an anonymous form in an attempt to avoid the need for an application to the court for leave. It is bad practice for expert witnesses who understand that their opinion is required for court proceedings to accept anonymous instructions and such breaches may lead to costs penalties. In *Re A (Family Proceedings: Expert Witnesses)* [2001] 1 FLR 723, the father made a secret video of contact taking place at a contact centre. His solicitors sent this to a psychologist with anonymised information about the family and instructions for a report. The father applied for residence exhibiting the report to his statement. The rules on disclosure and examination had not been broken because of the preservation of anonymity but Wall J strongly condemned the instruction.

9.5 DISCLOSURE OF DOCUMENTS TO EXPERT

Where a court has named the expert to be instructed in a case, it is not necessary to seek further leave to disclose documents to that expert (FPR 1991, r.4.23(1)(f)).

In cases where the court may be unlikely to grant leave for an examination or assessment of the child, leave of the court can be sought to place documentary evidence before an expert for an opinion on the papers only. If appropriate, an application for leave for an examination or assessment may then be reinforced by a letter or short report from the expert confirming that he considers an examination or assessment necessary.

9.6 LIMITING EXAMINATIONS OF THE CHILD

If leave for an examination is given, the court will usually try to limit the number of examinations to which the child is subjected. Where possible, the examination should be conducted by one expert agreed upon by all parties or there should be a single examination which the parties' respective experts are all invited to attend. Alternatively, the court may grant leave solely to the children's guardian to arrange an examination or assessment.

The dangers of the court granting a general leave, rather than leave for the instruction of the particular expert or experts, can be seen from *Re B (Child Sexual Abuse: Standard of Proof)* [1995] 1 FLR 904, in which following the grant of leave in general terms without limitations, 11 psychiatrists/psychologists became involved in the proceedings.

9.7 PRELIMINARY INVESTIGATIONS

FPR 1991, r.4.18(1) requires leave for the preparation of expert evidence 'for use in the proceedings'. This might allow for a preliminary examination or assessment of the child without leave (for instance, by the child's General Practitioner) for the purpose of obtaining advice as to whether it would be worth arranging for a comprehensive examination or assessment by an expert whose evidence would then be used in the proceedings.

However, given the reluctance for the court to allow children to be subjected to multiple examinations, it is anticipated that the rule will be widely interpreted so that such preliminary investigations will also require leave.

9.8 EXPERT EVIDENCE OBTAINED WITHOUT THE COURT'S LEAVE

Where evidence is obtained in disregard of FPR 1991, r.4.18(1), pursuant to an unauthorised examination or assessment:

- there is no absolute bar on the use of the material obtained and the court will consider whether to grant leave for it to be adduced;
- there may be circumstances in which it is in the interests of the child to admit such evidence;
- the court will require a full explanation as to how the examination or assessment came about and the evidence adduced;
- breach of FPR 1991, r.4.18(1) is likely to be treated as a very serious matter and may result in costs penalties.

9.9 THE EXPERT'S ROLE

The duty of the expert is to assist the court on matters within his or her expertise (CPR r.35.3(1)) and this duty overrides any obligation to the person instructing and/or paying the expert (CPR r.35.3(2)).

The expert must inquire and report upon any question of fact or opinion not involving questions of law or construction (RSC Order 40 r.1(1)).

An expert's opinion on any relevant matter on which he is qualified to give expert evidence will be admissible in evidence (Civil Evidence Act 1972) including:

- an issue in the proceedings in question (Civil Evidence Act 1972, s.3(3));
- an opinion on what may be the ultimate issue in the case (*Re M and R (Child Abuse: Evidence)* [1996] 2 FLR 195).

9.10 NATURE AND IDENTITY OF THE EXPERT

An expert may be specifically engaged to act in a therapeutic and mediatory role for the family. In *W* v. *W (Foreign Custody Order: Enforcement)* [2005] EWCA 1811 (Fam), a child psychiatrist was appointed to advise and assist on the issues arising in the proceedings and to approach his role as that of a mediator in a position to express and advocate the position of the children. With the mediatory aspect of his anticipated intervention in mind, the parties agreed that he should not necessarily file a report in the proceedings, although in the event, with the parties' consent, he did do so.

Where a parent has a treating psychiatrist it will usually be acceptable for a report to be commissioned from that expert. However, this may cause difficulties for the expert in continuing his role as treating psychiatrist as a result of disclosure obligations to both parties conferred on him or her by the role of joint expert.

It is important for the expert not to confuse the role of expert engaged to treat with the role of expert whose task is to compile a forensic report on the person concerned for the purpose of the proceedings (*Re B (Sexual Abuse: Expert's Report)* [2000] 1 FLR 871, where a child psychiatrist who was treating a girl in relation to whom there were allegations of sexual abuse by her father could not make a proper forensic contribution to the father's proceedings for enforcement of a contact order).

If the parties are unable to agree, the court will nominate the expert to be appointed, direct the questions to be asked of the expert and details of any instructions to the expert, and will direct that the parties will bear the expert's fees jointly or otherwise.

9.11 LETTER OF INSTRUCTION TO THE EXPERT

This should be drafted by the lead solicitor (usually the applicant's solicitor) and agreed with solicitors for all parties in accordance with the timescale of the order granting leave for the instruction. It is also the responsibility of the lead solicitor to keep the expert informed of relevant developments and provided with updating documentation.

The initial instruction letter should follow the requirements of Appendix C to the Public Law Protocol and contain:

- details of the parties and their legal representatives (including necessary contact details);
- a schedule of all documents filed in the proceedings and those documents appended to the letter;
- a chronology of events and of the proceedings;
- the specific questions the expert has been directed to address;
- a request for the expert to meet with the parties and the child(ren) as necessary;
- a statement emphasising to the expert that he or she is expected to meet with the parties and child(ren) and is free to discuss the case with any other instructed experts but a careful note must be taken of any discussions with professionals or parties, and any such discussions or correspondence must be disclosed and an explanation given of them in the conclusions reached in the expert's report;
- confirmation as to how the expert's fees are to be met, whether jointly or by one or more parties and as to whether one or more of the parties is publicly funded;
- a request for details of the expert's charging rate and method and an estimate of the likely cost of the expert's involvement in the case.

The letter of instruction and any relevant correspondence with and/or notes of attendance on the expert should be included in the court bundle.

9.12 INSTRUCTION OF A SECOND EXPERT

This issue was considered by the Court of Appeal in *GW and PW* v. *Oldham Metropolitan Borough Council* [2005] EWCA Civ 1247, where Wall LJ stated that a second opinion should 'normally only be permitted where the question to be addressed by the chosen expert goes to an issue of critical importance for the judge's decision in the case'.

This was based in part upon the Court of Appeal decision in *Daniels* v. *Walker* [2000] 1 WLR 1382 which considered the same issue in civil proceedings. The court directed that the joint instruction of an expert does not prevent one party 'for reasons which are not fanciful' seeking another report. The parties should:

(a) endeavour to instruct a single joint expert by an agreed letter;
(b) failing agreement on the terms of the letter, write separately to the joint expert;
(c) if one party for reasonable reasons is discontented with the report, he can put questions to the joint expert;
(d) if that does not resolve the position, then one or both parties may seek a direction as to the calling of further evidence and this will be considered on the basis of proportionality to the issues involved.

CHAPTER 10

CAFCASS and welfare reports

10.1 CHILDREN AND FAMILY COURT ADVISORY AND SUPPORT SERVICE (CAFCASS)

The Children and Family Court Advisory and Support Service (CAFCASS) was brought into being by the Criminal Justice and Court Services Act 2000. It combines the Family Court Welfare function provided by the Guardian Ad Litem and Reporting Officer Service, the Family Court Welfare Service and the Children's Branch of the Official Solicitor's Office. The unified CAFCASS service comes under the responsibility of the Lord Chancellor.

CAFCASS issued the National Standards of the Children and Family Court Advisory and Support Service on 3 April 2003. These service principles and standards include a complaints procedure and are available at www.cafcass.gov.uk.

The central functions of CAFCASS are to:

(a) safeguard and promote the welfare of children;
(b) give advice to any court about any application made to it in such proceedings;
(c) make provision for children to be represented in such proceedings; and
(d) provide information, advice and other support for children and their families.

The various roles for CAFCASS officers in private law children proceedings are as follows:

- Children and Family Reporter (CFR): preparation of welfare report (CA 1989, s.7(1)(a); FPR 1991, rr.4.11 and 4.11B);
- welfare officer: preparation of local authority welfare report (CA 1989, s.7(1)(b); FPR 1991, rr.4.11 and 4.11B);
- children's guardian: representation of child in 'specified proceedings' (CA 1989, ss.41–2; FPR 1991, rr.4.10, 4.11 and 4.11A);
- guardian ad litem (GAL): representation of child as a party (FPR 1991, rr.4.10, 4.11, 4.11A, 9.2 and 9.5).

The role of CAFCASS in private law children proceedings is changing. As set out in *Parental Separation: Children's Needs and Parents' Responsibilities: Next Steps*, in the future, CAFCASS will work with the courts at a local level to reduce report requests which will help to increase the role of CAFCASS in conciliation work. The aim of a reduction in written reports is to free CFRs actively to facilitate contact in the way envisaged by Munby J in *Re D (A Child) (Intractable Contact Dispute: Publicity)* [2004] 1 FLR 1226.

Written CAFCASS reports will continue to be made, although it is intended that they will be more focused and better targeted to address specific areas. Practitioners should be familiar with the requirements for written reports in addition to other powers and duties of CAFCASS officers and their relationship with the court.

10.2 WELFARE REPORTS

Section 7(1) of the Children Act 1989 (CA 1989) gives the court power, when it is 'considering any question with respect to a child under this Act', to ask an officer of CAFCASS (s.7(1)(a)) or officer of the local authority (s.7(1)(b)) 'to report to the court on such matters relating to the welfare of the child as are required to be dealt with in the report'.

Whenever the court considers ordering a welfare report, reference should be made to the Best Practice Note of January 1995, concerning best practice for the judiciary and family proceedings courts, and the specimen form for a 'Welfare Report Referral' annexed to that Note.

The referral to a CFR or welfare officer is entirely within the discretion of the court. The court may call for a welfare report either at the request of a party or of its own motion. Even in contested cases where the parties have requested a report, the court may decide not to order this.

If a direction for a CFR's report is made it should normally form part of a detailed directions order, including the filing of statements by the parties and any further evidence, and listing the matter for hearing.

Timetable for the welfare report

Although under CA 1989, s.7 the court 'asks' for the report, there is a duty under section 7(5) to comply with the request. Representations about who should be responsible for the report and what should be included should therefore be made before the report is ordered. The difficulty is that this is dependent upon a representative of CAFCASS or the local authority being at court when the direction is made.

If the court's request causes difficulties, the CFR will request directions to be given (FPR 1991, r.4.14 or FPC(CA 1989)R 1991, r.14). If directions are sought because of an inability to meet the court deadline for filing the report

(FPR 1991, r.14(3) and FPC(CA 1999)R 1991, r.13), the court will have to balance the prejudice which delay will cause to the welfare of the children under section 1(2) of the CA 1989 against the desirability of obtaining a relevant report, the child's welfare being the paramount consideration (*Re H (Minors) Welfare Reports* [1990] 2 FLR 172).

To avoid difficulty occurring, CAFCASS should be contacted to find out how long is required for the report and to fix the dates for the filing of the report and for the listing of the hearing with this information to hand (*Re H (A Minor) Times*, 1 April 1991), where the Court of Appeal approved this practice at the Royal Courts of Justice for use in the county court).

Duties of the CFR

Under FPR 1991, r.4.11, the CFR must:

- carry out his duties having regard to the delay principle in CA 1989, s.1(2) and the welfare checklist in CA 1989, s.1(3) (FPR 1991, r.4.11(1));
- make necessary investigations and must, in particular, interview persons he thinks appropriate or as the court directs and obtain appropriate professional assistance (for example, expert evidence) as the court directs (FPR 1991, r.4.11(2)); any medical examination or assessment requires leave of the court (FPR 1991, r.4.18(1));
- provide the court with such other assistance as required (FPR 1991, r.4.11(3)).

Unless the court expressly imposes limitations, the CFR will generally:

- visit the child's home and any proposed new home;
- interview the parties;
- interview anyone closely involved (for example, grandparents) and also local authority social workers with knowledge of the family or anyone else involved with the family who might be of assistance (for example, teacher or health visitor);
- meet the child, either alone or with parents or carers in order to ascertain, where possible, the child's wishes and feelings (see *Re R (A Minor) (Court Welfare Report)* [1993] Fam. Law 722 for the duty to see all relevant parties and wherever possible the child with each party; *Re P (Welfare Officer: Duty)* [1996] Fam. Law 664, where the welfare report was inadequate as the officer had seen the children only once at a meeting involving all parties at her office and the report contained no assessment of the relationships between the children and parents);
- where the principle of contact is in dispute, see the applicant parent alone with the child (Best Practice Note, January 1995).

The CFR should work as appropriate to the child's age and understanding, and the seriousness of the child's situation, and develop a comprehensive understanding of the child's needs in the light of the child's age and maturity.

Format of the welfare report

The report may be written or oral, as required by the court. In practice, it is usually written in accordance with the standard CAFCASS format and guidelines. If the proceedings are particularly urgent, a detailed written report is likely to be less important. If a wide range of issues are to be covered in the report, then it should be in writing.

Content of the welfare report

Section 7(2) of the CA 1989 provides for the Lord Chancellor to make regulations specifying matters which, unless the court orders otherwise, must be dealt with in a welfare report. No such regulations have yet been made. The CFR must therefore have regard to the CAFCASS National Standards and also any specific directions given by the court about the scope of the report. The standard welfare report referral form, which is used in conjunction with the guidance, enables the CFR to focus on the important issues as the request for a report should state the issues giving rise to the request. The CFR should also bring to the court's attention any other matters which he or she considers the court should take into consideration.

Opinion evidence

The report should set out all relevant information which the CFR has acquired through his or her investigations, clearly identifying the source of the information and distinguishing between matters of fact and opinion.

A CFR's report may include legitimate expressions of expert opinion and also the presentation of evidence but it must not usurp the fact-finding function of the court, for example by seeking to determine issues of credibility of witnesses or primary findings of fact (*Re B (A Minor), The Times*, 16 July 1990 and also *Re T* [1997] 2 FLR 55, where the CFR inappropriately assessed the credibility of the adults after the father had been accused of sexually abusing his son when this should have been an issue for the judge).

Hearsay

The welfare report and the CFR's evidence will often include reports of conversations with third parties (for example, relatives or teachers) and with the child and may also contain other statements traditionally viewed as inadmissible. Section 7(4) of the CA 1989 deals with statements and evidence which would otherwise be inadmissible and provides that, regardless of an enactment or rule of law which would otherwise prevent it from doing so, the court may take account of:

(a) any statement contained in the report; and
(b) any evidence given in respect of the matters referred to in the report, insofar as the statement or evidence is, in the opinion of the court, relevant to the question which it is deciding.

Section 7(4) of the CA 1989 enables the court to disregard all rules of evidence and to take into account any statement or evidence which is relevant to the question in issue. The court will decide what weight is appropriate to attach to each statement (Children (Admissibility of Hearsay Evidence) Order 1993, SI 1993/621). The CFR should identify hearsay in his report, and its source, and any reasons he has for agreeing with such opinions. The parties can then deal with any prejudicial hearsay evidence by calling the original maker of the statement to give evidence.

Confidentiality to witnesses

A CFR cannot guarantee confidentiality to any person to whom he speaks in the course of his investigations.The judge will decide whether or not evidence should be disclosed to the parties (*Re G (Minors) (Welfare Report: Disclosure)* [1993] 2 FLR 293). If information is to be kept confidential, the judge must be satisfied that real harm to the child will ensue and not the less stringent test of whether there is significant risk of harm (*Re M (Minors: Disclosure of Evidence)* [1994] 1 FLR 760).

Confidentiality of the welfare report

The Practice Direction [1994] FLR 356 at 3(D) requires reports to be endorsed with the following statement:

> This report has been prepared for the Court and should be treated as confidential. It must not be shown nor its content revealed to any person other than a party or adviser to such a party. Such legal adviser may make use of the report in connection with an application for legal aid.

This direction should be strictly observed, in the interests of the children concerned, and solicitors who supply copies of reports to parties should make it clear to them that the report is confidential and that to show it to anyone else is a contempt of court (*Re G (a Minor) (Welfare Officer's Reports)* [1989] Fam. Law 475).

The court has jurisdiction to grant leave for information in the report to be used in proceedings before another court (*Brown* v. *Matthews* [1990] 2 All

ER 155, where the other court was dealing with a claim to a beneficial interest in property formerly occupied as the matrimonial home).

Recommendations in the welfare report

The report should make clear recommendations or explain why recommendations cannot be made, relating such recommendations/explanations to the relevant factors of the welfare checklist under CA 1989, s.1(3) (FPR 1991, r.4.11(1)). The court:

- is not bound by any recommendation which the report makes (*Re F (Children) (Shared Residence Order)* [2003] 2 FLR 397; *Re G (Children) (Residence: Same Sex Partner)* [2005] 2 FLR 957);
- should give the recommendations proper consideration and give reasons if it chooses not to follow those recommendations (*Re J (Children) (Residence: Expert Evidence)* [2001] 2 FLR 44; *Re M (Residence)* [2005] 1 FLR 656);
- does not have to state specifically why it chose to depart from the recommendation, provided that the judgment as a whole, directly or by inference, discloses the reasons for the departure and those reasons are a sound basis for the exercise of judicial discretion (*Re V (Residence: Review)* [1995] 2 FLR 1010).

Addendum reports

Addendum reports should not normally be ordered and should not be necessary if timetabling has been effective. An addendum report may be ordered, for example, for the purpose of testing an agreement between the parties or where there has been a substantial change in circumstances.

Agreement reached before welfare report complete

If the parties reach agreement during the course of preparation of the report and the CFR concludes that this agreement is in the child's best interests, the report may be briefer than previously intended. However, it should include details of the CFR's enquiries, the nature of the dispute, details of the agreement and an indication of whether an order ought to be made. It should also cover any issues identified by the court.

The CFR may encourage the parties to settle their differences if the possibility of a settlement arises during the course of the CFR's investigations. However, the CFR should not act as a conciliator in helping the parties to a resolution at this stage. The function of conciliation or mediation should not be confused with that of preparation of a welfare report.

Filing the report

Where the court has directed that a written report be made, the report must be filed at the court's direction or, in the absence of a direction, at least 14 days before a hearing at which the CFR has been given notice that his report is to be considered (FPR 1991, rr.4.11B(2) and 4.13(1) and FPC(CA 1989)R 1991, rr.11(b)(2) and 13(1)). The report is then available for advance disclosure, and clarification of or expansion on its content can be achieved by the CFR giving oral evidence at the hearing as part of the report.

Under FPR 1991, r.4.11B(2), the CFR is obliged to file the report with the court and serve a copy on the parties and the children's guardian (if any). Common practice, however, is for the CFR to file the report and for the court then to provide the parties/guardian with a copy. The parties, or their representatives, should therefore be told when the report has been submitted to the court and litigants in person should be advised of their right to obtain a copy of the report from the court.

Attendance of the CFR at the hearing

A CFR is only obliged to attend a hearing, at which his or her report is to be considered, if required to do so by direction of the court (FPR 1991, r.4.11B(3), FPC(CA1989)R 1991, r.11B(3)). A party wishing to cross-examine a CFR should therefore seek a direction requiring the CFR's attendance. It should be noted that, by section 16 of the Criminal Justice and Court Services Act 2000 (CJCSA 2000), CFRs may now be cross-examined to the same extent as any witness. This change resulted from the incorporation into English law of Article 6 of the European Convention on Human Rights (the right to a fair trial). If directed by the court to attend and give evidence, a CFR or welfare officer is not entitled to refuse.

If a direction to a CFR to attend court is given, whether by the court's own motion or on the application of a party, it is advisable for the parties' solicitors to write to the CFR with a copy of the directions order directing his or her attendance at a court hearing rather than relying solely on the court office to ensure the CFR is notified.

Courts are encouraged to make the best use of a CFR's time by ensuring that the request for the CFR to attend any hearing is examined carefully and not granted as a matter of course. When a court does require a CFR to attend this should be arranged in accordance with the CFR's availability and the court should allow the CFR to give evidence first and then be released.

Where a CFR is required to attend the hearing, he should put before the court all information which he considers to be relevant and consider all orders available to the court (see CAFCASS Service Standards para. 3.13).

The attendance of the CFR at the hearing is necessary in the following circumstances:

- where a transfer of primary care of any child is contemplated by the court, contrary to the conclusion in the report, in which case the CFR's views on the transfer of residence should be sought (*Re T (a Minor) (Order as to Residence)* [1996] 2 FLR 352);.
- where a report makes an assertion without providing evidence in support and without the CFR attending court, in which case the court should either order the CFR to attend for cross-examination or refuse to admit the evidence (*Re L (A Child); Re V (A Child); Re M (A Child); Re H (Children) (Contact: Domestic Violence)* [2000] 2 FLR 334 at 351);
- where the court forms conclusions directly contrary to the CFR's recommendation it should also hear oral evidence from the CFR (*Re CB (Access: Attendance of Court Welfare Officer)* [1995] 1 FLR 622; *Re W (Residence)* [1999] 2 FLR 390).

In *Re CB (Access: Attendance of Court Welfare Officer)* [1995] 1 FLR 622, which concerned sexual abuse of a child by a Sex Offences Act 1997, Sched. 1 offender, it was said to be a defective exercise of the judge's discretion to reject clear recommendations and warnings in a report without hearing oral evidence from the CFR. The Court of Appeal said that where the CFR is not available in person at the hearing, the judge can adjourn the case and demand the presence of the CFR to put to the CFR the reasons why his or her recommendations are not agreed with and to obtain an explanation of the CFR's views.

In *Re C (Section 8 Order: Court Welfare Officer)* [1995] 1 FLR 617, the Court of Appeal made clear, however, that *Re CB* is not an absolute rule and the question of whether to adjourn a case to request the attendance of a CFR is a matter for the discretion of the judge who must carry out the balancing exercise required by the paramountcy of the child's welfare and the delay principle in CA 1989, s.1(2). The court should take into account factors such as how much further assistance the CFR can give, what difference his attendance is likely to make, and the extent to which it would be safe and proper to depart from any recommendations made.

The distinction between *Re CB* and *Re C* is that in *Re CB*, the CFR had made clear recommendations and warnings of the most serious kind and it was not proper to reject those recommendations in his absence, whereas in *Re C*, the report was an account of interviews which the CFR had carried out with both parents and with the child concerned but did not make firm recommendations in either direction, although the tenor of the considerations was in favour of the status quo (residence with the mother). In *Re C*, the Court of Appeal found that the judge had been entitled to exercise his discretion and to refuse the father's application for an adjournment in order for the CFR to attend.

Additional powers and duties of the CFR

A CFR has additional powers and duties (FPR 1991, r.4.11B and FPC(CA 1989)R 1991, r.11B) which include:

- notifying and explaining to the child such of the contents of the report as the CFR considers appropriate for the child's age and understanding (FPR 1991, r.4.11B(1));
- advising the court if he considers the joinder of a person as party would be likely to safeguard the child's interests (FPR 1991, r.4.11B(4));
- considering whether it is in the child's best interests to be made a party (FPR 1991, r.4.11B(5) and (6)).

Relationship between the court and the CFR

In *Re M (Disclosure: Children and Family CFR)* [2002] 2 FLR 893, Wall J commented on the relationship between the court and the CFR and concluded that:

1. CFRs are not 'officers of the court'. They are officers of CAFCASS with the duties and responsibilities laid upon them by CJCSA 2000, s.12, CA 1989, s.7 and FPR 1991, r.4.11.
2. CFRs are not under the control of the judiciary. Within the scope of their employment by CAFCASS, they are independent professionals who, at the request of the court, investigate issues identified by the court as relating to the welfare of the child in question and give the court any advice and assistance it requires. During the course of those investigations, they are free to exercise their professional judgment on those issues, and in particular do not need the court's permission to disclose information to local authority child protection workers.
3. The relationship between CFRs and the judiciary should be collaborative and cooperative. In particular, CFRs should not hesitate to seek directions from the judge in relation to issues which arise during the course of investigations.
4. CFRs should advise the court immediately if a child protection issue of gravity arises such as has required the CFR to notify the local authority. The CFR in such circumstances should seek the court's directions and any decision to terminate or continue the CFR's inquiries is for the court, not the CFR.

10.3 WELFARE REPORTS UNDER SECTION 7(1)(B) OF THE CA 1989

In private law cases, the court might choose to ask for a report from an officer of the local authority welfare officer where, for example, the local authority is already involved with the child following an allegation of abuse by one parent against the other. However, it may be preferable where a welfare officer is already closely involved with one of the parties to request a report of a CFR to avoid allegations of bias. This will also avoid future conflict where the local authority may wish to apply for an order itself and be joined as a party at a future date.

Procedural requirements

Where the court orders a welfare officer to report, the following procedural points apply:

- in an urgent case, the report is likely to be in the form of a statement or a letter setting out the important facts;
- discovery of relevant documentation to the report is required;
- the local authority will be expected to make the welfare officer who writes the section 7 report available to give evidence and be cross-examined, at the invitation of the court.

Reports from CFR and welfare officer

Sections 7(1)(a) and (b) of the CA 1989 are expressed as alternatives. However, it is possible for the court to request a report from a CFR in addition to a welfare officer, for example, to coordinate private law proceedings with child abuse investigations by the local authority (see *Re W (Welfare Reports)* [1995] 2 FLR 142 and *Re A and B (Minors) (No. 2)* [1995] 1 FLR 351). Equally, the court can request a further report by a CFR having received a welfare officer's report.

Welfare reports under section 7(1)(b)(ii) of the CA 1989

Under section 7(1)(b)(ii) of the CA 1989, the court can ask the local authority to arrange for such other person (other than an officer of the service) as the authority considers appropriate to report. The choice of the other person to be appointed is at the discretion of the local authority and the court has no power to control that appointment or to require the local authority to pay for expert evidence. It is not appropriate to use section 7(1)(b)(ii) to require the local authority to appoint an officer to obtain a report from a child psychiatrist (*Re K (Contact: Psychiatric Report)* [1995] 2 FLR 432).

10.4 REPORTS UNDER SECTION 37 OF THE CA 1989

The alternative to directing a local authority to report under CA 1989, s.7(1)(b) is the direction of the authority to report under CA 1989, s.37. The court can direct the local authority to investigate the child's circumstances under this section, where 'in any family proceedings in which a question arises with respect to the welfare of any child, it appears to the court that it may be appropriate for a care or supervision order to be made' in respect of the child.

The use of a section 37 report is not appropriate where the court is requesting information about an investigation which has already been made rather than instigating an investigation. A section 7 report is preferable in such circumstances (*Re A and B (Minors) (No. 2)* [1995] 1 FLR 351).

All cases in which a CA 1989, s.37(1) direction is made must be conducted in accordance with the Protocol for Judicial Case Management in Public Law Children Act Cases (June 2003). Appendix G to the Protocol sets out the recommended procedure for the termination of a section 37 request by the court.

In addition, reference should be made to the Best Practice Guidance on CA 1989, s.37(1), Directions of the Children Act Advisory Committee, published in its Annual Report 1992/93 (which also provides guidance on the request for a report from a local authority under CA 1989, s.7(1)(b)). The guidance was designed to stop the over-use of the section 37 procedure to facilitate the appointment of a children's guardian or to avoid the delay of a CFR's report in private law proceedings. It clarified that it is not lawful to make a section 37(1) direction unless it appears to the court that a care or supervision order is appropriate.

In *Re M (Intractable Contact Dispute: Interim Care Order)* [2003] 2 FLR 636, Wall J ordered an investigation under CA 1989, s.37, resulting in the issue of care proceedings by the local authority and the removal of the children from their mother under interim care orders. Wall J subsequently made a residence order to the father and a two-year supervision order to the local authority. The section 37 procedure was used to remove the children because they were suffering significant harm having been falsely persuaded, by the mother, that the father and paternal grandparents had physically and sexually abused them, with a resulting cessation of all contact with the father and his family. In a detailed judgment, Wall J set out general considerations for the use of the section 37 procedure:

1. Section 37 can only be used if, on the facts of the case, the court is satisfied that there are reasonable grounds for believing that the children are suffering or are likely to suffer significant harm under the CA 1989, s.31(2) threshold criteria.

2. The action contemplated (removal of the children from the residential parent's care either for an assessment or with a view to a change of residence) must be in the child's best interests.The consequences of the removal must be thought through. There must, in short, be a coherent plan of which temporary or permanent removal from the residential parent's care is an integral part.
3. Where the allegation is that the children have been sexually or physically abused by the absent parent, the court must have held a hearing in which those issues were addressed, and findings made about them.
4. The court must spell out its reasons for making the section 37 order very carefully, and a transcript (or a very full note) of the judgment should be made available to the local authority at the earliest opportunity.
5. The children should be separately represented. One of the prime categories for the tandem model of separate representation in private law proceedings is where all contact has ceased and the issue of contact has become intractable. Children in this situation frequently have an interest in the proceedings and in the outcome which is independent from the viewpoint being advanced by each of their parents (see also the guidance in *Re CE (Section 37 Direction)* [1995] 1 FLR 26 on the appointment of a guardian under CA 1989, s.37(1) below).
6. Preferably, the section 37 report should be supported by professional or expert advice. This advice does not necessarily have to come from a psychiatrist or psychologist. A competent CAFCASS report by a CFR should identify the problem.
7. Judicial continuity is essential. Apart from saving time and resources, this means applications can be made to the judge at short notice and he or she can keep tight control over it. The very fact of ordering a section 37 report involves an element of delay and to minimise this requires strict judicial control by continuity.
8. Undue delay must be avoided. The date of receipt of the report and the giving of further directions must be specified. If a guardian is required and CAFCASS cannot allocate one immediately, a guardian from another source should be appointed. This can either be a specialist solicitor who can then instruct an independent social worker to undertake the guardian role or an organisation such as the National Youth Advocacy Service (NYAS).
9. The case may need to be kept under review if the decision of the court is to move the children from one parent to another.The object of the care proceedings, following the section 37 report, is to remove the children from the significant harm they were suffering with the residential parent and to restore their relationship with their non-residential parent. The longer term aim is to enable the children to retain a good relationship with both parents.That objective is defeated if, having regained their relationship with the non-residential parent, they then lose it with the parent

from whose care they have been removed. The court should be satisfied that mechanisms are in place to address the issue of ongoing contact.

Practicalities

1. A copy of the CA 1989, s.37(1) or s.7(1)(b) order should be served on the local authority as soon as practicable (FPR 1991, r.4.26(3) and FPC(1989)R 1991, r.27(3)) and an immediate telephone notification should then be confirmed in writing.
2. The court should be clear about how, and by whom, the local authority is to be notified (*Re M (Intractable Contact Dispute: Interim Care Order)* [2003] 2 FLR 636).
3. The court must direct which documents filed in the proceedings should be served on the local authority (FPR 1991, r.4.26(4) and FPC(1989)R 1991, r.27(4)) and the applicant's solicitor should prepare a bundle for service as soon as possible.
4. The court must give reasons for the making of a section 37 order and a transcript or full note of the judgment should be made available to the local authority at soon as possible – a note agreed between solicitors will assist whilst a transcript is being obtained.
5. The judge should give detailed directions on the investigations to be carried out and a timescale for such investigations (*Re H (A Minor) (Section 37 Direction)* [1993] 2 FLR 541) without fettering the local authority in the execution of its statutory duty (*Re M (Official Solicitor's Role)* [1998] 2 FLR 815).
6. The court can make an interim care or supervision order at the same time as giving a direction for an investigation under CA 1989, s.37(1) where, for example, the children are in immediate physical danger.
7. The local authority should report to the court within eight weeks unless otherwise directed (CA 1989, s.37(4)).

10.5 APPOINTMENT OF A CHILDREN'S GUARDIAN UNDER SECTION 37(1) OF THE CA 1989

At present, private law children proceedings are not 'specified' proceedings under CA 1989, s.41. However, the definition of 'specified proceedings' under CA 1989, s.41(6) includes any proceedings 'in which the court has made, or is considering whether to make an interim care order' (CA 1989, s.41(6)(b)). Consequently, when a court has made a CA 1989, s.37(1) direction in private law proceedings they become 'specified' by virtue of CA 1989, s.41(6)(b) and 'the court shall appoint a guardian ad litem for the child concerned unless satisfied that it is not necessary to do so in order to safeguard his interests' (CA 1989, s.41(1)).

The appointment should not be automatic and the following should be borne in mind (*Re CE (Section 37 Direction)* [1995] 1 FLR 26):

1. Is it a case in which the court is actually making an interim order as opposed to giving consideration to making one? If so, the circumstances of the case are likely to be serious and unusual, and it may well be appropriate for the appointment of a children's guardian to be made immediately.
2. If the court is only considering making an interim order, what factors are there in the circumstances of the case which require the children's guardian to represent the child?
3. Given the timescale, will there in practice be time for the guardian to be informed of the issues in the case and to play a useful role?
4. Is there a specific role for the guardian in the investigation itself, particularly where a very short timescale for it is fixed?
5. Will the child's interests be properly safeguarded in the interim and during the investigation without a guardian?
6. Does the child have his or her own solicitor?

If the local authority decides not to apply for a care or supervision order following an investigation, the proceedings cease to be 'specified' but the appointment of the guardian subsists until terminated by the court.

Termination of the appointment

Termination should be a judicial act and must follow the procedure set out in the rules (FPR 1991, rr.4.10(9), 4.14 and FPC(1989)R 1991, rr.10(9), 14). The court should hear representations from the guardian and other parties.

The order for appointment should contain a direction that the question of the guardian's continuing involvement be reviewed on completion of the section 37 report and a directions appointment should be fixed shortly after the date the report is to be received. In *Re CE (Section 37 Direction)* [1995] 1 FLR 26, it was in the child's interests for the guardian to remain involved until the local authority's final assessment was in place and a final resolution could be ordered or sanctioned by the court. The court invoked its jurisdiction under FPR 1991, r.9.5 to appoint the guardian in private law proceedings.

An appointment should not be terminated where all contact has ceased and the dispute has become intractable as children should have separate representation in such a case (*Re M (Intractable Contact Dispute: Interim Care Order)* [2003] 2 FLR 636).

10.6 INDEPENDENT WELFARE REPORTS

Independent welfare reports may be ordered in an appropriate case. They may be of use, for example, where CAFCASS resources prevent a CFR from reporting for a significant period of time and the parties to private law children proceedings are in agreement that there should be an independent report and are willing to fund it or, if publicly funded, have obtained authority for the instruction.

Guidance as to such reports is contained in the Family Division: Independent Welfare Reports Practice Direction of 24 March 1983 [1983] FLR 450:

1. No person (other than the party who instructs the independent reporter) is under any obligation to discuss the case with or be interviewed by the independent reporter.
2. Where the child is a ward of court, the independent reporter should not interview the child without leave of the court.
3. The independent reporter may not see a report by a court welfare officer/CFR.This is confidential to the parties and the court.
4. The court welfare officer/CFR may not discuss the case with the independent reporter unless authorised by the court.
5. Where the court has ordered an enquiry and report from a court welfare officer/CFR the court should not depart from the usual practice of relying on that report or of ordering a further report by a different court welfare officer/CFR.

Particular problems were encountered with independent social work reports in *Re S (Expert Evidence)* [1998] Fam. Law 594, where the court relied upon them not knowing of certain material matters concerning the independent social worker, and in *Re C (Wardship: Independent Social Worker)* [1985] FLR 56, where the court had refused permission but the independent social worker had nevertheless been shown documents in the case in a serious, albeit unintentional, breach of confidentiality. Caution should therefore be exercised in the instruction of an independent reporter.

Practicalities

1. The court should look first to the instruction of a welfare officer/CFR before ordering an independent report (*Re C (A Minor) (Wardship Proceedings)* [1984] FLR 419) and, where a welfare officer/CFR has previously been instructed, it would be wrong to order a second report unless there were a good reason for showing that the welfare officer/CFR had not performed his duties adequately, or would not do so, or there were other reasons for being dissatisfied with the welfare officer's/CFR's approach (*Re P (A Minor) (Independent Welfare Officer)* [1989] 2 FLR 43).

2. Where an independent report is ordered, clear and specific directions should be given by the court as to the remit of the independent report and what the independent reporter is allowed or expected to do (*Re P (A Minor) (Independent Welfare Officer)* [1989] 2 FLR 43).
3. Great care should be taken in ensuring that the independent reporter is suitably qualified to undertake the report (*Re M (Adoption: International Adoption Trade)* [2003] 1 FLR 1111 where the independent social worker's conclusions displayed such a lack of elementary standards of professional care and competence as to render its author unfit ever to be involved in such work again).
4. The National Association for Guardians Ad Litem and Reporting Officers (NAGALRO) (www.nagalro.com) is a useful organisation for locating a qualified independent reporter and maintains a directory of independent social workers.

CHAPTER 11

Separate representation of children in private law proceedings

11.1 APPLICATIONS BY CHILDREN

Section 10(8) of the CA 1989

Children have the right to request leave to make an application for any CA 1989, s.8 order. The court may only grant leave under CA 1989, s.10(8) if it is satisfied that the child is of sufficient understanding to make the proposed application. This is the only factor to which the court is specifically directed and is addressed in more detail in relation to FPR 1991, r.9.2A at section 11.6 below.

The fact the child has sufficient understanding does not mean the court is bound to grant leave; it retains a discretion.

The following will be relevant to the exercise of the court's discretion:

- section 1(1) of the CA 1989, although there is a divergence of opinion as to whether this applies, and the welfare of the child is paramount, where the applicant for leave is the child himself (in *Re S (Contact: Application by Sibling)* [1998] 2 FLR 897, the court held that welfare is not paramount; however, it was held that the child's welfare is paramount in *Re C (A minor) (Leave to Seek Section 8 Orders)* [1994] 1 FLR 26 and that, even if the welfare of the child is not paramount, the best interests of the child are important in dealing with a leave application);
- the welfare checklist at CA 1989, s.1(3) as, although this does not strictly apply, the factors are likely to be relevant and useful;
- the likelihood of success of the proposed application;
- why the child is seeking to apply for an order to be made in favour of someone else rather than the application being made by that person directly (*Re SC (A Minor) (Leave to Seek Residence Order)* [1994] 1 FLR 96, where a girl of 14 years sought leave to apply for a residence order in favour of a family friend).

Procedure

Requests for leave by children should be made to the High Court (Practice Direction of 22 February 1993).

Under FPR 1991, r.4.3, a written request for leave should be made on Form C2 setting out the reasons for the application; and a draft of the application (Form C1) together with sufficient copies for service on each respondent should also be filed.

Decision on paper/at hearing

On considering a request for leave, the court under FPR 1991, r.4.3(2) must:

(a) grant the request; or
(b) list the matter for hearing.

The court does not have power to refuse leave on the papers. If the court is not convinced of the merits of the written request, it must direct a hearing.

Except in emergency cases, the interests of justice require that notice be given to all parties likely to be affected (*Re SC (A Minor) (Leave to Seek Residence Order)*[1994] 1 FLR 96); *Re W (Minor) (Contact Application: Procedure)* [1999] Fam. Law 853). Those who are likely to be potential respondents to the main application will be obvious candidates to receive notice at the application for leave stage. Regard should be had, when fixing the date of the hearing of the leave application, that those to whom notice has been given may well need an opportunity to seek legal advice.

In reaching its decision the court may:

- direct the assistance of a welfare report under CA 1989, s.7;
- determine factual issues;
- call for oral evidence including cross-examination (*Re A (A Minor) (Residence Order: Leave to Apply)* [1993] 1 FLR 425).

11.2 ATTENDANCE OF THE CHILD AT COURT

FPR 1991, r.4.16(1) requires the child, if he is a party, to be present at directions appointments unless the court otherwise directs. As it is not generally considered advisable for children to attend court, it may be appropriate to seek, at an early stage, a direction excusing the child from attendance at directions hearings.

There is no obligation on the child to attend hearings other than directions hearings but, if he is a party, he is entitled to do so unless excluded under FPR 1991, r.4.16(2) or otherwise by order of the court.

FPR 1991, r.4.16(2) empowers the court to exclude a party if:

(a) it considers it is in the interests of the child, having regard to the matters to be discussed or the evidence likely to be given; and
(b) the party is represented by a children's guardian or solicitor.

When considering the interests of the child under (a), the court is obliged to give the children's guardian, the solicitor for the child and, if he is of sufficient understanding, the child an opportunity to make representations.

11.3 SECTION 41 OF THE CA 1989: 'SPECIFIED PROCEEDINGS'

Section 122 of the Adoption and Children Act 2002 (ACA 2002) inserts into section 41 of the CA 1989 a new sub-section (6A) so as to include within 'specified proceedings' any proceedings for the making, varying or discharging of an order under CA 1989, s.8 (i.e. residence, contact, specific issue and prohibited steps orders). This widening of the definition of 'specified proceedings' will permit the appointment of a children's guardian in private law children cases. A children's guardian can already be appointed under CA 1989, s.41 where the proceedings become specified by virtue of CA 1989, s.41(6)(b) when a section 37 direction is made.

The government intended ACA 2002, s.122 to address three main concerns:

1. There was too stark a distinction between public law and private law cases.
2. Because of the importance of separate representation of children, it was necessary to provide for this in primary legislation.
3. Children should have access more frequently to separate representation (Rosie Winterton, Hansard, vol. 392, col. 108 (4 November 2002)).

Potentially, the effect is far-reaching as CA 1989, s.41(1) states that 'for the purpose of any specified proceedings, the court shall appoint an officer of [CAFCASS] for the child concerned unless satisfied that it is not necessary to do so in order to safeguard his interests'.

The Children Act Sub-committee of the Lord Chancellor's Advisory Board on Family Law took the view (in their *Report on the Separate Representation of Children in Public and Private Law Proceedings under the Children Act 1989*, Lord Chancellor's Department (1999)) that (para. 4.7):

> A decision by the court not to appoint a guardian ad litem in public law proceedings (a) should be very much the exception and (b) should only be taken when the facts clearly demonstrate that an appointment is not required to protect the child's interest.

The small minority of public law cases where the appointment of a guardian is not considered necessary to safeguard the child's interests include, for example, those where a child of sufficient age and understanding prefers to instruct a solicitor direct or where there is no conflict of interest and the child, being of sufficient age and understanding, supports the application (*Re J (A Minor) (Change of Name)* [1993] 1 FLR 699).

It seems unlikely that the presumption in favour of the appointment of a guardian in public law proceedings will apply equally in private law children proceedings. The expectation is that it will be utilised particularly in severely contested residence or contact disputes where the children's interests do not coincide or cannot be adequately represented by the parent (e.g., *Re H (Contact Order)* [2002] 1 FLR 22; *Re M (Intractable Contact Dispute: Interim Care Order)* [2003] 2 FLR 636).

Section 122 of the ACA 2002 came into force on 7 December 2004 (SI 2004/3203) but in order to be effective, amendments to the FPR 1991 are required and no such amendments have yet been made. The government has given no indication of when new rules will be made but has stated that they will be developed in the light of research evidence into whether children's needs are best met by representation through a solicitor and guardian and CAFCASS's proposals in 'Every Day Matters: New Directions for CAFCASS' (Hansard, written statement 11, 11 January 2006).

11.4 FPR 1991, RULES 9.2, 9.2A AND 9.5

At present, the representation of children in private law proceedings is governed by FPR 1991, rr.9.2, 9.2A and 9.5. These rules do not apply to children in 'specified proceedings' of which they are the subject.

Rule 9.2(1) sets out the general rule that, except where r.9.2A or any other rule provides otherwise, persons under disability may only begin and prosecute proceedings by a next friend and may only defend them by a guardian ad litem.

Rule 9.2A provides mechanisms whereby minors may, with the leave of the court, begin, prosecute or defend proceedings (r.9.2A(1)) or prosecute or defend the remaining stages of the proceedings without a next friend or guardian ad litem (r.9.2A(4)).

Rule 9.5 provides that if, in any family proceedings, it appears to the court that it is in the best interests of the child to be made a party, the court may appoint a guardian ad litem with authority to take part in the proceedings on the child's behalf from the following:

- an officer of CAFCASS or Welsh family proceedings officer;
- the Official Solicitor (if he consents); or
- some other proper person (if he consents).

11.5 FPR 1991, RULE 9.5

Under FPR 1991, r.9.5(2), a separate representation order for a child may be made (FPR 1991, r.4.14(3)(b)) either:

- by the court of its own motion; or
- on the application of a party to the proceedings (using Form C2); or
- on the application of the proposed guardian ad litem.

The court may at any time direct that an application be made by a party for a separate representation order and has discretion to stay the proceedings until the application has been made (FPR 1991, r.9.5(3)).

If a Children and Family Reporter (CFR) or welfare officer has been appointed to report in ongoing proceedings, he must consider whether it is in the child's best interests to be made a party and, if it is, he must notify the court of his opinion together with his reasons (FPR 1991, r.4.11B(5) and (6)).

The court's power under rule 9.5 is without prejudice to the rule 9.2A right of the child of sufficient understanding in certain circumstances to act without a guardian ad litem.

Guidance for a rule 9.5 appointment

The following are essential reading:

- President's Direction (Representation of Children in Family Proceedings pursuant to Family Proceedings Rules 1991 Rule 9.5) [2004] 1 FLR 1188;
- CAFCASS Practice Note (Appointment of Guardians in Private Law Proceedings) [2006] 2 FLR 143 which supersedes the (CAFCASS Practice Note) Representation of Children in Family Proceedings pursuant to FPR 1991 Rule 9.5 [2004] 1 FLR 1190;
- President's Guidance of 25 February 2005 (Appointment of Guardians in accordance with Rule 9.5) and the President's Practice Note of 5 April 2004;

President's Direction (Representation of Children in Family Proceedings pursuant to Family Proceedings Rules 1991 Rule 9.5) [2004] 1 FLR 1188 was issued following a gradual shift towards joining children as parties. It gives the following guidance:

1. Making a child a party to the proceedings is a step to be taken in only a minority of cases which involve an issue of significant difficulty.
2. Before taking such a step, consideration should be given to whether an alternative route might be preferable, such as asking a CAFCASS officer or Welsh family proceedings officer to carry out further work or by referring to children's services or possibly by obtaining expert evidence.

3. The decision whether or not to make the child a party to non-specified proceedings is exclusively that of the judge, in the light of the circumstances of the particular case.
4. The following 10 examples are offered, solely by way of guidance, as circumstances which may justify the making of a separate representation order:

   (a) where a CAFCASS officer has notified the court that in his opinion the child should be made a party;
   (b) where the child has a standpoint or interest which is inconsistent with or incapable of being represented by any of the adult parties;
   (c) where there is an intractable dispute over residence or contact, including where all contact has ceased, or where there is rational but implacable hostility to contact or where the child may be suffering harm associated with the contact dispute;
   (d) where the views and wishes of the child cannot be adequately met by a report to the court;
   (e) where an older child is opposing a proposed course of action;
   (f) where there are complex medical or mental health issues to be determined or there are other unusually complex issues that necessitate separate representation for the child;
   (g) where there are international complications outside child abduction, in particular, where it may be necessary for there to be discussions with overseas authorities or a foreign court;
   (h) where there are serious allegations of physical, sexual or other abuse in relation to the child or there are allegations of domestic violence not capable of being resolved with the help of the CAFCASS officer;
   (i) where the proceedings concern more than one child and the welfare of the children is in conflict or one child is in a particularly disadvantaged position;
   (j) where there is a contested issue about blood testing.

- Separate representation of the child may result in delay in the resolution of the proceedings contrary to section 1(2) of the CA 1989 and the court must take into account the risk of delay together with other factors adverse to the welfare of the child as part of its application of the paramountcy principle in section 1(1) of the CA 1989.
- The court's primary consideration will be the best interests of the child.
- When a child is made a party and a guardian is to be appointed, consideration should first be given to appointing a CAFCASS officer as guardian ad litem (GAL). Before appointing an officer, the court will cause preliminary enquiries to be made of CAFCASS. (Note that it is helpful for CAFCASS to know whether the court considers there is any reason why any CAFCASS officer who has dealt with the matter so far

should not continue to deal with it in the role of GAL. The decision as to which particular CAFCASS officer to appoint as GAL is a matter for CAFCASS.)

- The appropriate procedure and preferred form of order is set out in the CAFCASS Practice Note (Appointment of Guardians in Private Law Proceedings) [2006] 2 FLR 143 which supersedes the (CAFCASS Practice Note) Representation of Children in Family Proceedings pursuant to FPR 1991 Rule 9.5 [2004] 1 FLR 1190] accompanying the Practice Direction.
- If CAFCASS is unable to provide a GAL without delay, or if for some other reason the appointment of a CAFCASS officer is not appropriate, the court may appoint the Official Solicitor or some other 'proper person', in either case providing he consents.This could for example be a Children Panel Solicitor, the Children's Rights Officer for the NSPCC, the Family Rights Group or the National Youth Advisory Service (NYAS).
- The court may consider transferring cases proceeding in the county court to the High Court depending on the nature and complexity of the case and the importance of the issues involved.

The President's Direction of 2004 apparently led to an 'unanticipated and dramatic' increase in the number of GAL appointments in private law cases and, as a result, the President issued new guidance on 25 February 2005 – The Appointment of Guardians in accordance with Rule 9.5 – and the President's Practice Note of 5 April 2004, which took effect on 4 April 2005.

This limits the appointment of a GAL in a private law case to be made only:

(a) by a circuit judge; or
(b) in exceptional circumstances by a district judge (for example, where a case is urgent and there is no resident circuit judge); or
(c) a district judge of the Principal Registry of the Family Division.

The guidance of 25 February 2005 also states that:

- the case should be listed for a short directions hearing of no more than half an hour to consider whether the appointment of the GAL should be made;
- CAFCASS should be notified and invited to attend that hearing;
- if a GAL is not appointed, the case should be transferred back to the district judge;
- if a GAL is appointed, consideration should be given as to whether:
  - a circuit judge should retain the case;
  - the case is of sufficient complexity to be transferred to the High Court;
  - the case should still be dealt with by a district judge and transferred back.

The guidance from the President and CAFCASS followed a gradual shift towards joining more children to proceedings in the most difficult private law cases, particularly since the implementation of the Human Rights Act 1998. In private law proceedings, representation of the child's views has historically been primarily through the welfare report, if one is called for. However, in *Re A (Contact: Representation of Child's Interests)* [2001] 1 FLR 715, the Court of Appeal acknowledged that children were not always sufficiently seen and heard by the use of a welfare report and that, partly as a result of the European Convention on Human Rights becoming part of domestic law, the English courts were increasingly taking the view that children should be seen and heard and this would mean an increased use of guardians in certain private law cases.

Where the child's interests are quite separate from the parents in a marked degree, the child should be added as a party and a guardian ad litem appointed. In *Re H (Contact Order) (No. 2)* [2002] 1 FLR 22, Wall J stated per curiam:

> where the court is faced with contact issues as difficult as those which arise in this case, consideration should be given to the children being separately represented and, where appropriate, expert advice being sought on their behalf. In such cases children quite frequently have particular interests and standpoints which do not coincide with and are not necessarily capable of being adequately represented by their parents.Absence of separate representation in the present case means, in my judgment, that the court cannot give the children all the assistance they need.

Appointment of the GAL

The President's Direction of 2004 makes clear that CAFCASS are the first port of call for the appointment of the GAL and then other avenues can be explored. This stems from case law.

In *Re W (Contact: Joining Child as a Party)* [2003] 1 FLR 681, an order was made, early in the proceedings, joining the child as a party and appointing a solicitor with an independent social worker. On the recommendation of the social worker, the trial judge made a final order for no contact. The father applied for permission to appeal and, in granting permission to appeal and allowing the appeal to the extent of inviting CAFCASS to act on behalf of the child, the Court of Appeal held as follows:

1. It was wrong to appoint a solicitor and independent social worker.The normal course would be to request a CAFCASS report and only if the report is not adequate, should the issue of separate representation be considered.
2. CAFCASS should first be invited to provide a guardian to represent the child. If CAFCASS is unable to represent the child, it is then appropriate to consider whether a local guardian and local solicitor should be appointed to represent the child.

3. The trial judge erred in making a final order for no contact as the child had a right to a relationship with his father and the child's welfare demanded that efforts should be made to develop this relationship. The court process ought to have been used as a means of achieving this. CAFCASS were therefore invited to accept the guardianship of the child, to investigate the case, and to consider the propriety of involving a child psychiatrist or other mental health professional.

When alternative agencies are approached, care should be taken by parties other than the child to avoid any perception of bias. In *Re A (Contact: Representation of Child's Interests)* [2001] 1 FLR 715, the Court of Appeal agreed that the child should be separately represented and invited the Official Solicitor to be guardian ad litem (pre CAFCASS). NYAS had sought leave to intervene and act as guardian ad litem for the four and a half-year-old child at the request of the mother who had made allegations of sexual abuse against the father. The Court of Appeal commented that NYAS was a well known and well respected service and, in principle, there was no objection to the use of such a respectable charitable organisation to represent the child but, in this case, the Official Solicitor should be appointed as the father would perceive NYAS as acting on the mother's behalf because of the degree of contact which had already taken place between it and the mother's family. It was only a perception, however, and there was no doubt that NYAS would act independently.

Where an application is made to involve NYAS in proceedings, its consent will be required before any appointment can be finalised and it is often the case that NYAS should be consulted on the appointment in advance. Leave for disclosure of the papers to NYAS will be required for such a consultation. In *Re B (A Child)* [2006] EWCA Civ 716, the Court of Appeal held that the judge had been wrong to refuse an order for disclosure of the papers to NYAS to ascertain whether the child should be separately represented and the judge had given no weight to the real possibility that the child, properly advised, would wish to have contact with her father. In *Re H (A Child)* [2006] EWCA Civ 896, the Court of Appeal found that where in contact proceedings the criteria for involving NYAS had been made out, the judge should not exercise his discretion to refuse an application for the appointment of NYAS without consulting NYAS and inviting it to respond.

Duties of the GAL

The general duty of the GAL is to safeguard the interests of the child in the manner prescribed by rules of court (CA 1989, s.41(2)(b)). The guardian's role in safeguarding the child's interests is a protective one, but the child's interests may not coincide with the child's views, and therefore, although he must give full consideration to ascertaining the child's wishes and feelings, the guardian is not just a mouthpiece for the child.

The GAL must have regard to:

- the paramountcy principle in CA 1989, s.1(1) to ensure that the interests of the child are paramount;
- the need to minimise delay in accordance with the avoidance of delay principle in CA 1989, s.1(2);
- the statutory checklist in CA 1989, s.1(3)(a)–(f);
- the no order principle in CA 1989, s.1(5);
- the CAFCASS service principles and standards where a CAFCASS officer is appointed as GAL.

The GAL should:

- work in the manner and at a pace which are appropriate to the child's age and understanding, and the seriousness of the child's situation;
- develop a comprehensive understanding of the child's needs in the light of the child's age and maturity.

Where the appointed GAL is an officer of CAFCASS, FPR 1991, rr.4.11 and 4.11A apply as they apply to a children's guardian appointed under CA 1989, s.41 (FPR 1991, r.9.5(6)).

FPR 1991, r.4.11 (powers and duties of officers of the service) applies equally to GALs as to children's guardians and CFRs. The GAL must:

- carry out his duties having regard to the delay principle in CA 1989, s.1(2) and the welfare checklist in CA 1989, s.1(3) (FPR 1991, r.4.11(1));
- make necessary investigations and, in particular, interview persons he thinks appropriate or as the court directs and obtain appropriate professional assistance (e.g. expert evidence) as the court directs (FPR 1991, r.4.11.(2)); CAFCASS Service Standards require that the children's guardian will normally see all children who are the subject of proceedings on one or more occasions; he will also take all reasonable steps to see adult parties to the proceedings and any other relevant children and adults unless directed otherwise by the court; any medical examination or assessment requires leave of the court (FPR 1991, r.4.18(1));
- provide the court with such other assistance as required (FPR 1991, r.4.11(3)).

FPR 1991, r.4.11A (additional powers and duties of the children's guardian) gives the GAL additional powers which reflect his extra duties to represent the child in court and to obtain legal representation for the child. It sets out the GAL's substantive and case management responsibilities, including to:

- appoint a solicitor to represent the child unless such a solicitor has already been appointed;

- advise the child, as is appropriate having regard to his understanding;
- instruct the solicitor representing the child on all matters relevant to the child's interests, including possibilities for appeal, arising in the course of proceedings;
- attend all directions appointments and hearings in the proceedings;
- advise the court as to whether the child is of sufficient understanding for any purpose, including refusal to submit to medical treatment;
- advise the court as to the child's wishes;
- advise the court as to the appropriate forum and timetable;
- advise the court as to the available options for the child and the suitability of each option and what order should be made;
- be questioned by any party about oral or written evidence which he tenders to the court;
- notify any person, whose joinder as a party to the proceedings will be likely, in the guardian's opinion, to safeguard the child's interests of his right to apply to be joined;
- serve and accept service of documents on behalf of the child and advise the child with sufficient understanding of the content of such documents.

Conflict of interests between children

Where a guardian has been appointed to represent more than one child, and finds that the children's interests conflict, there is nothing in the rules which prevents the guardian representing all the children. The guardian will need to identify and define the interests of each child before conducting a balancing exercise between the interests of each child and giving a view as to where the balance lies (*Re T and E (Children's Proceedings: Conflicting Interests)* [1995] 1 FLR 581).

The GAL's report

The requirements for the report replicate the requirements for a CFR's report under CA 1989, s.7. The report should set out all relevant information which the guardian has acquired through his enquiries, making clear the source and distinguishing between matters of fact and opinion.

The children's guardian must, unless the court directs otherwise, not less than 14 days before the date fixed for the final hearing of the proceedings, file a written report advising on the child's interests and serve a copy of the filed report on the parties (FPR 1991, r.4.11(A)(7)). If the circumstances justify, for example, if a guardian would be unable to prepare a written report in time, the court may sanction the giving of an oral report (FPR 1991, r.4.11A(5)).

Evidence

The GAL's function is not to adopt a judicial role and he should not assess material which is outside his expertise (for example, sexual abuse allegations).

If, as in *B* v. *B (Child Abuse: Contact)* [1994] 2 FLR 713, the guardian is faced with allegations of sexual abuse, then Wall J said that it is the function of the court and not the guardian to decide whether abuse occurred. The guardian should present a fair and balanced assessment of the material factors and base his recommendations on alternative premises, namely, whether a finding of abuse is made or not. The guardian:

(a) should limit any report to factual observations and assessments which are within his professional expertise as a social worker; and
(b) should always seek expert evidence on the interpretation of controversial material relating to allegations of sexual abuse.

It has been suggested that it may be advisable for his report and evidence to acknowledge expressly that the decision is a matter for the court (*Re N (A Minor) (Sexual Abuse: Video Evidence)* [1996] 2 FLR 214).

The operation of the hearsay rule is excluded in relation to any statement contained in the report and any evidence given in respect of the matters referred to in the report (CA 1989, s.41(11)). Any other rule of law or enactment which would prevent admissibility is also disapplied. The admissibility of such evidence is a matter for the court.

Recommendations

The report should make clear recommendations (or explain why recommendations cannot be made) which draw on relevant aspects of the section 1(3) welfare checklist. It should explain the basis upon which those recommendations have been made, including reasons both for and against them. In his recommendations, the guardian should consider how the child's needs should best be met. His report should refer to the child's wishes and feelings in the light of his age and understanding.

The court is not bound to follow the recommendations of the guardian but it must give reasons for doing so. The need for the court to explain why it is rejecting the guardian's report applies equally where the report is based on a combination of the expert evidence and the guardian's own experience and knowledge of the child (*Re M (Residence)* [2002] 2 FLR 1059).

In *Re K (Supervision Orders)* [1999] 2 FLR 303, Wall J stated that where the local authority and the parents have reached a sensible agreement which clearly protects the child, and is in no sense collusive, a guardian should think long and hard before he seeks to upset the agreement or put forward alternative contentious proposals. Nevertheless, the court should not exclude the guardian's evidence on the points in question.

Wall J's recommendations, in a public law context, must apply equally to private law proceedings where the parents have reached an agreement between themselves.

Report to the child

The GAL must ensure that any decision made by the court is notified to the child if he considers it appropriate to the child's age and understanding (FPR 1991, r.4.11A(10)).

The GAL should usually see the child after the proceedings and explain the outcome in a manner that is appropriate to the child's age and understanding. If he does not do so, he must record his reasons (CAFCASS Service Standards, para. 3.17).

Termination of the appointment

Termination should be a judicial act and must follow the procedure set out in the rules (FPR 1991, rr.4.10(9), 4.14).

The court should hear representations from the guardian and other parties.

Appointment of the child's solicitor

Where the children's guardian is a CAFCASS officer (authorised by CAFCASS in accordance with Criminal Justice and Court Services Act 2000 (CJCSA 2000), s.15(4) or a Welsh family proceedings officer) and he intends to act as the child's solicitor in the proceedings, he is not required to appoint a solicitor for the child, unless the child wishes to instruct a solicitor direct and either the children's guardian or the court considers that the child has sufficient understanding to do so (FPR 1991, r.4.11A(2)). As a CAFCASS practitioner, he will need to have regard to the CAFCASS Service Standards.

The court may exceptionally appoint someone to act both as GAL and as solicitor for the child (*Re K (Replacement of Guardian ad Litem)* [2001] 1 FLR 663).

Role of the child's solicitor

The child's solicitor's role is different from that of the children's guardian. In particular, the solicitor does not have the investigatory or social work roles placed on the guardian, although the solicitor should have regard to the CAFCASS Service Standards.

The relationship between the guardian and the solicitor instructed by him should be one of partnership on every aspect of the case, including definition of issues, the nature of the investigation, the need to instruct experts and the conclusions to be presented to the court.

The solicitor's client is the child and the solicitor takes instructions from the child rather than the children's guardian, unless the child is either insufficiently mature to instruct direct, or is sufficiently mature and his instructions do not conflict with the guardian's views. Where a mature child is in conflict with the guardian, the child will give instructions to the solicitor and they must be followed, even if they are contrary to the child's interests as perceived by the solicitor.

Where it appears to the children's guardian that the child (a) is instructing his solicitor direct, or (b) intends, and is capable of, conducting the proceedings on his own behalf, he must inform the court at the next directions appointment or, if there is none fixed, the guardian should immediately take out an appointment for directions. Thereafter, he performs his statutory duties and takes such part in the proceedings as the court directs. The guardian may, with the court's leave, have legal representation of his own in the conduct of those duties (FPR 1991, r.4.11A(3)).

In such a situation, or where the children's guardian finds there is likely to be a conflict between his recommendations and the child's views and the child is, or may be, capable of conducting the proceedings on his own behalf, it has been suggested by Wall J in *Re M (Minors) (Care Proceedings: Conflict of Children's Wishes: Instruction of Expert Witnesses)* [1994] 1 FLR 749 that the guardian should:

(a) take an early opportunity to discuss the likely difficulties with the solicitor instructed on behalf of the child and;
(b) either take out a summons for directions for the point to be resolved or, where a summons for directions is already fixed, bring the matter to the attention of the court and the other parties at the directions appointment. If there is an issue about the child's capacity to give coherent and consistent instructions or to conduct the proceedings on his own behalf, that issue should be resolved by the court. The court may make a direction that the children's guardian should have separate legal representation, either upon application by the guardian or by the court of its own motion.

If the child's detachment from the GAL occurred at a late stage in the proceedings, the court may consider that the GAL should present a case as if he were a party to the proceedings. This ensures a neutral view of the best interests of the child is advanced as the GAL remains bound by CA 1989, s.41(2)(b) and his purpose is to safeguard the interests of the child. Alternatively, the court may allow the GAL to retain only a small role or may terminate the appointment under FPR 1991, r.4.10(9).

In the ordinary case, where conflict arises, the solicitor first appointed continues as the representative of the child, putting forward the views, wishes and feelings of the child client, whilst the GAL will obtain alternative representation.

The Law Society has issued guidance regarding the circumstances where it may be necessary for a solicitor to break confidentiality against the child client's wishes. The solicitor must be able to justify any breach of confidentiality and should seek appropriate advice.

Sources of guidance for solicitors acting for children

- The Resolution (formerly the Solicitors Family Law Association), *Guide to Good Practice for Solicitors Acting for Children* (6th Edition) will assist practitioners, particularly those acting for, or contacted by, children in proceedings (both public and private law) where there is or may be a conflict between the guardian and the mature child (www.resolution.org.uk).
- The Law Society (2006) *Family Law Protocol* (2nd Edition) Law Society Publishing, Chapter 3 'Children Private Law' available in hard copy and at www.guide-on-line.lawsociety.org.uk;
- The Law Society (2004) *Good Practice in Child Care Cases*, Law Society Publishing (available in hard copy and at www.lawsociety.org.uk);
- The Law Society and CAFCASS (February 2004) *Guidance on Working Relationship between Children Panel Solicitors and Children's Guardians* (www.lawsociety.org.uk);
- Lord Chancellor's Advisory Committee (June 2003) S*tatement of Good Practice in the Appointment of Solicitors Where it Falls to the Court to Do So in Specified Proceedings.*

11.6 FPR 1991, RULE 9.2A

FPR 1991, r.9.2A(1) provides that where a child is entitled to begin, prosecute or defend proceedings he may do so without a next friend or GAL:

(a) where he has obtained the leave of the court for that purpose; or
(b) where a solicitor:
  - considers that the minor is able, having regard to his understanding, to give instructions in relation to the proceedings; and
  - has accepted instructions from the minor to act for him in the proceedings and, where the proceedings have begun, is so acting.

Removal of a GAL

FPR 1991, r.9.2A(4) provides for the removal of a next friend or GAL where a child wishes to prosecute or defend the remaining stages of proceedings without such assistance. The child may apply to the court for leave for the removal to be affected.

Form of the application for leave

The child applies for leave by:

(a) filing a written request setting out the reasons for the application: no particular form is required but it is suggested that Form C2 should be used in existing proceedings or on a request for leave to bring proceedings (exhibiting a Form C1 draft application); or
(b) making an oral request for leave at any hearing in the proceedings.

The application for leave may be granted on paper, under FPR 1991, r.9.2A(3)(a), and it is therefore advisable to set out full reasons for the application when making a written request as the need for a hearing may be obviated.

Where the court does direct a hearing under FPR 1991, r.9.2A(3)(b), this will be ex parte. The request for leave to dispense with the need for a next friend or GAL is a matter between the child and the court (and the next friend/GAL if one is already acting). The other parties to the proceedings (or proposed parties) have no standing. However, the court retains discretion to hear representations from the child's parents or others in the interests of justice (*Re S (A Minor) (Independent Representation)* [1993] 2 FLR 437).

Revocation of leave

The court may wish to revoke leave under FPR 1991, r.9.2A(8), and to direct that a GAL be re-appointed using its power under FPR 1991, r.4.14(2)(d), in two main types of case:

- where the complexity of the proceedings have materially increased so that, without altering the court's assessment of the level of the child's understanding, it concludes that it is insufficient in the changed circumstances;
- through experiencing how the child conducts the case, the court may decide it was wrong to grant leave initially.

Sufficient understanding

An application for leave, under either rule 9.2A(1)(a) or 9.2A(4), is granted where the child concerned has 'sufficient understanding' to participate as a party in the proceedings without a next friend or GAL (FPR 1991, r.9.2A(6)).

Even where a child has retained a solicitor, the solicitor may still wish to seek the court's leave if he is unsure of whether the FPR 1991, r.9.2A(1)(b)(i) test is satisfied, or is unwilling to accept the responsibility of deciding this for himself. In any event, the court, rather than the solicitor, has the right to decide whether a child who comes before it as a party has the necessary ability, having regard to his understanding, to instruct a solicitor (*Re CT (A Minor) (Wardship: Representation)* [1993] 2 FLR 278).

The decision as to whether a child has sufficient understanding is based on an assessment of the evidence, of the understanding of the individual child in the context of the proceedings in which he seeks to participate (*Re S (A Minor) (Independent Representation)* [1993] 2 FLR 437).

In deciding what qualifies as 'sufficient understanding' the courts have commonly encountered the following circumstances:

1. The conflict between children's rights and welfare: a judicious balance should be struck between, first, a child's right, as a human being with an individual mind and will, to express his own views and emotions which should command serious attention and, secondly, the need to protect a child's interests because he is liable to be vulnerable and impressionable, lacking the maturity to weigh the long term against the shorter, lacking the insight and imagination to gauge reactions in himself and others, and lacking the experience to measure the probable against the possible (*Re S (A Minor) (Independent Representation)* [1993] 2 FLR 437). *Mabon* v. *Mabon* [2005] 2 FLR 1017 involved an application for leave to remove a guardian by three boys aged 17, 15 and 13 years old. The application was refused by the trial judge on grounds of delay, emotional damage to the children, and exposure to the harshness of the litigation process. In allowing the children's appeal Thorpe LJ in the Court of Appeal stated as follows:

   (a) The tandem model of representation of children in family proceedings of guardian ad litem and solicitor is the 'Rolls Royce' model which is the envy of many other jurisdictions. However, its overall approach is paternalistic as the guardian's first priority is to advocate the welfare of the child and his second is the child's wishes and feelings. Where the two conflict, FPR 1991, r.9.2A(6) provides for the mandatory grant of the application to remove the guardian provided the child has 'sufficient understanding'.

   (b) The court must, 'in the case of articulate teenagers, accept that the right to freedom of expression and participation outweighs the paternalist judgment of welfare'.

   (c) In testing sufficiency of understanding, welfare has a place and if direct participation would pose an obvious risk of harm to the child, which the child is incapable of comprehending, then the judge is entitled to find that sufficient understanding has not been demonstrated. But judges must be equally alive to the risk of emotional harm that might arise from denying the child knowledge of and participation in the proceedings.

2. The nature of the issues: in *Re S (A Minor) (Independent Representation)* [1993] 2 FLR 437, Sir Thomas Bingham MR commented that 'Different children have different levels of understanding at the same age. And understanding is not absolute. It has to be assessed relatively to the proceedings. Where any sound judgment on these issues calls for insight and imagination which only maturity and experience can bring, both the court and the solicitor will be slow to conclude that the child's understanding is sufficient'.
3. The disturbed child: in *Re H (A Minor) (Care Proceedings: Child's Wishes)* [1993] 1 FLR 440 it was said that 'a child must have sufficient rationality within the understanding to instruct a solicitor'. It may well be that the level of emotional disturbance is such as to remove the necessary degree of rationality that leads to coherent and consistent instruction'.
4. The child whose views are influenced or manipulated by adult family members: while the evidence may point to a strong influence which associates upon the child's views, the question is whether that influence has been so intense as to destroy the child's capacity to give coherent instructions (*Re H (A Minor) (Role of Official Solicitor)* [1993] 2 FLR 5522).
5. The factor of litigation disturbance: in *Re C (Residence: Child's Application for Leave)* [1995] 1 FLR 927, Stuart-White J stated that the question to be asked is whether lack of objectivity and insight is a function of the youth of the applicant or a function of the individual child or adult caught up in a distressing dispute, it being the experience of the courts that many adult individuals find it difficult to be wholly objective in such matters.

CHAPTER 12

Human rights and children's rights

The two most important international rights instruments for domestic child law in the United Kingdom are the United Nations Convention on the Rights of the Child (CRC) and the European Convention on Human Rights and Fundamental Freedoms (ECHR).

12.1 UNITED NATIONS CONVENTION ON THE RIGHTS OF THE CHILD

The CRC was ratified by the United Kingdom in 1991. It has not been incorporated directly into UK law but does influence developing domestic law as a set of considerations to be used when evaluating legislation, policy-making and administrative action. The CRC is a comprehensive statement of children's rights. The particularly important articles in the context of child contact applications are:

- Article 2(1): the right of all children to the application of the CRC rights without exception or discrimination;
- Article 3(1): the best interests of the child being of primary consideration in all actions concerning children whether undertaken by public or private social welfare institutions, courts of law, administrative or legislative bodies;
- Article 9(3): the right of the child who is separated from one or both parents to maintain personal relations and direct contact with both parents on a regular basis, except if it is contrary to the child's best interests;
- Article 12(1): the right of the child who is capable of forming his or her own views to express those views freely in all matters affecting the child, the views of the child being given weight in accordance with the age and maturity of the child;
- Article 12(2): the opportunity to be provided to the child to be heard in any traditional and administrative proceedings affecting the child, either directly, or through a representative or an appropriate body, in a manner consistent with the procedural rules of national law.

12.2 EUROPEAN CONVENTION ON HUMAN RIGHTS AND FUNDAMENTAL FREEDOMS

The ECHR was implemented into UK domestic law by virtue of the Human Rights Act 1998 (HRA 1998) on 2 October 2000. It does not specifically address children's rights although children, as human beings, have rights under the ECHR in the same way as adults. The ECHR has influenced, and is influencing, domestic children law in the United Kingdom. Key ECHR articles in the context of private children law are:

- Article 6 (right to a fair trial);
- Article 8 (right to respect for private and family life);
- Article 14 (prohibition of discrimination).

Article 8 (right to respect for private and family life)

Article 8 has assumed central importance in private law disputes over contact. It provides that:

(a) everyone has the right to respect for his private and family life, his home and his correspondence;

(b) there should be no interference by a public authority with the exercise of this right except as is in accordance with the law and is necessary in a democratic society in the interests of national security, public safety or the economic wellbeing of the country, for the prevention of disorder or crime, for the protection of health or morals, or the protection of the rights and freedoms of others.

In practice, the dispute usually centres around whether an interference is 'necessary' in that it meets a pressing social need and is proportionate to the legitimate aim pursued. There is a margin of appreciation, or measure of discretion, available to member states as the European Court of Human Rights (the European Court) recognises that practice will not be identical across the board. Where there is common practice between states, however, the permitted margin will be narrow. The European Court accepts a wider margin of appreciation in residence cases, for example, while contact cases are subject to much stricter scrutiny.

Right to contact

Article 8 rights include:

- the substantive right to contact; and
- the procedural right to sufficient involvement in the proceedings and a decision which is based on relevant and sufficient reasons to found that decision.

Article 8 has significantly influenced UK domestic law by placing a positive obligation on member states to ensure adequate machinery is in place to facilitate contact, even if a child is refusing it, and any resistance on the child's part must be investigated by an expert. The Children and Adoption Act 2006 (CAA 2006) is designed to address some of the problems surrounding the enforcement of contact orders which led Munby J to conclude that the English courts could no longer complacently assume that the conventional domestic approach met the standards required by Articles 6 and 8 of the ECHR in *Re D (Intractable Contact Dispute: Publicity)* [2004] 1 FLR 1226.

12.3 THE SUBSTANTIVE RIGHT UNDER ARTICLE 8

The European Court specifically addressed the right of a parent to maintain contact with a child in *Hokkanen* v. *Finland* [1996] 1 FLR 289. The father agreed to the care of his daughter by maternal grandparents after the death of his wife. The grandparents subsequently refused to return the child and did not comply with custody and access orders. The Finnish Appeal Court transferred custody to the grandparents and declined to enforce access orders after the child had expressed her views against it. The father argued before the European Court that forcible measures should have been more readily resorted to. The European Court held that:

- Article 8 includes the right of a parent to have measures taken to reunite with the child, and there is an obligation on relevant authorities to take action to ensure this, and that such measures apply equally in the context of transfer of care by private agreement as to public care cases;
- national authorities must do their utmost to facilitate cooperation with orders but the rights and freedoms of all parties concerned must be taken into account and, more particularly, the best interests of the child and his or her rights under Article 8 and where contact with a parent might threaten those interests or interfere with those rights, national authorities must strike a fair balance between them;
- the non-enforcement of access was a breach of the father's Article 8 rights until the child reached an age of sufficient maturity to express her own views that access was not in accordance with her wishes.

The right of a child to maintain contact, as opposed to repudiating it, was not specifically mentioned in *Hokkanen* but there is no doubt that the ECHR also acknowledges this right.

Hokkanen was followed by decisions on the substantive right to family life in *Ignaccolo-Zenide* v. *Romania* (Application No. 31679/96) (2002) 31 EHRR 7; *Nuutinen* v. *Finland* (Application No. 32842/96) (2002) 34 EHRR 15; *Glaser* v. *United Kingdom* (Case No. 32346/96) [2001] 1 FLR 153; *Yousef* v. *The Netherlands* (Application No. 33711/96) [2003] 1 FLR 210; *Sylvester* v.

Austria (Application Nos 36812/97 and 40104/98) [2003] 2 FLR 210; *Hansen* v. *Turkey* (Application No. 36141/97) [2004] 1 FLR 142; *Kosmopoulou* v. *Greece* (Application No. 60457/00 [2004] 1 FLR 800; *Lebbink* v. *The Netherlands* (Application No. 45582/99) [2004] 2 FLR 463; *Maire* v. *Portugal* (Application No. 48206/99) [2004] 2 FLR 653; *Sawadka* v. *Poland* (Application No. 48542/99) [2005] 2 FLR 897.

The cases since *Hokkanen* have developed the following particular issues covered below.

Acceptance of coercive measures to enforce contact

The question for the European Court is often whether national authorities have taken all necessary steps to facilitate reunion as can reasonably be demanded in the special circumstances of the case.

The European Court has approved realistic coercive measures against the resident parent to ensure compliance with contact orders which, although undesirable in the sensitive area of obliging children to reunite with a parent, must not be ruled out in the event of non-compliance or unlawful behaviour by the other parent (*Ignaccolo-Zenide* v. *Romania* (2001) 31 EHRR 7; *Hansen* v. *Turkey* [2004] 1 FLR 142).

In *Zawadka* v. *Poland* [2005] 2 FLR 897, the father complained of a breach of his Article 8 rights on the basis that contact had not been enforced with adequate assistance from the Polish authorities. The Polish court removed the father's parental rights on the basis that he had abused his rights in the past and been uncooperative with courts, including having repeatedly failed to comply with court orders himself and having shown a complete disregard for the child's wellbeing and health. Despite his behaviour the European Court held that there had been a violation of the father's Article 8 rights and that:

(a) although the obligation of the national authority to take measures to facilitate contact was not absolute, the issue was whether or not the authority had taken all necessary steps to facilitate contact as could reasonably be demanded in the circumstances of each case;
(b) the state could not argue that lack of cooperation between the parents was the circumstance which could exempt the authorities from their positive obligations under Article 8;
(c) refusal of assistance by a state authority vested with powers to assist the parties and to retain effective compliance with judicial orders on contact arrangements was incompatible with the positive obligations of the state under Article 8.

The failure of a party to progress his own case is therefore not an excuse for the failure of the state to progress and enforce an application for contact.

The exact nature of the coercive measures which a state should implement to give effect to the substantive Article 8 rights to family life are unclear but clearly coercive measures, such as enforcement orders for unpaid work requirements under the CAA 2006, are permissible and even encouraged to ensure compliance with court orders.

Ensuring respect for the rule of law

National authorities must strike a fair balance between the interests of the parties, on the one hand, and the wider public interest in national courts ensuring compliance with their orders and the general interest in ensuring respect for the rule of law, on the other (*Hokkanen* v. *Finland* [1996] 1 FLR 289; *Hansen* v. *Turkey* (Application No. 36141/97) [2004] 1 FLR 142).

Importance of the effect of effluxion of time

The European Court recognises that in cases concerning a person's relationship with his or her child, there is a duty to exercise exceptional diligence in view of the risk that the passage of time may result in a de facto determination of the case (*Hoppe* v. *Germany* [2003] 1 FLR 384).

Future relations between parent and child should not be determined by the mere effluxion of time and the lapse of time may be caused to a large extent by the ineffective and unacceptable method of the authorities in handling the case (*W* v. *United Kingdom* (1998) 10 EHRR 29 at para. 65; *Sylvester* v. *Austria* [2003] 2 FLR 210).

Delay caused by the court process may well result in a liability of the state to pay compensation to a party whose Article 8 rights have been interfered with and, as a result, effective measures for timetabling cases and for the enforcement of contact orders have become increasingly important.

Rights v. Welfare

Prior to the implementation of the Human Rights Act 1998, concerns were expressed about the erosion of the welfare principle in the face of parental claims for protection of substantive rights under Article 8 to family life, particularly apparent in relation to contact with children.

There is an inevitable conflict between the rights-based approach of the ECHR and the welfare approach of the Children Act 1989 (CA 1989). Although the implementation of the ECHR has not had the feared effect of eroding the welfare principle, it has, when coupled with social change accentuating the involvement of the non-primary carer in the child's life, had an impact on the approach of the UK domestic courts to contact applications.

The non-erosion of the welfare principle is largely a result of:

- the absolute refusal of the UK government and domestic courts to abandon or erode the primacy of section 1(1) of the CA 1989; and

- the acceptance by the European Court of a more welfare-based approach than was perhaps initially contemplated.

UK case law on Rights v. Welfare

To some extent, UK domestic law sidestepped the issue of the conflict between rights and welfare from the beginning by declaring that welfare trumps rights and that there is nothing in the European jurisprudence to contradict this.

Although decided prior to the implementation of the HRA 1998, *Re KD (A Minor) (Access: Principles)* [1988] 2 FLR 139 is still referred to as good law (Thorpe LJ in *Payne* v. *Payne* [2001] 1 FLR 1052). In *Re KD*, the House of Lords held that there is a general proposition that a natural parent has a claim to access to his or her child to which the court will pay regard and it would not be inappropriate to describe such a claim as a 'right'. Equally, a normal assumption is that a child will benefit from continued contact with his natural parent but both the right and the assumption will be displaced if the interests of the child indicate otherwise (Lord Oliver). The House of Lords found nothing in the decision of *R* v. *United Kingdom, The Times*, 9 July 1987, in which the European Court clearly recognised that a parent has a substantive right of access to his child, to suggest otherwise.

In *Re B (Adoption: Natural Parent)* [2002] 1 FLR 196, Lord Nichols of Birkenhead in the House of Lords took the view that where a court finds that an order is in the child's best interests, this identifies the pressing social need and represents the court's considered view of proportionality required by Article 8(2). The difficulty with this decision is that to suggest that the child's welfare will always justify an interference with an individual's Article 8 rights, no matter how substantial the interference or weak the case on welfare, ignores Article 8 requirements. The child's welfare must be a 'relevant and sufficient' reason to justify a violation in the circumstances of the particular case and should be examined in every case.

Prior to, and since, the implementation of the HRA 1998, the English courts have taken the view that as the jurisprudence of the European Court incorporates and stresses the importance of the welfare principle, they can largely ignore the more technical demands of Article 8(2). However, the court should always examine whether an interference with Article 8 rights is necessary and proportionate even where it is alleged to be in the best interests of the child.

The approach of the English courts has been to assume that any order which fulfils the requirements of the CA 1989 automatically fulfils the requirements of Article 8(2). In *Re H (Contact Order (No. 2)* [2002] 1 FLR 22, Wall J said that every case involves the courts balancing the rights of the participants to the application (including the children who are the subjects of it) and arriving at a result which is in the interests of those children (or least detrimental to it) and proportionate to the legitimate aim being pursued. Wall J considered that a proper application of the CA 1989, s.1(3) checklist is equivalent to the balancing exercise required in the application of Article 8 which is then a useful cross-check to ensure that the proposed order is in accordance with the law, necessary for the protection of the rights and freedoms of others and proportionate.

European Court case law on Rights v. Welfare

Hokkanen emphasised the importance of striking a fair balance between the right of a parent to contact and the interests of the child and the child's rights under Article 8.

Since *Hokkanen*, the European Court has put this higher in saying that the interests of the child are particularly to be taken into account (*Hansen* v. *Turkey* (Application No. 36141/97) [2004] 1 FLR 142), and of particular importance which, depending on the nature and seriousness, may override those of the parent (*Elsholz* v. *Germany* [2000] 2 FLR 486).

In *Hoppe* v. *Germany* [2003] 1 FLR 384, where the applicant father was granted limited access to his daughter by the German court because the previous extensive access had caused the child a conflict of loyalty with which she could not cope. The European Court dismissed the father's claim that the decision violated his Article 8 rights and found that the decision to reduce access, albeit an interference, was legitimate and necessary, the courts having properly taken into account the child's best interests.

There is also a stronger line of authority advancing the interests and rights of children. In *Yousef* v. *The Netherlands* [2003] 1 FLR 210, the European Court said that where the rights under Article 8 of parents and those of the child are at stake, the child's rights must be of paramount consideration and, if any balancing of interests is necessary, the interests of the child must prevail.

The welfare principle has therefore been protected by the European Court stressing that countries have wide margins of appreciation when assessing how necessary an interference is and also by the repeated referral to the crucial importance of the best interests of the child which may override the rights of the parent and, in particular, that the parent cannot be allowed measures which would harm a child's health or development.

In private law disputes, an order restricting parental rights can be justified by reference to the child's best interests as long as both parents have been involved in the decision-making process, the restriction is proportionate to the legitimate aim pursued and a fair balance is struck between all competing interests.

Balancing rights: parents and children

A way of accommodating the welfare principle within the ECHR and, more particularly Article 8, has been found but it cannot disguise the underlying problem of the differences in requirements of Article 8 and the welfare principle. Before the implementation of the HRA 1998, the court was only required to identify the child's best interests, albeit in the context of a presumption of contact, but the court must now specifically address parental rights under Article 8(1) and any infringement must be justified by reference to Article 8(2). The child's own rights must also be considered together with the issue of his or her welfare and the approach of the court can often be simply to assume that the child's rights are incompatible with the child's welfare.

It has been noted that the welfare principle provides inadequate protection of parental rights whilst the rights-based approach fails to provide a solution in the situation of a clash between the competing rights of each parent and the child, with no indication of how such rights should be weighted.

Press freedom case law offers an example of how to conduct the balancing exercise of Article 8 rights effectively (*Re S (A Child) (Identification: Restrictions on Publication)* [2005] 1 AC 593) and emphasises the importance of the right of the child of sufficient understanding, the *Gillick* competent child (*Gillick* v. *West Norfolk AHA* [1986] 1 FLR 224), to personal autonomy and the right of the child to knowledge of his or her own development and history, which is central to psychological and moral integrity and feelings of self-worth (*Torbay NBC* v. *NGN ex parte Roddy* [2003] EWHC 2927 (Fam)).

Article 8(1) protects the child's right to family and private life, which includes the right to identity and personal development and to establish and develop relationships with other beings (*Niemietz* v. *Germany* (1993) 16 EHRR 97; *Botta* v. *Italy* (1998) 26 EHRR 241; *Bensaid* v. *United Kingdom* (2001) 33 EHRR 205; *Pretty* v. *United Kingdom* (2002) 35 EHRR 1; *Gaskin* v. *United Kingdom* (1990) 12 EHRR 36). These rights should not be forgotten or overlooked in the context of contact proceedings where the non-enforcement of contact may deny or limit them.

The European Court clearly recognises the long-term importance of a child's relationship with his or her biological parents, even where the child has not already established a proper relationship with the birth parent. Article 8(1) provides this protection regardless of whether the parents were married when the child was born.

12.4 THE PROCEDURAL RIGHT UNDER ARTICLE 8

In addition to the substantive right to respect for family life, the European Court recognises a procedural right which is inherent within Article 8 (*W* v.

United Kingdom (Application No. 9749/82) (1988) 10 EHRR 29) to ensure that a party has sufficient involvement including:

(a) information and opportunity necessary to put his or her case;
(b) that the reasons for the decision and the evidence on which it is based must themselves be relevant and sufficient to found that decision.

European Court case law

The high point of the European Court case law on this procedural aspect is *Elsholz* v. *Germany* [2000] 2 FLR 486. The case involved unmarried parents. The father had contact with the child until she was almost five years old when contact was withdrawn, apparently at the child's request. The German court refused to order contact as the father's relationship with the mother was so strained that if contact were ordered it would be against the mother's will and would put the child into a situation of loyalty conflict which she could not cope with and which would affect her wellbeing. The German court found that further contact with the father would disrupt the child's undisturbed development and the recommendation of an expert psychological opinion by the German Youth Office was refused.

The European Court held that although the best interests of the child are of crucial importance, a fair balance must be struck between the interests of the child and those of the parents. Depending on the nature and seriousness of the case, the interests of the child may override those of the parent and, in particular, a parent cannot be allowed measures which would harm a child's health or development. The European Court noted, however, that the German court had relied on the statement of a five-year-old child and took account of a strained parental relationship whilst not considering which party was responsible for the tensions in that relationship. The European Court found that these reasons, although relevant, were insufficient to explain why the German court had not obtained the expert advice recommended by the Youth Office and that there had been a violation of the father's Article 8 rights.

The European Court has retreated somewhat from *Elholz* with the decision in *Hoppe* v. *Germany* (Application No. 28422/95) [2003] 1 FLR 384 and the appeal to the Grand Chamber of the European Court in *Sahin* v. *Germany*; *Sommerfeld* v. *Germany* (Application Nos 0943/96 and 31871/96 [2003] 2 FLR 671). In *Sahin*, the issue was whether the child should have been met and heard by the court as well as by a psychologist and in *Sommerfield* it was whether the child should have been met and heard by a psychologist as well as by the court.

In *Sahin*, the Chamber of the European Court found that the German court's failure to hear the child revealed an insufficient involvement of the applicant in the access proceedings and that the German court should not have been satisfied with the expert's vague statements about the risks inherent in questioning the child, without even contemplating the possibility for special arrangements in view of the child's young age.

The Grand Chamber, by contrast, found on the appeal in *Sahin* that, having heard the psychological expert opinion on the question of whether contact with the applicant was in the child's interests, it was for the German court to assess the evidence before it. The Grand Chamber felt it would be going too far to say that domestic courts are always required to hear a child in court on the issue of access to a parent, depending on the specific circumstances of each case, having due regard to the age and maturity of the child concerned. The Grand Chamber found that the German court had not overstepped its margin of appreciation when relying on the findings of the child psychologist, even though the judge had not asked the child direct questions about her relationship with her father.

In *Sommerfield*, the Chamber of the European Court found that the failure to order a psychiatric report on the possibilities of establishing contact revealed the father was not sufficiently involved.

The Grand Chamber, again by contrast, found in *Sommerfield* that as the court had the benefit of direct contact with the child it could evaluate her evidence without the need for expert involvement.

Despite the decision of the Grand Chamber in *Sahin* and *Sommerfield*, there remains a strong right to 'sufficient involvement' (*Kosmopoulou* v. *Greece* [2004] 1 FLR 800, where the European Court found the applicant mother had not been sufficiently involved in the decision-making process by the state to provide the requisite protection of her rights under Article 8(1) to contact with her daughter and, in particular, that there had been a failure to have independent experts' reports and too much attention had been paid to reports produced by indviduals instructed by the father).

UK case law

The procedural right under Article 8 has impacted on UK domestic law and will continue to do so in the future.

In *Re S* [2004] 1 FLR 1279, the Court of Appeal directed a psychological assessment of the whole family as the possible key to a reconsideration of future contact, after the judge had ordered indirect contact and debarred the father from making any further applications under section 8 for one year. The Court of Appeal took the view that 'good-enough parents' should have a relationship with their children for their own benefit and the benefit of the children and the attempt to promote contact between the child and the non-resident parent should not be abandoned until it was clear that the child would not benefit from continuing the attempt.

In *Re G (A Child)* [2006] EWCA Civ 348, the Court of Appeal held that where a father had been refused direct contact with his daughter, the court was wrong to refuse to direct that CAFCASS meet with the child to discuss contact issues, as there was an obligation on the courts to pursue all avenues towards the resumption of direct contact.

The right to sufficient involvement extends to children whether parties to, or the subject of, the proceedings. In UK domestic law, there is now a recognition of the need for separate representation of children (*Re T (Contact: Alienation: Permission to Appeal)* [2003] 1 FLR 531) and the involvement of therapeutic experts in difficult contact cases.

It should be noted, however, that where the judge reaches the conclusion that family proceedings in relation to issues of contact can go no further, he has the right and duty to bring such proceedings to an end to eliminate any case which only operates to prolong other cases waiting to be heard. The Court of Appeal has upheld two first instance decisions on such grounds.

In *Re C-P* [2006] EWCA Civ 120, the judge made a final order for no contact at a hearing listed as a directions hearing, taking into consideration psychological reports and abusive letters and text messages the father had sent to the mother resulting in the child's reluctance to have contact with her father. The Court of Appeal held there had been no unfairness to the father in the judge taking this course, that the judge had a wide discretion as to how the proceedings should be conducted and if he reached the conclusion the proceedings had come to the end of the road he had a right and duty to bring them to an end there and then. The Court of Appeal also noted that the parties had been legally represented and the hearing, albeit listed for directions, lasted over an hour.

In *Re D* [2006] EWCA Civ 349, the parties agreed contact by consent to continue until the substantive hearing. The judge treated a directions hearing as a final hearing and converted the interim order into a final order. The mother appealed, claiming that this denied her the opportunity to give oral evidence at a final hearing and denied the court the full range of reports and consequently there had been a breach of Article 6. The Court of Appeal refused to accept that there had been a breach of Article 6 and stated that the judge was entitled to reach this conclusion but any judge, when doing so, should give full reasons explaining his decision and why it is justifiable on grounds of proportionality.

12.5 COMPATIBILITY OF THE CAA 2006 WITH THE ECHR

Under HRA 1998, s.9, the Minister in charge of a Bill is required to make a statement about the compatibility of that Bill with Convention rights before its Second Reading. The following was stated in relation to the Children and Adoption Act 2006:

CONTACT ACTIVITY – DIRECTION OR CONDITION

- Article 6 is not breached as the requirement would not of itself mean that the case before the court would not be concluded in due course.
- Article 8 rights engaged by the making of a contact activity direction, condition or FAO, will not be infringed as the direction or condition would be justified since:
  - it pursues a legitimate objective;
  - would be in accordance with the law; and
  - would be a proportionate response, in that it would be a reasonable way to facilitate an outcome which is in the best interests of the child.

Enforcement orders

- Article 6 will not be infringed by the implementation of appropriate procedural safeguards.
- Article 8 rights engaged will not be infringed due to the range of matters of which the courts will have to be satisfied before imposing such orders.
- Article 4 (prohibition of slavery and forced labour) rights are not breached because unpaid work requirements do not amount to forced or compulsory labour as:
  - they would not be unjust or oppressive as sections 11I to 11M include provision for warning the individual of the consequences of failing to comply with the contact order (sections 11I and 11K);
  - the court must be satisfied that making the enforcement order is necessary to secure compliance with the contact order and is proportionate (section 11L);
  - they fall within the exception in Article 4.3(d) of the ECHR (work or service which forms part of normal civic obligations) since it is in the general interest of the community, as well as of the individuals involved, particularly the child, to ensure that contact orders are obeyed;
  - it is normal in our society to expect and require people to comply with court orders.

12.6 PROCEDURE ON AN APPLICATION TO THE COURTS OF ENGLAND AND WALES UNDER THE HRA 1998

A human rights point may be brought before the courts of England and Wales in the following ways:

- as a free-standing issue, which will be by way of judicial review proceedings to the Administrative Court and CPR Part 54;
- in existing proceedings, when a party who seeks to rely on any provision of or right arising under the HRA 1998 or seeks a remedy available under that Act must state that fact in his originating document or answer (Family Proceedings Rules 1991 (FPR 1991), r.10.26(2)(a)) and in his originating document or answer must (FPR 1991, r.10.26(2)(b)):

  - give precise details of the Convention right which it is alleged has been infringed and details of the alleged infringement;
  - specify the relief sought;
  - state if the relief sought includes a declaration of incompatibility;
- if the issue arises after the commencement of proceedings, the application should be amended to include the human rights point under FPR 1991, r.10.26(3); the amendment should be made as soon as possible and, in any event, not less than 28 days before the hearing.

Form of application/answer

In private law children applications, reference to the HRA 1998 point should be included in the Form C1 application.

'Answer' under FPR 1991, r.10.26(1) does not include an acknowledgement of service and it is therefore suggested that a respondent should cross apply on Form C1 or use Form C2 (for an order in existing family proceedings) to state the issue raised.

Application for declaration of incompatibility

An application may be made under HRA 1998, s.4 to declare primary or secondary legislation incompatible with the provisions of the ECHR (as defined under HRA 1998, s.1). If such an issue is raised:

- the application must be dealt with in the High Court (HRA 1998, s.4(5)) so the application must either be made to the High Court or transferred there;
- notice must be given to the Crown to consider joinder as a party to the application (CPR r.19.4A and FPR 1991, r.10.26(6)).

An application may be made claiming that there has been a failure in a judicial act to be compatible with the provisions of the ECHR (as defined under HRA 1998, s.1). Such a claim may only be made by way of appeal or judicial review where an appeal may not be made (HRA 1998, s.9); and notice must be given to the court with a view to joinder (CPR r.19.4A and FPR 1991, r.10.26(18)).

12.7 APPLICATIONS FOR LEAVE TO REMOVE CHILDREN FROM THE JURISDICTION

In a private children law context, the conflict between rights and welfare is perhaps nowhere more pronounced than in the field of applications for leave to remove children from the jurisdiction, and the consequent loss of regular contact with the non-resident parent. In such cases, the courts' avoidance of the technical requirements of Article 8 is at its most obvious and the difficult balancing exercise required by Article 8 is generally dealt with by subsuming the child's welfare, which is paramount, within the rights and welfare of the primary carer.

The current law on leave to remove applications is set out in *Payne* v. *Payne* [2001] 1 FLR 1052, in which the Court of Appeal approved and confirmed the earlier decision of *Poel* v. *Poel* [1971] WLR 1469. In *Payne*, the mother originated from New Zealand and the father from England. The mother and child moved to New Zealand when the child was about 14 months old, the father having taken a job temporarily in Kuala Lumpar. When that job ended, the father joined the family in New Zealand. There was a dispute between the parties as to whether there had been an agreement about settling in New Zealand long term. The father applied for the return of the child to the United Kingdom after the marriage broke down which was ordered by the New Zealand court under the Hague Convention on the Civil Aspects of International Child Abduction 1980. On return to England, the mother obtained a residence order with defined contact to the father. The mother's subsequent application for leave to remove the child to New Zealand was upheld by the Court of Appeal.

The *Payne* guidelines

In the Court of Appeal, Thorpe LJ set out the following four step process which is the basis of the current approach in leave to remove cases:

1. Pose the question: is the mother's application genuine in the sense that it is not motivated by some selfish desire to exclude the father from the child's life? Then ask if the mother's application is realistic, by which I mean founded on practical proposals both well researched and investigated? If the application fails either of these tests refusal will inevitably follow.
2. If, however, the application passes these tests then there must be a careful appraisal of the father's opposition: is it motivated by genuine concern for the future of the child's welfare or is it driven by some ulterior motive? What would be the extent of the detriment to him and his future relationship with the child were the application to be granted? To what extent would that be offset by extension of the child's relationships with the maternal family and home land?
3. What would be the impact on the mother, either as a single parent or as a new wife, of the refusal of her realistic proposal?
4. The outcome of the second and third appraisals must then be brought into an overriding review of the child's welfare as the paramount consideration, directed by the statutory checklist in so far as appropriate.

Thorpe LJ emphasised that in relation to step (3) the importance of the emotional and psychological wellbeing of the primary carer should not be diminished and that, in any evaluation, the welfare of the child is the paramount consideration and great weight must be given to that factor. In *Payne*, the crucial findings of the trial judge were that the mother would be devastated, isolated and depressed to a degree which could well damage the child if she were not able to return to New Zealand.

Butler-Sloss LJ also laid down the following guidelines in *Payne*:

1. The welfare of the child is always paramount.
2. There is no presumption created by CA 1989, s.13(1)(b) in favour of the applicant parent.
3. The reasonable proposals of the parent with a residence order wishing to live abroad carry great weight.
4. Consequently, the proposals have to be scrutinised with care and the court needs to be satisfied that there is a genuine motivation for the move and not the intention to bring contact between the child and the other parent to an end.
5. The effect upon the applicant parent and the new family of the child of a refusal of leave is very important.
6. The effect upon the child of the denial of contact with the other parent and in some cases his family is very important.
7. The opportunity for continuing contact between the child and the parent left behind may be very significant.

No presumption of removal

In *Payne*, the elevation of the approach in favour of the primary carer seeking to remove the child into a presumption of removal (previously indicated in *MH* v. *GP (Child: Emigration)* [1995] 2 FLR 106 and *Re C (Leave to Remove from the Jurisdiction)* [2000] 2 FLR 457) was rejected on the basis that it would run the risk of violating the respect for family life to which the father, in addition to the mother and child, was entitled, together with the father's right to a fair trial, under Articles 8 and 6 of the ECHR. However, the court also rejected the father's arguments that the approach in *Poel* was incompatible with the ECHR relying on the European Court's recognition of the paramountcy principle albeit not expressed in the language of the CA 1989.

Thorpe LJ referred to *Re KD (A Minor) (Access: Principles)* [1988] 2 FLR 139 (see above) in support of this proposition. He held that the advent of the ECHR into domestic law did not necessitate a revision of the fundamental approach to relocation applications, which had always been to apply the child's welfare as the paramount consideration and that supporting the reasonable proposal of the primary carer is an important factor in the assessment of welfare. Thorpe LJ's view was that in a united family the right to family life is a shared right but once a family disintegrates the separate members' rights can only be to a fragmented family life and the absent parent has the right to participation to the extent and in what manner the complex circumstances of the individual case dictate.

Impact of refusal on the emotional and psychological stability of the primary carer

The *Payne* approach was very much based on the acceptance of a child's need for emotional and psychological security and stability and that this cannot be ensured unless the primary carer herself is emotionally and psychologically stable and secure. This has been reasserted in subsequent cases.

In *Re B* [2005] 2 FLR 239, the Court of Appeal indicated that emotional and psychological wellbeing of the primary carer was a significant element but also, and importantly, that there is no difference in principle between lifestyle cases and return cases involving foreign nationals wanting to return to their home countries.

In *Re G* [2005] 2 FLR 166, the Court of Appeal concluded that the failure to establish psychiatric damage if permission were refused was not itself a ground for refusing permission. In this case, however, the court insisted on practical arrangements for schooling and contact being confirmed prior to the child's departure.

Impact of refusal on the new family

The *Payne* approach regarding the impact of refusal on the new family has been reaffirmed in two linked cases: *Re B (Removal from Jurisdiction; Re S (Removal from Jurisdiction)* [2003] 2 FLR 1043. Both cases involved mothers wishing to relocate to join spouses in, respectively, South Africa and the Philippines. Appeals against refusals of leave were allowed by the Court of Appeal clarifying that:

(a) the 'natural gravitation' of a new family had an important bearing on the outcome of the case;
(b) where a mother cared for a child within a new family, the impact of refusal on the new family altogether had to be carefully evaluated;
(c) under both (a) and (b) above, the welfare of the children could not be achieved unless the new family had the ordinary opportunity to pursue its goals and make its choices without unreasonable restriction.

Common case categories

In leave to remove applications, the reasons given by the parent seeking to remove a child from a jurisdiction generally fall into three categories:

1. Remarriage: *Poel* v. *Poel*; *Re H (Application to Remove from Jurisdiction)* [1998] 1 FLR 848, in which the father of a five-year-old child had played

an unusually large role in her care but, despite recognising that the balance was on a knife edge, the court allowed the mother's application to remove the child; *Re C (Leave to Remove from Jurisdiction)* [2000] 2 FLR 245, in which, more unusually, the mother's application for leave to remove the child was refused as, despite the benefits of the plan, the harm done by its frustration was found to be outweighed by a greater harm flowing from the severe reduction of the father's contact; *Re B (Remove from Jurisdiction)*; *Re S (Remove from Jurisdiction)* [2003] 2 FLR 1043.

2. Career/lifestyle choice: *Nash* v. *Nash* [1973] 2 All ER 704; *Re B (Leave to Remove: Impact of Refusal)* [2005] 2 FLR 239.
3. Return home: *A* v. *A (Child: Removal from the Jurisdiction)* [1980] 1 FLR 380; *Payne* v. *Payne* (above); *Re G (Removal from Jurisdiction)* [2005] 2 FLR 166.

Points to address in the application

An application for leave to remove a child from the jurisdiction will not be successfully obtained simply by arguing that the applicant will suffer extreme depression and unhappiness, with arguably disastrous results for the child, if her application is refused. This is one argument only and the court will be concerned with this but also a variety of other issues. A leave to remove application should include the following:

- the history of arrangements for care of the child: in *Payne*, Butler-Sloss LJ stated that the reasonable proposals of a parent with a residence order wishing to remove a child from the jurisdiction would carry great weight; logically, therefore, weight should also be attached to the wishes of an applicant who has been the primary carer of the child for a number of years even in the absence of a residence order;
- the motivation of the applicant: this is the starting point for the court under Thorpe LJ's four stage test in *Payne* and if this motivation is merely to prevent contact with the non-resident parent, then the application will fail; where the motivation is to return home, pursue employment and/or accompany a new spouse or future partner, this will be regarded as valid motivation for the removal;
- practical arrangements, for example, housing, schooling and financial support in the new jurisdiction or in the United Kingdom if the application is refused and the applicant is required to remain in this jurisdiction;
- the nature of the jurisdiction to which relocation is planned, for example, whether it is politically stable;
- proposals for contact arrangements with the non-resident parent if the application to remove the child is approved: this should be subject to careful consideration in every case; an applicant offering good and sustainable contact arrangements will assist the court in deciding in her favour;

- where there is a risk of an application for leave to remove the child from the jurisdiction, it may be of benefit to a non-resident parent to apply for a shared residence order, provided only that such an application stands a realistic prospect of success, in order to establish a historical pattern of shared parenting. The courts are increasingly willing to make orders for shared residence in non-exceptional circumstances and to reflect the fact that parents are equal and have equal duties and responsibilities to their children. However, a shared residence order will not necessarily mean a strictly equal division of time spent by a child with each parent and in reality one parent is likely still to be regarded as the primary carer for the purposes of any subsequent application for leave to remove the child from the jurisdiction.

Refusal of application for leave to remove

It has been argued that the devastating unhappiness and depression caused to the non-resident parent, usually the father, who is left behind is not given proper consideration, whilst weight is readily attached to the consequences for the applicant, usually the mother, if her application is refused. There is support for the proposition that leave to remove is too easily granted to an applicant who can argue that the welfare of the child is the court's paramount consideration and that her welfare is inextricably bound up with the welfare of the child. The decision in an applicant's favour is not guaranteed, however, as recent cases show.

In *Re Y* [2004] 2 FLR 330, Hedley J refused an application for leave to remove a five and a half-year-old child when his mother, who was a foreign national, wished to return to her home, despite finding that she had good and valid reasons for the return and that her motivation was entirely genuine. The decision was largely based on the child having been the subject of a shared care arrangement since the parties separated. Hedley J made a shared residence order after refusing the mother's application.

In *Re R* [2005] 1 FLR 687, Baron J refused an application by a mother to remove the children to France (despite the feasibility of contact if the children relocated to that jurisdiction) because of concerns about (a) the mother's plans not being sufficiently considered but based on an assumption that life would improve if she returned to France; (b) her relationship with her French relatives not having been sufficiently tested under crisis; (c) her emotional stability as she had a tendency to act 'on a whim' and there was a possibility that the removal to France would not work out in reality; and (d) that contact would be adversely affected between the children and their father and grandparents.

In *Re N* [2006] EWCA Civ 357, the mother's application to remove the children to Turkey was refused at first instance. Her appeal was allowed by the Court of Appeal on an application to send the children to family abroad for a two-week holiday. She did not appeal the refusal of her application for leave to remove the children entirely.

Procedure on application for leave to remove

Leave to remove applications are made in accordance with FPR 1991, r.4.4 and brought under either CA 1989, s.13(1)(b) where there is a residence order in force, or CA 1989, s.8 in the absence of a residence order.

The application is therefore subject to the paramountcy principle in section 1(1) and, where the application is under section 8, the welfare checklist in CA 1989, s.1(3). Although technically an application bought under section 13(1) is not subject to the welfare checklist, the trial judge should nevertheless take the precaution of regarding the checklist factors when carrying out his welfare appraisal (*Payne* v. *Payne* [2001] 1 FLR 1052).

The application can be made in any court. However, where the application is for leave to remove a child permanently from the jurisdiction, it should be transferred for determination either in the county court or the High Court, depending on the complexity and difficulty of the decision.

12.8 RELOCATION WITHIN THE UNITED KINGDOM

The removal of a child from England and Wales to Scotland does not require an application for leave to remove the child from the jurisdiction, since Scotland is part of the United Kingdom (*Re T (A Child)* (28 June 2001)).

Relocation within the United Kingdom may not require the primary carer to apply for leave. However, the relocating parent may still have to defeat either:

- a challenge to relocation by the application of the left behind parent for a prohibited steps order under CA 1989, s.8; or
- the imposition of a condition to any residence order under CA 1989, s.11(7) that the parent seeking to relocate remains in the current area of residence in the United Kingdom.

In *Re H (Children) (Residence Order: Condition)* [2001] 2 FLR 1277, the Court of Appeal held that the welfare of the child is always paramount and that the test to be applied for external or internal relocation is that laid down in *Payne*. However, the test is less stringent in cases of internal relocation than external relocation (*Re S (Child) (Residence Order: Condition)* [2001] 3 FCR 154).

CHAPTER 13

Child contact and public authorities

13.1 INTRODUCTION

It is not only parents who have responsibilities and duties to children. Local authorities also have obligations and statutory duties towards children. There are different categories of children in respect of these obligations. The first category is 'looked after children' who are either children in the care of a local authority under an interim care order or post-proceedings, a full care order. The category also includes those children who are being provided accommodation by the local authority outside of the province of a care order. The second and more elusive category is 'children in need'. Lastly, there are other services which a local authority can provide and should be available to all children whether or not they are deemed to be in need.

Whereas many looked after children will invariably be or will have been the subject of public law proceedings children in need can include children who are involved in private law proceedings of some description or whose parents are caught up in familial conflict. Although practitioners advising on contact issues are unlikely to need an amplified knowledge of local authority obligations, it is useful to have an underlying grasp of the area. This is primarily because, where a local authority does become involved in the lives of children or parents whom the solicitor is advising in relation to contact, the private law/public law divide can close (often rather suddenly) and a parent may require assistance in this regard. This might be so particularly in circumstances where child protection measures have been commenced or a local authority has convened a child protection case conference. Such action can swiftly transform the case into care proceedings and appropriate advice should be given to clients as necessary (see further L. Goldthorpe with P. Monro, *Child Law Handbook*, Law Society Publishing (with the Association of Lawyers for Children) (2005)).

Practitioners also need to be aware of those circumstances where their parent clients require assistance from the local authority towards their child. It is important for the practitioner to be attuned to these situations and to be able to make appropriate referrals or furnish initial advice to clients who may not otherwise be aware of the help or relief that a local authority could provide. For this reason a brief consideration of local authorities and their duties is given in this chapter although it is not a comprehensive account of this area.

13.2 CHILDREN IN NEED

'Children in need' is defined by section 10(17) of the Children Act 1989 (CA 1989) as being where:

> (a) he is unlikely to achieve or maintain, or to have the opportunity of achieving or maintaining, a reasonable standard of health or development without the provision for him of services by a local authority under this Part;
> (b) his health or development is likely to be significantly impaired, or further impaired without the provision for him of such services; or
> (c) he is disabled.

Section 17(11) clarifies that health relates to physical or mental health, whereas development means 'physical, intellectual, emotional, social or behavioural development' which is broad. While the CA 1989 does not specify who should determine whether or not a child is in need, in practice it will fall to the local authority to conduct an assessment of the child under its powers (CA 1989, Sched. 2 Part 1 para. 3) to determine the issue. This could be of the local authority's own volition or where a parent insists on an assessment. There will be occasions where it is clear to the local authority that a child is in need and the assessment will be as to services that can be provided. Equally, there may be cases where the local authority might dispute the parent's contention that their child is in need and therefore the authority may need some persuading to perform an assessment to determine that question. Paragraph 3 of CA 1989, Sched. 2, Part 1 merely states that the authority 'may' assess and where there is entrenched reluctance from the local authority to do so, the issue could possibly be the subject of a public law or human rights challenge.

It is clear, then, that there may be children who come within the definition of children in need but yet continue to live within the family. Those family members may have engaged a solicitor in respect of contact issues. Where a solicitor is so instructed (or in relation to any private law proceedings) it is good practice to be able to advise or offer a signpost to a client who has a child who could come within the definition and therefore qualify for services from their local authority.

13.3 SERVICES FOR CHILDREN IN NEED

Section 17 of the CA 1989 gives the main statutory footing for the provision of services for children in need, their families and other persons. The general duty is at section 17(1) and states that:

> it shall be the general duty of every local authority (in addition to the other duties imposed on them by this Part):
>
> (a) to safeguard and promote the welfare of children within their area who are in need; and
> (b) so far as is consistent with that duty, to promote the upbringing of such children by their families,
>
> by providing a range and level of services appropriate to those children's needs.

The form of services may include providing accommodation, giving assistance in kind or, in exceptional circumstances, in cash (CA 1989, s.17(6)). With reference to this general duty (provision of services), there is a list of specific duties and powers that local authorities 'shall have' in Part 1 of Schedule 2 to the CA 1989. That list is subject to a power of amendment by the Secretary of State. This does not prevent the local authority from providing services where appropriate to children which are not set out in that list. Of note, however, is paragraph 8, which lists specific provision for 'children living with their families', such as advice, counselling, home help, holiday assistance and activities.

In so exercising its functions under CA 1989, s.17, any service that the authority provides may be provided for the family of a child in need or for any member of his family so long as it is provided with a view to safeguarding or promoting the child's welfare. Prior to the Children Act 2004 (CA 2004), CA 1989, s.17 made no reference to the wishes and feelings of the child in respect of the local authority's consideration of provision of services for either the child or his or her family. Section 53(1) of the CA 2004 has remedied this gap by inserting a new sub-section 4A into section 17. It provides that:

> Before determining what (if any) services to provide for a particular child in need in the exercise of functions conferred on them by this section, a local authority shall, so far as is reasonably practicable and consistent with the child's welfare:
>
> (a) ascertain the child's wishes and feelings regarding the provision of those services; and
> (b) give due consideration (having regard to his age and understanding) to such wishes and feelings of the child as they have been able ascertain.

Clearly there will be children who are too young to be able to directly express their wishes and feelings to a social worker. Arguably, reasonable steps will need to be taken even in the case of young children to attempt to ascertain their wishes and feelings. For children who are able to express a view, a local authority would be in clear breach of its duties under the section if it failed to perform exercises which sought to ascertain the child's wishes and feelings or to give them due consideration its the decision-making process. Although this does place upon the local authority an additional task when considering each case for services, it is fundamental one and one that speaks well to the rhetoric of children's rights. As the CA 2004 is in its very initial stages and this sub-section is a new creature, it will take some time before we see whether local authorities are treating the duty with the significance it deserves.

13.4 CHALLENGING LOCAL AUTHORITIES

Where a parent has sought the assistance of a local authority by the way of services and is dissatisfied with the response or decision, he or she can seek to challenge that decision.

Complaints/representations

The most common method will be either to make representations to the local authority or seek to involve a more senior member of staff than the original decision-maker. A step further will be to make a formal complaint. Every local authority must have a complaints procedure for children's matters (CA 1989, s.26(3)), which should be followed when initiated by a complainant lodging his or her complaint. Parents of 'children in need' are one category of the group who qualify as complainants under the section. Where the dispute between the parents and the local authority relates to the question of whether or not the child is in fact in need, with the local authority possibly arguing he or she is not (and thereby not warranting the provision of services), the parent may need to follow the non-children-specific complaints procedure: the Local Authority Social Services Complaints (England) Regulations 2006, SI 2006/1681 (replacing the Complaints Procedure Directions 1990 made pursuant to the Local Authority Social Services Act 1970). The new regulations for complaints came into force on 1 September 2006.

Where possible, it would appear prudent to bring, and state that the complaint is being brought, under the CA 1989, s.26(3) footing as this avenue requires the consideration of the matter to have the involvement of an independent person (not a member of that local authority); this feature would usually serve to benefit the complainant or to assist him or her to accept more easily any negative outcome of the complaint-handling process. The representations or complaint should be dealt with and processed in accordance with the Children Act 1989 Representations Procedure (England) Regulations 2006, SI 2006/1738 which came into force on 1 September 2006.

Children's Commissioner

The Children's Commissioner, a role created by the CA 2004 (Part 1) can *inter alia* investigate into and report on a child's individual case where it raises issues of public policy which are also relevant to other children. However, he cannot do this if it would be a duplication of the work of another person and he must also consult the Secretary of State before holding any inquiry. The CA 2004 also permits the Secretary of State to direct the Children's Commissioner to hold an inquiry. It is unlikely that practitioners would have frequent recourse to the Children's Commissioner. However, if on careful assessment it appears that the issues of an individual case are compelling and have significant wider interest, parents or practitioners may wish to make representations to the Commissioner asking that an inquiry be held.

Local Government Ombudsman

The office of the Local Government Ombudsman (LGO) was created by the Local Government Act 1974. The LGO is independent and impartial and his task is to investigate complaints of injustice arising from maladministration by local authorities and certain other bodies. It will not usually criticise the merits of a decision which has been taken properly yet the examples given of what will be considered to be maladministration are wide and will encompass delay, incorrect action, lack of action, lack of reply, broken promises and failure to follow procedures or the law. Where circumstances fall to be decided in line with statutory guidance and there is a failure on the part of a local authority to do so, this is an example of a complaint which the LGO should investigate.

A complaint to the LGO will be expected to have been brought within 12 months of the decision complained of. The LGO retains discretion to look at complaints brought outside this period and will have regard to the seriousness of the injustice when making a decision to consider an out of time complaint. It is normally expected that the local authority in question will have been given notice of the problem, which should be in the form of a formal complaint to the authority itself. The authority should have had a reasonable period in which to investigate and respond to the complaint. The LGO deems a reasonable opportunity 12 weeks from the date of the written complaint to the authority. It should not be the case that a complainant has to exhaust the entire internal complaints procedure before bringing his or her matter to the attention of the LGO. However, it may be preferable to allow this to happen prior to making a complaint to the LGO. There will be other times where the usual 12-week 'reasonable opportunity' to be given to the local authority will cause prejudice. In these situations, representations will need to be made on an exceptional basis to the LGO in order to argue why he should become involved sooner. Examples given are circumstances where time is of the essence, vulnerability of a person, or where an entire system of administration has collapsed.

The LGO has no discretion to investigate a complaint once the complainant has commenced court proceedings, started an appeal to a government minister or started an appeal to a statutory body. Neither will he look behind the outcomes of decisions of any of those persons or bodies. He will not usually investigate a complaint where the complainant has an alternative right or remedy with which he could avail himself. However, if such avenues are available but have not yet been pursued, the LGO will consider the question of whether or not he is willing to investigate; in each case the question will be decided on its own merits, taking into account various factors. During the process of investigation, the LGO can undertake various tasks, such as examine the authority's files, visit the complainant and collect information from third parties. At the outcome stage, and if the LGO finds adversely against the local authority, he can ask the authority to make amends by taking action, such as making an apology, paying compensation or improving procedures. More information about LGO complaints can be found at www.lgo.org.uk.

Judicial review

Judicial review is an area of administrative law. It is a complex area and will not have any general relevance to family proceedings. It is the method by which decisions of those performing administrative functions (legislative, executive, judicial or adjudicatory) can be challenged and therefore is of great importance to those seeking to challenge local authority decisions. The principles of judicial review cannot be considered in full here. However, in brief, judicial review is available to review the decision-making process of the body being challenged. The petitioner can seek certain orders from the court but the court charged with considering judicial review proceedings does not take on the same role as an appellate court. The grounds for judicial review, i.e. the basis of any challenge, are that the body being challenged acted either illegally, irrationally or improperly. The court will only usually hear judicial review proceedings where the applicant has exhausted all remedies available.

The application for judicial review is a two-stage process. At the permission stage, a decision is taken as to whether or not permission will be granted to the applicant to apply for judicial review. The application for permission should be brought promptly and within three months of the date from when the decision being challenged was taken, unless the court considers that there is good reason to extend that period. Where permission on the papers is not granted, an application to renew can be made and the matter will be listed for an oral hearing. If permission is granted, interim relief sought at that stage may be granted and thereafter the matter proceeds to a full hearing where the substantive matter is considered by the court.

Care contact orders

The law regarding children who are in care and contact between them and other persons is not subject to the private law sections of the CA 1989. Contact in these circumstances is viewed to be distinct and is governed primarily by CA 1989, s.34 and regulations. When any care order is made, any section 8 orders that were in existence in relation to that child are discharged and no further section 8 orders (save for a residence order) can be made while the child remains in the care of a local authority. If a residence order is made in respect of a child subject to a care order, the residence order would discharge the care order.

The subject matter of contact with children in care is substantial in its own right and outside the scope of this book. The underlying principle is that the local authority should permit reasonable contact between a child in care and his or her parents. What will be 'reasonable' will largely be dictated by the circumstances of the individual case. There are provisions which give a discretion to the local authority to refuse contact and likewise provisions where prescribed persons (or others who have obtained leave of the court) can make an application to the court for an order for contact with the child in care. The court also has a power to make such an order of its own accord, including an order (on the application of the local authority or the child) authorising the local authority to refuse to allow contact between the child and a named person in the order. These orders of the court can be made subject to certain conditions as the court sees fit (for example, that a particular person should not be present during a contact session or that contact takes place in a contact centre). It is also recognised that the court can order contact even after it has been satisfied that a care order should be made. In some cases this will be wholly inappropriate, whereas, in others, it may be in the best interests of the child to continue having contact with his or her birth family, but in all cases the court is under a duty to consider the issue of contact upon making a care order (CA 1989, s.34(11)(a)). These decisions can be difficult, especially in cases where it is appropriate to find a suitable long-term placement and ensure that nothing impedes that objective.

13.5 CHILD CONTACT AND IMMIGRATION

The interface between these two jurisdictions is often easily overlooked. It is important for family lawyers to have an awareness that the two areas do at times cross paths and essential that they are able to access information about immigration law where necessary and in the interests of their client. It is also useful for practitioners to be able to flag up where a client might need immigration advice (quite distinct from any family law advice) and therefore an appropriate referral should be made.

Although not commonplace, the circumstances which involve an interplay between child contact law and immigration are:

(a) a parent client is the respondent to an application for contact by a person who is subject to immigration control (i.e. a person who is not a British citizen or does not have indefinite leave to remain in the United Kingdom);
(b) a parent client is subject to immigration control and seeks advice on applying for or otherwise securing contact with his or her child;
(c) the practitioner is instructed by a non-parent family member subject to immigration control who seeks contact with a child to whom he or she is related;
(d) the practitioner is consulted by an immigration practitioner for advice about child contact proceedings in the United Kingdom for their client who seeks entry into the United Kingdom for this purpose.

Inevitably, in family cases which involve components of immigration law, it will be sensible and logical for the family matter to be dealt with first (whether by the court or settled otherwise). In the family court, the paramountcy principle (see Chapter 1) applies whereas immigration law has no equivalent principle. Where the family court has considered the best interests of the child, this can be presented to the immigration officials as bearing weight. It is vital to bear in mind that the family courts have no jurisdiction to decide upon or otherwise seek to influence a party's immigration status: this is strictly the domain of the Secretary of State for the Home Department and the immigration tribunals where appeals are pursued (e.g., see *Findlay* v. *Matondo* [1993] 1 AC 542). However, often the family court may wish to be appraised of and to give consideration to the immigration status of the child and/or the parties.

Where family lawyers act in circumstances where their client is seeking contact with a child but is subject to immigration control, the family court should be informed of any pending or anticipated application or appeal to the immigration authorities for an extension of leave to remain or any other form of application. This is necessary because the court should not be influenced by the fact that a parent has limited leave to remain and therefore is due to leave the United Kingdom. It should not be assumed that the parent will be forced to leave and that their application to extend leave will be refused. These are matters for the Home Secretary and not for the judge hearing the contact proceedings.

In the same way that the family court is unable to make a decision over a parent's immigration status, similarly the Home Secretary does not have the power to decide a contact application. However, as the Home Secretary does not have to consider the child's interests as paramount, he or she can obliquely influence contact proceedings by deciding unfavourably upon a parent's immigration application. Contact orders of the family court are of relevance to immigration authorities pursuant to:

- the Immigration Directorate's Instructions in which, at Chapter 8, Annex M, paragraph 9, it is stated at that 'children who are subjects of court orders made under the Children's [sic] Act 1989 in the United Kingdom, may still be removed or deported from the United Kingdom. However, the existence of any such order is a factor which should be taken into account'; and
- Article 6 of the ECHR, where fair trial and hearing rights come into play insofar as it is arguable that the Home Secretary in prudently making immigration decisions should await the conclusion of child contact proceedings where the order sought may be pertinent to the decision that he or she is to make.

Family practitioners should note that they may be called upon by an immigration adviser for their mutual client to assist with supporting evidence where they seek to extend or obtain discretionary leave for that client from the Immigration and Nationality Directorate pending an outcome from the contact proceedings.

The President of the Family Division introduced a Protocol on Communicating with the Home Office in June 2004 ([2004] 1 FLR 638 and [2004] Fam. Law 608). The Protocol is not reciprocal as it only concerns the making of a request for information from the Home Office. Where the family practitioner seeks to provide information about contact proceedings to the Home Office in order to assist their client (or a mutual client with an immigration lawyer), the giving of such information will therefore be subject to the rules of disclosure, which are complex. See a more detailed discussion at section 14.2.

As a result of the increased awareness of children's rights and the potential benefits of contact for the child with the non-resident parent, the Immigration Rules were amended. The amended provisions are contained within the Immigration Rules (IR) (HC 395), under Part 7 'Other Categories'. Paragraphs 246 – 248 deal with leave to enter the United Kingdom as a person exercising rights of 'access' to a child resident in the United Kingdom. Provisions for leave to remain owing to the need to exercise rights of access come under paragraphs 248A – 248C and indefinite leave to remain provisions at paragraphs 248D – 248F. Although provisions were introduced in October 2000, contact is described as 'access'.

Practitioners should be alert to the motivation for seeking a contact order. If acting for a party who is opposed to contact, it may be useful to consider the merits of any allegations that the party seeking contact is only doing so to obtain an order which will assist him or her in regularising immigration status. Conversely, it might be the case that the parties are in effect in agreement that contact should take place and the resident party seeks to assist the immigration application of the non-resident parent. These questions should be looked at. It is clear that a party seeking to enter the United Kingdom to have contact with their child will need to prove he has a right to contact. This can only be in the form of a residence or contact order granted in the United Kingdom or a certificate issued by a district judge which confirms that person's intention to maintain contact with the child (IR, para. 246(iii)). In situations where the parties are both in agreement, an application to have a consent order formalised through the family court might gain more sympathy from the court than an unnecessary (uncontested) application for a contact order. Where a party has obtained some form of leave to enter under the 'exercising rights to access' provisions and seeks to make an application for indefinite leave to remain, the applicant does not necessarily need to seek any further order from the family court if he can provide a statement from the other parent or from the supervisor of contact (if contact is supervised) stating that he is maintaining contact with the child (IR, para. 248A(iii)(c)).

CHAPTER 14

Professional conduct in children cases

14.1 INTRODUCTION

As far as public law cases are concerned, the Law Society issued a guide *Good Practice in Child Care Cases* in 2004. There is no corresponding guide for contact and, more generally, private law cases. The rules relating to conduct are found in the following sources:

- *The Guide to the Professional Conduct of Solicitors 1999*, published by the Law Society (the Guide);
- Law Society (2006) *Family Law Protocol (2nd edition)* Law Society Publishing; and
- Resolution's (formerly the Solicitors Family Law Association) republished *Guides to Good Practice* (Spring 2006).

Solicitors will naturally be expected to practise in accordance with the Guide. There are, however, certain sections which are of particular note to child contact cases. This chapter sets out pertinent aspects of which those handling child contact cases should be aware. Practitioners will have to bear in mind that only the most common aspects are covered here and it may be that other issues arise which will have to be tackled with reference to the materials set out above. The Law Society operates a Professional Ethics telephone helpline which may be of use to solicitors presented with such situations.

14.2 CONFIDENTIALITY

The Guide sets out at Principle 16.01 the general rule of confidentiality that all solicitors owe to their clients. The circumstances in which the duty can be overridden are given at Principle 16.02. Of most relevance to child contact cases will be paragraph 4 of that Principle. This sets out those exceptional circumstances involving children where a solicitor should consider overriding the duty of confidentially owed to clients and disclose information to an appropriate authority. Where such circumstances arise, these raise significant issues for the solicitor, as to override confidentiality may also be a breach of the basic principle (see Solicitors' Practice Rule 1(c)) 'duty to act in the best interests of the client'.

In such a situation, the solicitor with conduct must decide. By way of an example, the Guide states 'there may be situations where an adult discloses abuse either by himself or herself or by another adult against a child but refuses to allow any disclosure. The solicitor must consider whether the threat to the child's life or health, both mental and physical, is sufficiently serious to justify a breach of the duty of confidentiality'. Clearly the principle imports a mode of proportionality which must be employed in deciding these questions.

14.3 APPROPRIATE ADVICE TO CLIENTS

From the inception of the case, it is vital that the practitioner asks appropriate questions in order to give appropriate advice. Instructions may need to be taken sensitively.

Domestic violence

Domestic violence as a substantive topic is covered in Chapter 6. The practitioner must ascertain whether there has been or is a risk of any domestic abuse as soon as possible. Taking instructions as to any allegations of current or past domestic abuse (whether or not relating to the present contact matter) may shed light on why a parent has chosen to behave or conduct themselves in a particular way. Where a client has not allowed contact with the non-resident parent as a result of concerns surrounding domestic abuse, these will need to be set out in a witness statement in the proceedings (see Chapter 6). The credibility of a client can be seriously damaged if he or she does not raise significant issues such as domestic abuse at the initial stages of proceedings but then later chooses to raise them when facing allegations by the other party which appear to present a view of that parent being hostile to allowing contact for no reason.

The Family Law Protocol advises that solicitors should:

- signpost clients to appropriate agencies for their clients themselves or their children;
- encourage clients to inform appropriate authorities where allegations of domestic abuse are discovered;
- screen for domestic abuse, rather than merely rely on the client to raise it; it might be necessary for the solicitor to give information as to the meaning of domestic abuse, notably the change to the definition of harm to include 'impairment suffered from seeing or hearing the ill-treatment of another'.

In respect of file management there may be cases where a client is in fear of his or her safety or for some other reason has asked that the solicitor does not divulge certain information to the other party or their solicitor. In such circumstances, the solicitor's practice should ensure that there are adequate measures to ensure that any person handling the file (for example, in the absence of the solicitor with conduct) heeds the client's instructions. Appropriate clear markings on the files should be made. Where a client resides in a hostel or refuge for those who have suffered domestic abuse, the solicitor must be familiar with protocols that the refuge operates with regard to correspondence and comply with them strictly.

Where a client has good cause not to wish for disclosure of his or her address or that of the child, to the other party (which would ordinarily be disclosed through service of the application form on the respondent), a Form C8 can be completed which indicates that the address will not be disclosed without order of the court.

Further guidance for working with clients in contact cases where allegations of domestic abuse are a feature are contained in the Guidelines for Good Practice on Parental Contact in Cases where there is Domestic Violence. The Guidelines were produced by the Children Act Sub-Committee of the Lord Chancellor's Advisory Board on Family Law.

Previous contact proceedings

Initial instructions should establish an outline of the background to any previous contact proceedings, whether or not these came before the court. This may have a real significance to conducting the present contact matter and previous findings of fact may influence the present case. These considerations can only be focused on if sufficient information is given as to the previous dispute.

The solicitor should consider obtaining the file of papers from any previous legal adviser. Issues of previous advice on the 'same matter' are also relevant to publicly funded advice (see Chapter 15).

Abduction

This area of child law is specialised. Solicitors must be able to act on any concerns that a client has as to the risk of child abduction and refer to a solicitor with adequate expertise if necessary. The Family Law Protocol at paragraph 3.4 sets out a useful summary of areas of concern and sets out the issues of which solicitors should be aware.

14.4 EXPERTS

Where the instruction of experts is concerned, practitioners should have regard to the following matters:

1. Parties must seek permission from the court before instructing any experts, whether on a joint basis or otherwise.
2. The expert so instructed should have relevant and recent experience. It is good practice to obtain a CV of the expert.
3. Permission from the court should be sought if any expert is to assess the child.
4. Joint instruction of experts should be encouraged and any letter of instruction to a joint expert should be agreed with the other party's legal representatives in advance (if possible) of dispatch. Usually the drafting of the letter will be the responsibility of one of the solicitors – the lead solicitor for the purpose of the instruction.

See Chapter 9 for further information on the instruction of experts. Further reading in relation to experts in private law proceedings can be found in the Family Law Protocol, para.3.11.

CHAPTER 15

Public funding

15.1 INTRODUCTION

Public funding of legal work for contact cases is available through the government's legal aid scheme. The issues surrounding publicly funded work are intricate and continuously evolve. For that reason it is not possible to discuss every aspect within this book. What follows is a guide to practitioners as to public funding issues insofar as they relate to the conduct of a child contact case.

Public funding in England and Wales is operated by the Legal Services Commission (LSC) which came into being on 1 April 2000, replacing the Legal Aid Board pursuant to the Access to Justice Act 1999. The LSC manages the funds. To do so it created the Criminal Defence Service and the Community Legal Service through which criminal and civil legal work is respectively funded. The LSC provides legal services to those who are eligible by, in the main, contracting that work to suppliers who are (generally speaking) solicitors' firms or not-for-profit organisations. The suppliers provide the legal advice and representation with the LSC retaining auditing functions and administering checks and balances in regard to costs, eligibility assessment and administrative aspects. The LSC Manual contains comprehensive guidance and regulations covering all elements relating to public funding. It comprises four hefty volumes; although not easy to navigate, practitioners should familiarise themselves with the Manual's layout and sections to access information as and when this is necessary.

Financial eligibility of the client seeking advice is a factor in the determination of whether or not public funding can be provided. In some cases, the assessment is undertaken by the practitioner and in others by the LSC upon receipt of the appropriate forms (CLSMEANS forms).

Volume 3 of the Manual contains the LSC's Funding Code (the Code) which was written and amended pursuant to sections 8 and 9 of the Access to Justice Act 1999. Part 1 of the Code (vol. A) deals with the criteria for decision-making as to whether the LSC will fund services and Part 2 (vol. B) comprises the procedures that are applied.

Types of public funding

There are various levels of service which exist to publicly fund legal work. These are:

- Legal Help;
- Help at Court;
- General Family Help;
- Legal Representation (Investigative Help or Full Representation);
- Help with Mediation;
- Family Mediation.

NB Legal Representation by way of Investigative Help is not available for family work - only Full Representation can be applied for.

A discretion exists for the Lord Chancellor to make specific orders or directions for other services as he sees fit but any supplier seeking to provide a client with publicly funded legal assistance cannot do so unless that assistance is provided in compliance with one of the above levels of service. The supplier must also comply with the rules that apply to that level of service. Failure to conduct and administer publicly funded cases correctly and efficiently can lead to penalties, including those relating to remuneration to the supplier on particular cases and, in extreme circumstances, the withdrawal of the franchise contract. As far as the conduct of contact cases is concerned, the only levels of service that will generally apply are: Legal Representation (Full Representation); General Family Help; Family Mediation; Help with Mediation; and Legal Help. There is no specific level of public funding that exists only for contact cases. The varied issues which may be embodied in a contact case are those that are deemed to fall within the category of 'family proceedings' which are covered by the Code (Part A, s.11). The test as to whether an issue in dispute will be one that comes within the LSC's definition of family proceedings is whether or not the dispute arises out of family relationships. There is no doubt that child contact proceedings fall squarely within this definition. The 'standard criteria' are the starting point for any application for funding. They are found at Part A, section 4 of the Code and relate to elementary points (e.g. financial eligibility of applicant, reasonable conduct, compliance with the LSC contract, scope and details of identity of the client and supplier).

15.2 LEGAL HELP

This is the first rung of service permitting advice and assistance (see AJA 1999, s.4(2)). Express exclusions from this level of service are:

- issuing or conducting any court proceedings;
- advocacy or instructing an advocate;

- mediation or arbitration as a service itself (however note that Legal Help can be given in relation to mediation or arbitration and fees of a mediator or arbitrator can be incurred as a disbursement under Legal Help); and
- the giving of general information about the law, legal system and availability of legal services (save for where provision of such information is incidental to the actual provision of assistance in a specific case).

NB a family mediator's fees will normally not be permitted to be incurred as a disbursement to Legal Help given that a specific level of service (Family Mediation) is designed and available for the provision of mediation in family matters.

Criteria for provision

Provision of Legal Help is subject to a means assessment of the client and his or her partner which the supplier executes. Reference should be made to the current Keycard (periodically reissued by the LSC). The assessment has three components: gross monthly income test, disposable monthly income test and a capital test. Where the assisted person's financial circumstances are in excess of limits prescribed by the current Keycard, that person will not be eligible for Legal Help. Those who are in receipt of income support, income-based job seeker's allowance or guaranteed state pension credit will be 'passported' and therefore qualify automatically both on income and capital grounds.

Legal Help should only be provided to the client if the matter passes the 'sufficient benefit' test. The test requires that there should be sufficient benefit to the client, having regard to circumstances of the matter (including the client's personal circumstances). The test is ongoing in that where a supplier takes the view that the client no longer meets the test, further work should cease. Other potential sources of funding should be contemplated in order for the supplier to determine the reasonableness of funding the matter from the Community Legal Service Fund.

The LSC operates a general rule (Part B, s.B3.3 of the Code) holding that Legal Help cannot be provided to the client if it was provided within six months of being previously provided on the same matter (whether by that supplier or another). This may be an especially relevant consideration in contact cases where negotiations are undertaken by a solicitor (funded under Legal Help) and the arrangements for contact subsequently break down within six months of the Legal Help form having been signed. The two main exceptions to the rule are where the circumstances have changed materially between the present time and the previous provision of Legal Help or the client is reasonably dissatisfied with the first solicitor. There are other exceptions with which solicitors should become familiar. The reasons and circumstances will have to be set out on the form to justify the client seeking Legal Help notwithstanding the general rule.

15.3 FAMILY MEDIATION

This service provides mediation of a family dispute and will cover an assessment of whether mediation is suitable in the client's particular situation. Those with an LSC contract to provide mediation are bound by a Code of Practice (see Part B, s.D5 of the Code). Of note is that the mediator should have arrangements in place to ensure that parties only take part in the mediation if they are willing and not influenced by fear, violence or other harm and arrangements which encourage consideration as to whether children should have the opportunity to express their wishes and feelings in the mediation.

Criteria for provision

There are two stages:

(a) an 'intake assessment', i.e. whether or not mediation is suitable to the nature of the dispute, the parties themselves and all the circumstances; and

(b) substantive mediation, which can be provided only if the above is answered affirmatively.

Procedure and practice

1. The solicitor or the client should contact the mediation service (the LSC mention, for example, one deemed competent by the UK College of Family Mediators). Full details are provided of the client and the other party (or that party's solicitor, if known).
2. The mediation service will contact the other party to ascertain whether he or she is willing to attend an assessment.
3. The service is also responsible for checking the client's financial eligibility (Form CLSMEANS7) but it is wise for the solicitor to check this as it will potentially affect the solicitor's ability to provide other levels of publicly funded services to the client.
4. If the other party is willing, the mediation service arranges a meeting and notifies both parties (or their solicitors). The appointment should be offered within 15 days of the date the service was first contacted.
5. Where a joint assessment meeting is not possible or a party has requested a separate meeting, the second of the two meetings should be held within

20 days of the date of first contact with the service. The second meeting can only be held outside the 20 days if the client agrees to this.

6. A domestic abuse screening should be undertaken by the service as soon as possible after the initial contact.
7. A client who fails to attend the assessment without providing a good reason in advance will only be given a second appointment if it is reasonable in the particular circumstances.
8. Where it is the other party who failed to attend, the client should be offered the opportunity to deny a second appointment being offered to the other party. Where this happens, the service will deem mediation unsuitable and Form CLSAPP7 should be completed and signed accordingly.
9. Where the other party fails to attend a second appointment meeting, the service should regard mediation as unsuitable, again completing Form CLSAPP7.
10. Mediation will also be judged unsuitable where the other party does not respond to a request to attend a meeting within 10 working days of the service being first contacted, refuses to attend an appointment or does attend a meeting and the mediator decides mediation is not suitable with regard to the dispute, the parties and all circumstances. Form CLSAPP7 is completed and returned to the solicitor or the client.
11. If mediation is deemed unsuitable for whatever reason the client can, through his or her solicitor, apply for General Family Help or Legal Representation.
12. If mediation is suitable, the client can access Family Mediation and Help with Mediation.
13. The requirement to attend mediation will also be applied where a public funding certificate is already in place and an application is made for an amendment to the certificate to include assistance on additional matters. However, it is likely that contact and residence proceedings will be viewed to be similar for the purposes of mediation and so a change of scope to include 'contact' in what were previously 'residence' proceedings will not necessarily require mediation to be attempted once again.
14. Where mediation does begin and subsequently breaks down, Form CLSAPP7 must be completed outlining which issues are still in dispute. Any certificate issued by the LSC is likely to be limited to provide scope for only assistance in respect of those outstanding matters.
15. It is perfectly acceptable that, for example, contact issues may be deemed unsuitable for mediation (therefore allowing an application for Legal Representation), whereas financial issues continue to be mediated.

Further guidance is available at Part C, s.20.9 of the Code. Regard to this section should be had in those situations where a client has already sought mediation voluntarily and then consults a solicitor (self-referrals).

15.4 HELP WITH MEDIATION

This will authorise help and advice to the client who is receiving Family Mediation or assistance in drawing up any agreement reached through mediation. Where appropriate it will cover work to have an agreement incorporated into a court order. This, of course, will not necessarily apply to all agreements reached in mediation.

Criteria for provision

The prerequisite for this level of service is that the client is participating in Family Mediation or has reached an agreement or settlement in Family Mediation and needs assistance by way of this level of service. Help with Mediation will be refused if the service is not necessary in the circumstances or if Legal Help is the more appropriate level of service. Like Legal Help, Help with Mediation is subject to the sufficient benefit test.

The LSC give an example that 'a difference between parents concerning handover arrangements for contact or contact times between the absent parent and his or her child which is subject to mediation would not normally require this level of assistance' (Part C, s.20.10(16) of the Code). The general position is that the case should require substantial legal advice in support of ongoing mediation. Where solicitors will simply need to exchange letters to embody the arrangement reached during mediation, this can be undertaken under Legal Help. Where a solicitor advises that the agreement should be formalised by way of a court order, the LSC require that this action should be subject to the 'reasonable private paying client' test (the test is one of reasonableness, where the proceedings are those that a reasonable client paying for legal advice or representation on a private basis would take).

Procedure and practice

1. This level of service cannot commence prior to the client receiving Family Mediation. Therefore any advice to a client about options available to resolve a contact dispute fall to be provided under the Legal Help scheme.
2. A client who has already undertaken Family Mediation will have already met the means assessment, thus this will not need to be decided again. The solicitor should ensure for file management that he or she has had sight of Form CLSMEANS7 or a letter from the mediator confirming financial eligibility.
3. Help with Mediation is provided via a certificate from the LSC which must be applied for on Form CLSAPP4.

4. The level of service is not intended to encompass negotiation work; advice is permitted only to the client and does not include correspondence with the other party or their solicitors.
5. The solicitor may attend mediation sessions to advise during the mediation process. This is, however, stated to be exceptional and is subject to an application for prior authority from the LSC.
6. If the scope of advice changes (i.e. the nature of matters in dispute during mediation changes) an application for amendment of the certificate will need to be made on Form CLSAPP8.
7. Any assistance given in drafting a final agreement or confirming agreement by way of court order, which flows from a joint memorandum of understanding between the parties, is not an opportunity for the solicitor to re-open the contents of the memorandum or negotiate a new agreement. In circumstances where the client is unhappy with the memorandum having taken advice from the solicitor, he or she may return to mediation.
8. The LSC state that it will be more unusual in children cases for an application to be made to court for a consent order than in ancillary relief cases.
9. Help with Mediation is extinguished when mediation itself breaks down. Any advice following this should be properly given under Legal Help.

15.5 GENERAL FAMILY HELP

This level of service is similar to Legal Help but is restricted to family matters. Its generality means that any legal assistance can be provided as long as it relates to a family dispute. This is said to include assistance in 'resolving that dispute through negotiation or otherwise'. Its scope covers not only that which falls within Legal Help but also:

- issuing proceedings;
- representation in proceedings where necessary in order to secure the early resolution of a family dispute; and
- assistance to obtain a consent order following a settlement in whole or part.

Representation at a contested final hearing is not permitted under this level of service but it may cover all work short of that stage in the conduct of the case. If faced with a contested final hearing, it will be incumbent on the solicitor to have ensured that an application for Legal Representation has been submitted and approved by the LSC in advance of that hearing.

Criteria for provision

The level of service may be refused if mediation is more appropriate than General Family Help and if the case should have first been referred to a mediator to decide whether mediation is suitable. At any point where the mediator deems that mediation is either unsuitable or has broken down and certifies the Form CLSAPP7 accordingly, the 'mediation first test' is met for purposes of an application for General Family Help. The exemptions to this general rule are contained within 'the Procedures' which can be found at Part B, s.C29 of the Code. These are:

(a) urgent or emergency applications;
(b) where there is no mediator available to the parties to hold the assessment meeting (there are further categories which fall within this exemption, see Part C, s.20.16(5) of the Code);
(c) where proceedings have commenced and the client of the supplier is a respondent who has received notice of a court date which is within eight weeks of the date of the notification;
(d) the applicant has a reasonable fear of domestic abuse from another party to the mediation and therefore is unwilling to participate in mediation as a result of that fear; or
(e) where the applicant has received Legal Help from a FAInS accredited adviser in respect of the matter for which he or she now seeks to apply for General Family Help (see section 15.10).

General Family Help will only be granted if Legal Help is not more appropriate. Examples are where protracted negotiations are not suitable to be conducted under Legal Help or there is a need to issue proceedings following failed negotiations. For most cases it will be appropriate to have given initial advice and sought instructions with the possibility of attempting negotiations with the other side under Legal Help before it is clear that General Family Help is required to continue work on the matter. A client simply stating that the other side is unwilling to negotiate is unlikely to convince the LSC to grant a certificate for General Family Help as a matter of course; a precursor is that some investigation into these issues has been carried out at the Legal Help stage first.

The cost benefit consideration will be the reasonable privately paying client test. Where it becomes clear that the prospects of success are such that were an application for Legal Representation to be made, it would be refused, a certificate for General Family Help will not be allowed to continue.

Procedure and practice

1. An application on Form CLSAPP3 is made to the LSC for a certificate. However, solicitors who are FAInS accredited (see sections 15.9 and

15.10) can self-grant certificates for General Family Help under devolved powers.

2. The scope of the certificate will correspond with the dispute in question. Where the dispute changes or new disputes arise, the certificate must be amended to obtain additional scope to cover these disputes. This is done via Form CLSAPP8.
3. If the need for Legal Representation arises, this does not require a fresh application. A Form CLSAPP8 application should be submitted to convert the existing General Family Help certificate into one for Legal Representation.
4. In the usual way, certificates will be limited as to both scope and costs and these must not be exceeded without grant of an application to extend. Where an extension to the costs limitation is required but it is apparent that the resolution of the issue or issues will only be reached at a final contested hearing, consideration should be given to conversion of the certificate to Legal Representation.
5. Consideration of cost benefit analysis should again feature before making any application to the court for a consent order following agreement through negotiation. This is said to be exceptional in children cases because of the 'no order' principle (see Chapter 1).

15.6 LEGAL REPRESENTATION

This covers litigation and advocacy services, help which would usually be provided in the course of representation (to include that which is preliminary or incidental to proceedings) and help in relation to reaching or giving effect to any compromise with a view to avoiding or ceasing proceedings.

Criteria for provision

The LSC will have regard to the following when considering applications for Legal Representation:

1. Alternative funding: whether other sources of funding are available to the client (e.g. insurance) or another person or body can be reasonably expected to fund or bring proceedings. This latter aspect will not usually apply in contact cases as it cannot be reasonable to expect any other person than the parent seeking or responding to an application for contact to fund or bring the case.
2. Alternatives to litigation: the only consideration applicable in relation to contact issues will be that the LSC will normally expect alternative dispute resolution to have been tried before litigation. This will include both:

(a) reasonable attempts at resolving the dispute, through negotiation or otherwise (e.g. usually funded under General Family Help); and
(b) specifically mentioned at Part A, s.11.11.1 of the Code is that Legal Representation in private law children cases (including contact) will be refused unless the case is first referred to a mediator for the intake assessment (see section 15.3) and the outcome is negative in that mediation is deemed by a mediator as unsuitable or inappropriate. (Note also the exemptions at section 15.5.)

3. Other levels of service: an application can be refused if the proceedings appear premature or there is a more appropriate level of service under the Code.
4. The need for representation (a reasonableness test) will be considered, taking into account, for example, the nature and complexity of the issues, existence of other proceedings or interests of other parties in the proceedings to which the application relates.
5. The standard criteria at Part A, s.5.7 of the Code do not apply to Full Representation in family proceedings as there are category specific criteria at section 11.11 for private law cases. The prospects of success should not be 'poor' (Part A, s.11.11.5 of the Code) and section 11.11.6 creates its own cost benefit test for private law children cases which is virtually identical to the test for cost benefit in the standard criteria for unquantifiable claims, i.e. that funding will only be given if the likely benefits to be gained for the client justify the likely costs, such that a reasonable private paying client would be willing to fund taking or defending the proceedings in all the circumstances.

'Prospects of success' in respect of family cases is an assessment of whether there is likely to be a 'successful outcome'. In private law children cases, this is said to be the likelihood of 'obtaining what the client would regard as a significant improvement in the arrangements for the children'. It is an objective test so falls to 'reasonableness' consideration and should take into account all the client's circumstances.

Procedure and practice

The application is made on Form CLSAPP3 and should be submitted with the relevant means form. It can be provided under devolved powers (see section 15.9). The above details ('criteria for provision') will need to be addressed on the application form to show that the client and the circumstances meet the various requirements for Legal Representation.

15.7 ENFORCEMENT PROCEEDINGS

At the time of writing, the position of the LSC is that Legal Representation for enforcement of Children Act 1989, s.8 orders 'will only be granted where enforcement is appropriate and justified and likely to be successful'. It remains to be seen whether the LSC will make changes to the Funding Code or procedures following the implementation of the Children and Adoption Act 2006 (CAA 2006).

At present, Legal Representation is unlikely to be granted to defend enforcement proceedings. The application for funding would need to be able to demonstrate that the circumstances of the case are so exceptional as to justify the representation and that there would be a significant benefit to the client. However, note that another level of service, Help at Court (which has not been discussed elsewhere in this book as it is usually not applicable to family proceedings) is available. It is stated that this level of service may be more appropriate where the client has no legal defence to the application for enforcement but may need assistance in mitigation.

Where there is a likelihood of committal, this will usually justify the grant of Legal Representation. Again, it will be interesting to see whether the new enforcement provisions in the CAA 2006 will be treated as a form of deprivation of liberty which the LSC will deem to justify Legal Representation in relation to such proceedings.

15.8 PUBLIC FUNDING FOR A CHILD

As far as contact cases are concerned, the most typical circumstance when a child is made a party to the proceedings will be pursuant to an order made under FPR 1991, r.9.5 (see Chapter 11). In these situations, the LSC will accept the application to be made and signed by the solicitor for the child. The correspondence address for the application should be the firm's address and in this regard the solicitor is treated as agent for the child.

The standard criteria relating to alternative sources of funding will not come into play where a professional guardian is appointed by the court to act for a child in that it will not be considered that the costs of instructing a solicitor should be borne from the guardian's expenses.

15.9 DEVOLVED POWERS

Suppliers with a contract from the LSC to provide Licensed Work in the Family category, i.e. Legal Representation, General Family Help or Help with Mediation, will have the following devolved powers:

- Emergency Representation (covered at Part C, s.12 of the Code): the only level of service permitted to be given in an emergency is Legal Representation. There are sections on the application form which will need to be completed;
- General Family Help: the devolved power to grant these certificates is only available to FAInS accredited solicitors (see section 15.10).

When devolved powers are exercised, the reporting restriction will apply. This usually holds that the main application and means forms must be submitted to the LSC within five working days following exercise of the power (Part C, s.12.4(20) of the Code).

15.10 FAInS

The Family Advice and Information Networks (FAInS) scheme is a pilot scheme which seeks to develop publicly funded family work. Advisers participating become accredited as FAInS practitioners. As a result they gain additional devolved powers and enhanced payment. The aims are:

(a) to bring together expert services to protect children from harm and the risk of social exclusion;
(b) to facilitate the dissolution of broken relationships, in ways which minimise distress to parents and children, and which promote family relationships and cooperative parenting;
(c) to provide tailored information and access to services that may assist in resolving disputes, or may assist those who are trying to save their relationship;
(d) to provide a mechanism for piloting new structures for CLS funded family services.

The FAInS philosophy seems to have set the direction for the future of family work. It lays emphasis on a socio-legal approach, requiring the adviser to consider his or her role as a case manager for the client, part of which involves the development of a personal action plan and making referrals for the client where these are identified to be needed.

15.11 THE FUTURE OF PUBLIC FUNDING

Changes in the administration and schemes available under the umbrella are continuous. Such changes are often dictated by cost saving but very often flow from changes in the political climate and changes concerning the different areas of law.

In relation to family work in general, the LSC has directed its service towards early diagnosis and resolution of disputes. The LSC have indicated an intention to pilot a scheme of Collaborate Law (see section 8.12). In addition, a separate pilot scheme is to be launched in four regional areas which will remove Legal Help, Help with Mediation and General Family Help and replace those services with an all-encompassing level of service entitled 'Family Help'. The LSC states that 'it would be the single vehicle for funding the non-adversarial resolution of family disputes'. It can be seen as a follow-on from the FAInS approach in that it is to place greater emphasis on early diagnostic work, negotiation and mediation (see section 15.10). It is intended that there will be a further relaxation of reporting requirements with this level of service so that suppliers can exercise devolved powers and initially only require minimal information to be supplied to the LSC.

The knock-on effect will be that applications for Legal Representation will be 'more strictly controlled'. At the time of writing the LSC are consulting (following Lord Carter's review of legal aid procurement) on a wholesale restructuring of public funding in family work.

APPENDIX 1

Children and Adoption Act 2006, Part 1, Part 3 and Schedules

PART 1

ORDERS WITH RESPECT TO CHILDREN IN FAMILY PROCEEDINGS

Contact with children

1 Contact activity directions and conditions

After section 11 of the Children Act 1989 (c. 41) insert –

'11A Contact activity directions

(1) This section applies in proceedings in which the court is considering whether to make provision about contact with a child by making –
 (a) a contact order with respect to the child, or
 (b) an order varying or discharging a contact order with respect to the child.

(2) The court may make a contact activity direction in connection with that provision about contact.

(3) A contact activity direction is a direction requiring an individual who is a party to the proceedings to take part in an activity that promotes contact with the child concerned.

(4) The direction is to specify the activity and the person providing the activity.

(5) The activities that may be so required include, in particular –
 (a) programmes, classes and counselling or guidance sessions of a kind that –
  (i) may assist a person as regards establishing, maintaining or improving contact with a child;
  (ii) may, by addressing a person's violent behaviour, enable or facilitate contact with a child;
 (b) sessions in which information or advice is given as regards making or operating arrangements for contact with a child, including making arrangements by means of mediation.

(6) No individual may be required by a contact activity direction –
 (a) to undergo medical or psychiatric examination, assessment or treatment;
 (b) to take part in mediation.

(7) A court may not on the same occasion –
 (a) make a contact activity direction, and
 (b) dispose finally of the proceedings as they relate to contact with the child concerned.

(8) Subsection (2) has effect subject to the restrictions in sections 11B and 11E.

(9) In considering whether to make a contact activity direction, the welfare of the child concerned is to be the court's paramount consideration.

11B Contact activity directions: further provision

(1) A court may not make a contact activity direction in any proceedings unless there is a dispute as regards the provision about contact that the court is considering whether to make in the proceedings.

(2) A court may not make a contact activity direction requiring an individual who is a child to take part in an activity unless the individual is a parent of the child in relation to whom the court is considering provision about contact.

(3) A court may not make a contact activity direction in connection with the making, variation or discharge of a contact order, if the contact order is, or would if made be, an excepted order.

(4) A contact order with respect to a child is an excepted order if –

(a) it is made in proceedings that include proceedings on an application for a relevant adoption order in respect of the child; or

(b) it makes provision as regards contact between the child and a person who would be a parent or relative of the child but for the child's adoption by an order falling within subsection (5).

(5) An order falls within this subsection if it is –

(a) a relevant adoption order;

(b) an adoption order, within the meaning of section 72(1) of the Adoption Act 1976, other than an order made by virtue of section 14 of that Act on the application of a married couple one of whom is the mother or the father of the child;

(c) a Scottish adoption order, within the meaning of the Adoption and Children Act 2002, other than an order made –

(i) by virtue of section 14 of the Adoption (Scotland) Act 1978 on the application of a married couple one of whom is the mother or the father of the child, or

(ii) by virtue of section 15(1)(aa) of that Act; or

(d) a Northern Irish adoption order, within the meaning of the Adoption and Children Act 2002, other than an order made by virtue of Article 14 of the Adoption (Northern Ireland) Order 1987 on the application of a married couple one of whom is the mother or the father of the child.

(6) A relevant adoption order is an adoption order, within the meaning of section 46(1) of the Adoption and Children Act 2002, other than an order made –

(a) on an application under section 50 of that Act by a couple (within the meaning of that Act) one of whom is the mother or the father of the person to be adopted, or

(b) on an application under section 51(2) of that Act.

(7) A court may not make a contact activity direction in relation to an individual unless the individual is habitually resident in England and Wales; and a direction ceases to have effect if the individual subject to the direction ceases to be habitually resident in England and Wales.

11C Contact activity conditions

(1) This section applies if in any family proceedings the court makes –

(a) a contact order with respect to a child, or
(b) an order varying a contact order with respect to a child.

(2) The contact order may impose, or the contact order may be varied so as to impose, a condition (a 'contact activity condition') requiring an individual falling within subsection (3) to take part in an activity that promotes contact with the child concerned.

(3) An individual falls within this subsection if he is –
(a) for the purposes of the contact order so made or varied, the person with whom the child concerned lives or is to live;
(b) the person whose contact with the child concerned is provided for in that order; or
(c) a person upon whom that order imposes a condition under section 11(7)(b).

(4) The condition is to specify the activity and the person providing the activity.

(5) Subsections (5) and (6) of section 11A have effect as regards the activities that may be required by a contact activity condition as they have effect as regards the activities that may be required by a contact activity direction.

(6) Subsection (2) has effect subject to the restrictions in sections 11D and 11E.

11D Contact activity conditions: further provision

(1) A contact order may not impose a contact activity condition on an individual who is a child unless the individual is a parent of the child concerned.

(2) If a contact order is an excepted order (within the meaning given by section 11B(4)), it may not impose (and it may not be varied so as to impose) a contact activity condition.

(3) A contact order may not impose a contact activity condition on an individual unless the individual is habitually resident in England and Wales; and a condition ceases to have effect if the individual subject to the condition ceases to be habitually resident in England and Wales.

11E Contact activity directions and conditions: making

(1) Before making a contact activity direction (or imposing a contact activity condition by means of a contact order), the court must satisfy itself as to the matters falling within subsections (2) to (4).

(2) The first matter is that the activity proposed to be specified is appropriate in the circumstances of the case.

(3) The second matter is that the person proposed to be specified as the provider of the activity is suitable to provide the activity.

(4) The third matter is that the activity proposed to be specified is provided in a place to which the individual who would be subject to the direction (or the condition) can reasonably be expected to travel.

(5) Before making such a direction (or such an order), the court must obtain and consider information about the individual who would be subject to the direction (or the condition) and the likely effect of the direction (or the condition) on him.

(6) Information about the likely effect of the direction (or the condition) may, in particular, include information as to –
(a) any conflict with the individual's religious beliefs;
(b) any interference with the times (if any) at which he normally works or attends an educational establishment.

(7) The court may ask an officer of the Service or a Welsh family proceedings officer to provide the court with information as to the matters in subsections (2) to (5); and it shall be the duty of the officer of the Service or Welsh family proceedings officer to comply with any such request.

(8) In this section 'specified' means specified in a contact activity direction (or in a contact activity condition).

11F Contact activity directions and conditions: financial assistance

(1) The Secretary of State may by regulations make provision authorising him to make payments to assist individuals falling within subsection (2) in paying relevant charges or fees.

(2) An individual falls within this subsection if he is required by a contact activity direction or condition to take part in an activity that promotes contact with a child, not being a child ordinarily resident in Wales.

(3) The National Assembly for Wales may by regulations make provision authorising it to make payments to assist individuals falling within subsection (4) in paying relevant charges or fees.

(4) An individual falls within this subsection if he is required by a contact activity direction or condition to take part in an activity that promotes contact with a child who is ordinarily resident in Wales.

(5) A relevant charge or fee, in relation to an activity required by a contact activity direction or condition, is a charge or fee in respect of the activity payable to the person providing the activity.

(6) Regulations under this section may provide that no assistance is available to an individual unless –

(a) the individual satisfies such conditions as regards his financial resources as may be set out in the regulations;

(b) the activity in which the individual is required by a contact activity direction or condition to take part is provided to him in England or Wales;

(c) where the activity in which the individual is required to take part is provided to him in England, it is provided by a person who is for the time being approved by the Secretary of State as a provider of activities required by a contact activity direction or condition;

(d) where the activity in which the individual is required to take part is provided to him in Wales, it is provided by a person who is for the time being approved by the National Assembly for Wales as a provider of activities required by a contact activity direction or condition.

(7) Regulations under this section may make provision –

(a) as to the maximum amount of assistance that may be paid to or in respect of an individual as regards an activity in which he is required by a contact activity direction or condition to take part;

(b) where the amount may vary according to an individual's financial resources, as to the method by which the amount is to be determined;

(c) authorising payments by way of assistance to be made directly to persons providing activities required by a contact activity direction or condition.

11G Contact activity directions and conditions: monitoring

(1) This section applies if in any family proceedings the court –

(a) makes a contact activity direction in relation to an individual, or
(b) makes a contact order that imposes, or varies a contact order so as to impose, a contact activity condition on an individual.

(2) The court may on making the direction (or imposing the condition by means of a contact order) ask an officer of the Service or a Welsh family proceedings officer –
(a) to monitor, or arrange for the monitoring of, the individual's compliance with the direction (or the condition);
(b) to report to the court on any failure by the individual to comply with the direction (or the condition).

(3) It shall be the duty of the officer of the Service or Welsh family proceedings officer to comply with any request under subsection (2).'

2 Monitoring contact

After section 11G of the Children Act 1989 (c. 41) (as inserted by section 1) insert –

'11H Monitoring contact

(1) This section applies if in any family proceedings the court makes –
(a) a contact order with respect to a child in favour of a person, or
(b) an order varying such a contact order.

(2) The court may ask an officer of the Service or a Welsh family proceedings officer –
(a) to monitor whether an individual falling within subsection (3) complies with the contact order (or the contact order as varied);
(b) to report to the court on such matters relating to the individual's compliance as the court may specify in the request.

(3) An individual falls within this subsection if the contact order so made (or the contact order as so varied) –
(a) requires the individual to allow contact with the child concerned;
(b) names the individual as having contact with the child concerned; or
(c) imposes a condition under section 11(7)(b) on the individual.

(4) If the contact order (or the contact order as varied) includes a contact activity condition, a request under subsection (2) is to be treated as relating to the provisions of the order other than the contact activity condition.

(5) The court may make a request under subsection (2) –
(a) on making the contact order (or the order varying the contact order), or
(b) at any time during the subsequent course of the proceedings as they relate to contact with the child concerned.

(6) In making a request under subsection (2), the court is to specify the period for which the officer of the Service or Welsh family proceedings officer is to monitor compliance with the order; and the period specified may not exceed twelve months.

(7) It shall be the duty of the officer of the Service or Welsh family proceedings officer to comply with any request under subsection (2).

(8) The court may order any individual falling within subsection (3) to take such steps as may be specified in the order with a view to enabling the officer of the Service or Welsh family proceedings officer to comply with the court's request under subsection (2).

(9) But the court may not make an order under subsection (8) with respect to an individual who is a child unless he is a parent of the child with respect to whom the order falling within subsection (1) was made.

(10) A court may not make a request under subsection (2) in relation to a contact order that is an excepted order (within the meaning given by section 11B(4)).'

3 Contact orders: warning notices

After section 11H of the Children Act 1989 (c. 41) (as inserted by section 2) insert –

'11I Contact orders: warning notices

Where the court makes (or varies) a contact order, it is to attach to the contact order (or the order varying the contact order) a notice warning of the consequences of failing to comply with the contact order.'

4 Enforcement orders

(1) After section 11I of the Children Act 1989 (as inserted by section 3) insert –

'11J Enforcement orders

(1) This section applies if a contact order with respect to a child has been made.

(2) If the court is satisfied beyond reasonable doubt that a person has failed to comply with the contact order, it may make an order (an 'enforcement order') imposing on the person an unpaid work requirement.

(3) But the court may not make an enforcement order if it is satisfied that the person had a reasonable excuse for failing to comply with the contact order.

(4) The burden of proof as to the matter mentioned in subsection (3) lies on the person claiming to have had a reasonable excuse, and the standard of proof is the balance of probabilities.

(5) The court may make an enforcement order in relation to the contact order only on the application of –

(a) the person who is, for the purposes of the contact order, the person with whom the child concerned lives or is to live;

(b) the person whose contact with the child concerned is provided for in the contact order;

(c) any individual subject to a condition under section 11(7)(b) or a contact activity condition imposed by the contact order; or

(d) the child concerned.

(6) Where the person proposing to apply for an enforcement order in relation to a contact order is the child concerned, the child must obtain the leave of the court before making such an application.

(7) The court may grant leave to the child concerned only if it is satisfied that he has sufficient understanding to make the proposed application.

(8) Subsection (2) has effect subject to the restrictions in sections 11K and 11L.

(9) The court may suspend an enforcement order for such period as it thinks fit.

(10) Nothing in this section prevents a court from making more than one enforcement order in relation to the same person on the same occasion.

(11) Proceedings in which any question of making an enforcement order, or any other question with respect to such an order, arises are to be regarded for the purposes of section 11(1) and (2) as proceedings in which a question arises with respect to a section 8 order.

(12) In Schedule A1 –
 (a) Part 1 makes provision as regards an unpaid work requirement;
 (b) Part 2 makes provision in relation to the revocation and amendment of enforcement orders and failure to comply with such orders.

(13) This section is without prejudice to section 63(3) of the Magistrates' Courts Act 1980 as it applies in relation to contact orders.

11K Enforcement orders: further provision

(1) A court may not make an enforcement order against a person in respect of a failure to comply with a contact order unless it is satisfied that before the failure occurred the person had been given (in accordance with rules of court) a copy of, or otherwise informed of the terms of –
 (a) in the case of a failure to comply with a contact order that was varied before the failure occurred, a notice under section 11I relating to the order varying the contact order or, where more than one such order has been made, the last order preceding the failure in question;
 (b) in any other case, a notice under section 11I relating to the contact order.

(2) A court may not make an enforcement order against a person in respect of any failure to comply with a contact order occurring before the person attained the age of 18.

(3) A court may not make an enforcement order against a person in respect of a failure to comply with a contact order that is an excepted order (within the meaning given by section 11B(4)).

(4) A court may not make an enforcement order against a person unless the person is habitually resident in England and Wales; and an enforcement order ceases to have effect if the person subject to the order ceases to be habitually resident in England and Wales.

11L Enforcement orders: making

(1) Before making an enforcement order as regards a person in breach of a contact order, the court must be satisfied that –
 (a) making the enforcement order proposed is necessary to secure the person's compliance with the contact order or any contact order that has effect in its place;
 (b) the likely effect on the person of the enforcement order proposed to be made is proportionate to the seriousness of the breach of the contact order.

(2) Before making an enforcement order, the court must satisfy itself that provision for the person to work under an unpaid work requirement imposed by an enforcement order can be made in the local justice area in which the person in breach resides or will reside.

(3) Before making an enforcement order as regards a person in breach of a contact order, the court must obtain and consider information about the person and the likely effect of the enforcement order on him.

(4) Information about the likely effect of the enforcement order may, in particular, include information as to –
(a) any conflict with the person's religious beliefs;
(b) any interference with the times (if any) at which he normally works or attends an educational establishment.
(5) A court that proposes to make an enforcement order may ask an officer of the Service or a Welsh family proceedings officer to provide the court with information as to the matters in subsections (2) and (3).
(6) It shall be the duty of the officer of the Service or Welsh family proceedings officer to comply with any request under this section.
(7) In making an enforcement order in relation to a contact order, a court must take into account the welfare of the child who is the subject of the contact order.

11M Enforcement orders: monitoring

(1) On making an enforcement order in relation to a person, the court is to ask an officer of the Service or a Welsh family proceedings officer –
(a) to monitor, or arrange for the monitoring of, the person's compliance with the unpaid work requirement imposed by the order;
(b) to report to the court if a report under paragraph 8 of Schedule A1 is made in relation to the person;
(c) to report to the court on such other matters relating to the person's compliance as may be specified in the request;
(d) to report to the court if the person is, or becomes, unsuitable to perform work under the requirement.
(2) It shall be the duty of the officer of the Service or Welsh family proceedings officer to comply with any request under this section.

11N Enforcement orders: warning notices

Where the court makes an enforcement order, it is to attach to the order a notice warning of the consequences of failing to comply with the order.'

(2) Schedule 1 (which contains a Schedule to be inserted before Schedule 1 to the Children Act 1989 (c. 41)) has effect.

5 Compensation for financial loss

After section 11N of the Children Act 1989 (as inserted by section 4) insert –

'11O Compensation for financial loss

(1) This section applies if a contact order with respect to a child has been made.
(2) If the court is satisfied that –
(a) an individual has failed to comply with the contact order, and
(b) a person falling within subsection (6) has suffered financial loss by reason of the breach,

it may make an order requiring the individual in breach to pay the person compensation in respect of his financial loss.
(3) But the court may not make an order under subsection (2) if it is satisfied that the individual in breach had a reasonable excuse for failing to comply with the contact order.

(4) The burden of proof as to the matter mentioned in subsection (3) lies on the individual claiming to have had a reasonable excuse.

(5) An order under subsection (2) may be made only on an application by the person who claims to have suffered financial loss.

(6) A person falls within this subsection if he is –

(a) the person who is, for the purposes of the contact order, the person with whom the child concerned lives or is to live;

(b) the person whose contact with the child concerned is provided for in the contact order;

(c) an individual subject to a condition under section 11(7)(b) or a contact activity condition imposed by the contact order; or

(d) the child concerned.

(7) Where the person proposing to apply for an order under subsection (2) is the child concerned, the child must obtain the leave of the court before making such an application.

(8) The court may grant leave to the child concerned only if it is satisfied that he has sufficient understanding to make the proposed application.

(9) The amount of compensation is to be determined by the court, but may not exceed the amount of the applicant's financial loss.

(10) In determining the amount of compensation payable by the individual in breach, the court must take into account the individual's financial circumstances.

(11) An amount ordered to be paid as compensation may be recovered by the applicant as a civil debt due to him.

(12) Subsection (2) has effect subject to the restrictions in section 11P.

(13) Proceedings in which any question of making an order under subsection (2) arises are to be regarded for the purposes of section 11(1) and (2) as proceedings in which a question arises with respect to a section 8 order.

(14) In exercising its powers under this section, a court is to take into account the welfare of the child concerned.

11P Orders under section 11O(2): further provision

(1) A court may not make an order under section 11O(2) requiring an individual to pay compensation in respect of a failure by him to comply with a contact order unless it is satisfied that before the failure occurred the individual had been given (in accordance with rules of court) a copy of, or otherwise informed of the terms of –

(a) in the case of a failure to comply with a contact order that was varied before the failure occurred, a notice under section 11I relating to the order varying the contact order or, where more than one such order has been made, the last order preceding the failure in question;

(b) in any other case, a notice under section 11I relating to the contact order.

(2) A court may not make an order under section 11O(2) requiring an individual to pay compensation in respect of a failure by him to comply with a contact order where the failure occurred before the individual attained the age of 18.

(3) A court may not make an order under section 11O(2) requiring an individual to pay compensation in respect of a failure by him to comply with a contact order that is an excepted order (within the meaning given by section 11B(4)).'

Family assistance orders

6 Provision as to family assistance orders

(1) Section 16 of the Children Act 1989 (c. 41) (family assistance orders) is amended as follows.

(2) In subsection (3) (requirements for making an order), omit paragraph (a) (requirement that circumstances of case be exceptional).

(3) After subsection (4) insert –

'(4A) If the court makes a family assistance order with respect to a child and the order is to be in force at the same time as a contact order made with respect to the child, the family assistance order may direct the officer concerned to give advice and assistance as regards establishing, improving and maintaining contact to such of the persons named in the order as may be specified in the order.'

(4) In subsection (5) (maximum duration of order) for 'six months' substitute 'twelve months'.

(5) For subsection (6) substitute –

'(6) If the court makes a family assistance order with respect to a child and the order is to be in force at the same time as a section 8 order made with respect to the child, the family assistance order may direct the officer concerned to report to the court on such matters relating to the section 8 order as the court may require (including the question whether the section 8 order ought to be varied or discharged).'

Risk assessments

7 Risk assessments

After section 16 of the Children Act 1989 (c. 41) insert –

'16A Risk assessments

(1) This section applies to the following functions of officers of the Service or Welsh family proceedings officers –

(a) any function in connection with family proceedings in which the court has power to make an order under this Part with respect to a child or in which a question with respect to such an order arises;

(b) any function in connection with an order made by the court in such proceedings.

(2) If, in carrying out any function to which this section applies, an officer of the Service or a Welsh family proceedings officer is given cause to suspect that the child concerned is at risk of harm, he must –

(a) make a risk assessment in relation to the child, and

(b) provide the risk assessment to the court.

(3) A risk assessment, in relation to a child who is at risk of suffering harm of a particular sort, is an assessment of the risk of that harm being suffered by the child.'

Transitional provision

8 Transitional provision

(1) This section applies to any contact order under section 8 of the Children Act 1989 made before, and in force on, the relevant date.

(2) For so long as a contact order to which this section applies continues in force on and after the relevant date without being varied, the circumstances in which a notice under section 11I of the Children Act 1989 is to be attached to the contact order include –
(a) where an application for such a notice to be attached to the contact order is made by a person who, as regards the order, falls within any of paragraphs (a) to (d) of section 11J(5) of the Children Act 1989;
(b) where, in any family proceedings, a question arises with respect to the contact order.
(3) Where the person proposing to apply under subsection (2)(a) is the child with respect to whom the contact order was made, subsections (6) and (7) of section 11J have effect in relation to the application under subsection (2)(a) as they have effect in relation to an application under section 11J for an enforcement order.
(4) If a failure to comply with a contact order to which this section applies occurs while the contact order continues in force as described in subsection (2), each of sections 11K(1) and 11P(1) of the Children Act 1989 is to have effect, in relation to the failure, as if for paragraphs (a) and (b) there were substituted 'a notice under section 11I relating to the contact order'.
(5) In this section 'relevant date' means the day on which sections 3 to 5 come into force.

PART 2

ADOPTIONS WITH A FOREIGN ELEMENT

[*Not reproduced here*]

PART 3

MISCELLANEOUS AND FINAL

Miscellaneous provisions

15 Minor and consequential amendments and repeals

(1) Schedule 2 (minor and consequential amendments) has effect.
(2) Schedule 3 (repeals) has effect.

Final provisions

16 Regulations and orders

(1) Any power to make regulations conferred by this Act on the Secretary of State is exercisable by statutory instrument.
(2) The power to make and revoke an order under section 9(4) is also exercisable by statutory instrument.
(3) A statutory instrument mentioned in subsection (1) or (2) is to be subject to annulment in pursuance of a resolution of either House of Parliament.
(4) Regulations made under this Act may make different provision for different purposes.
(5) A power to make regulations under this Act (as well as being exercisable in relation to all cases to which it extends) may be exercised in relation to –
(a) those cases subject to specified exceptions, or
(b) a particular case or class of case.

17 Short title, commencement and extent

(1) This Act may be cited as the Children and Adoption Act 2006.

(2) Except as provided in subsection (3), the preceding provisions of this Act shall come into force on such day as the Secretary of State may by order made by statutory instrument appoint; and different days may be appointed for different purposes.

(3) Section 13, so far as relating to adoptions and prospective adoptions in relation to which the National Assembly for Wales may charge a fee under section 91A of the Adoption and Children Act 2002 (c. 38), shall come into force on such day as the National Assembly for Wales may by order made by statutory instrument appoint; and different days may be appointed for different purposes.

(4) Before making an order under subsection (2) the Secretary of State must consult the National Assembly for Wales.

(5) Before making an order under subsection (2) bringing sections 9 to 12 into force, the Secretary of State must consult the Department of Health, Social Services and Public Safety in Northern Ireland.

(6) Subject to subsections (7) and (8), this Act extends to England and Wales only.

(7) The amendment or repeal of an enactment has the same extent as the enactment to which it relates.

(8) The following provisions of this Act extend also to Northern Ireland –

(a) sections 9 to 11;

(b) section 12(1) to (5) and (7);

(c) section 16;

(d) this section.

SCHEDULES

SCHEDULE 1

Section 4

ENFORCEMENT ORDERS

Before Schedule 1 to the Children Act 1989 (c. 41) insert-

'SCHEDULE A1

ENFORCEMENT ORDERS

PART 1

UNPAID WORK REQUIREMENT

General

1 Subject to the modifications in paragraphs 2 and 3, Chapter 4 of Part 12 of the Criminal Justice Act 2003 has effect in relation to an enforcement order as it has effect in relation to a community order (within the meaning of Part 12 of that Act).

References to an offender

2 Subject to paragraph 3, references in Chapter 4 of Part 12 of the Criminal Justice Act 2003 to an offender are to be treated as including references to a person subject to an enforcement order.

Specific modifications

3 (1) The power of the Secretary of State by order under section 197(3) to amend the definition of 'responsible officer' and to make consequential amendments includes power to make any amendments of this Part (including further modifications of Chapter 4 of Part 12 of the Criminal Justice Act 2003) that appear to the Secretary of State to be necessary or expedient in consequence of any amendment made by virtue of section 197(3)(a) or (b).

(2) In section 198 (duties of responsible officer) –

(a) in subsection (1) –

(i) at the end of paragraph (a) insert 'and', and

(ii) omit paragraph (c) and the word 'and' immediately preceding it, and

(b) after subsection (1) insert –

'(1A) Subsection (1B) applies where –

(a) an enforcement order is in force, and

(b) an officer of the Children and Family Court Advisory and Support Service or a Welsh family proceedings officer (as defined in section 35 of the Children Act 2004) is required under section 11M of the Children Act 1989 to report on matters relating to the order.

(1B) The officer of the Service or the Welsh family proceedings officer may request the responsible officer to report to him on such matters relating to the order as he may require for the purpose of making a report under section 11M(1)(c) or (d); and it shall be the duty of the responsible officer to comply with such a request.'

(3) In section 199 (unpaid work requirement) –

(a) in subsection (2) (minimum and maximum hours of unpaid work) for paragraph (b) substitute –

'(b) not more than 200.',

(b) omit subsections (3) and (4), and

(c) in subsection (5) for the words from the beginning to 'of them' substitute 'Where on the same occasion and in relation to the same person the court makes more than one enforcement order imposing an unpaid work requirement'.

(4) In section 200 (obligations of person subject to unpaid work requirement), for subsection (2) substitute –

'(2) Subject to paragraphs 7 and 9 of Schedule A1 to the Children Act 1989, the work required to be performed under an unpaid work requirement imposed by an enforcement order must be performed during a period of twelve months.

(2A) But the period of twelve months is not to run while the enforcement order is suspended under section 11J(9) of the Children Act 1989.'

(5) Section 217 (requirement to avoid conflict with religious beliefs, etc) is omitted.

(6) In section 218 (availability of arrangements in local area), subsection (1) (condition for imposition of unpaid work requirement) is omitted.

(7) Section 219 (provision of copies of relevant order) is omitted.

(8) The power of the Secretary of State to make rules under section 222 in relation to persons subject to relevant orders may also be exercised in relation to persons subject to enforcement orders.

(9) The power of the Secretary of State by order under section 223(1) to amend the provision mentioned in section 223(1)(a) includes power to amend this Part so as to make such modifications of Chapter 4 of Part 12 of the Criminal Justice Act 2003 as appear to the Secretary of State to be necessary or expedient in consequence of any amendment of the provision mentioned in section 223(1)(a).

PART 2

REVOCATION, AMENDMENT OR BREACH OF ENFORCEMENT ORDER

Power to revoke

4 (1) This paragraph applies where a court has made an enforcement order in respect of a person's failure to comply with a contact order and the enforcement order is in force.

(2) The court may revoke the enforcement order if it appears to the court that –

(a) in all the circumstances no enforcement order should have been made,

(b) having regard to circumstances which have arisen since the enforcement order was made, it would be appropriate for the enforcement order to be revoked, or

(c) having regard to the person's satisfactory compliance with the contact order or any contact order that has effect in its place, it would be appropriate for the enforcement order to be revoked.

(3) The enforcement order may be revoked by the court under sub-paragraph (2) of its own motion or on an application by the person subject to the enforcement order.

(4) In deciding whether to revoke the enforcement order under sub-paragraph (2)(b), the court is to take into account –

(a) the extent to which the person subject to the enforcement order has complied with it, and

(b) the likelihood that the person will comply with the contact order or any contact order that has effect in its place in the absence of an enforcement order.

(5) In deciding whether to revoke the enforcement order under sub-paragraph (2)(c), the court is to take into account the likelihood that the person will comply with the contact order or any contact order that has effect in its place in the absence of an enforcement order.

Amendment by reason of change of residence

5 (1) This paragraph applies where a court has made an enforcement order in respect of a person's failure to comply with a contact order and the enforcement order is in force.

(2) If the court is satisfied that the person has changed, or proposes to change, his residence from the local justice area specified in the order to another local justice area, the court may amend the order by substituting the other area for the area specified.

(3) The enforcement order may be amended by the court under sub-paragraph (2) of its own motion or on an application by the person subject to the enforcement order.

Amendment of hours specified under unpaid work requirement

6 (1) This paragraph applies where a court has made an enforcement order in respect of a person's failure to comply with a contact order and the enforcement order is in force.

(2) If it appears to the court that, having regard to circumstances that have arisen since the enforcement order was made, it would be appropriate to do so, the court may reduce the number of hours specified in the order (but not below the minimum specified in section 199(2)(a) of the Criminal Justice Act 2003).

(3) In amending the enforcement order under sub-paragraph (2), the court must be satisfied that the effect on the person of the enforcement order as proposed to be amended is no more than is required to secure his compliance with the contact order or any contact order that has effect in its place.

(4) The enforcement order may be amended by the court under sub-paragraph (2) of its own motion or on an application by the person subject to the enforcement order.

Amendment to extend unpaid work requirement

7 (1) This paragraph applies where a court has made an enforcement order in respect of a person's failure to comply with a contact order and the enforcement order is in force.

(2) If it appears to the court that, having regard to circumstances that have arisen since the enforcement order was made, it would be appropriate to do so, the court may, in relation to the order, extend the period of twelve months specified in section 200(2) of the Criminal Justice Act 2003 (as substituted by paragraph 3).

(3) The period may be extended by the court under sub-paragraph (2) of its own motion or on an application by the person subject to the enforcement order.

Warning and report following breach

8 (1) This paragraph applies where a court has made an enforcement order in respect of a person's failure to comply with a contact order.

(2) If the responsible officer is of the opinion that the person has failed without reasonable excuse to comply with the unpaid work require-

ment imposed by the enforcement order, the officer must give the person a warning under this paragraph unless –

(a) the person has within the previous twelve months been given a warning under this paragraph in relation to a failure to comply with the unpaid work requirement, or

(b) the responsible officer reports the failure to the appropriate person.

(3) A warning under this paragraph must –

(a) describe the circumstances of the failure,

(b) state that the failure is unacceptable, and

(c) inform the person that, if within the next twelve months he again fails to comply with the unpaid work requirement, the warning and the subsequent failure will be reported to the appropriate person.

(4) The responsible officer must, as soon as practicable after the warning has been given, record that fact.

(5) If –

(a) the responsible officer has given a warning under this paragraph to a person subject to an enforcement order, and

(b) at any time within the twelve months beginning with the date on which the warning was given, the responsible officer is of the opinion that the person has since that date failed without reasonable excuse to comply with the unpaid work requirement imposed by the enforcement order,

the officer must report the failure to the appropriate person.

(6) A report under sub-paragraph (5) must include a report of the warning given to the person subject to the enforcement order.

(7) The appropriate person, in relation to an enforcement order, is the officer of the Service or the Welsh family proceedings officer who is required under section 11M to report on matters relating to the enforcement order.

(8) 'Responsible officer', in relation to a person subject to an enforcement order, has the same meaning as in section 197 of the Criminal Justice Act 2003 (as modified by paragraph 2).

Breach of an enforcement order

9 (1) This paragraph applies where a court has made an enforcement order ('the first order') in respect of a person's failure to comply with a contact order.

(2) If the court is satisfied beyond reasonable doubt that the person has failed to comply with the unpaid work requirement imposed by the first order, the court may –

(a) amend the first order so as to make the requirement more onerous, or

(b) make an enforcement order ('the second order') in relation to the person and (if the first order is still in force) provide for the second order to have effect either in addition to or in substitution for the first order.

(3) But the court may not exercise its powers under sub-paragraph (2) if it is satisfied that the person had a reasonable excuse for failing to comply with the unpaid work requirement imposed by the first order.

(4) The burden of proof as to the matter mentioned in sub-paragraph (3) lies on the person claiming to have had a reasonable excuse, and the standard of proof is the balance of probabilities.

(5) The court may exercise its powers under sub-paragraph (2) in relation to the first order only on the application of a person who would be able to apply under section 11J for an enforcement order if the failure to comply with the first order were a failure to comply with the contact order to which the first order relates.

(6) Where the person proposing to apply to the court is the child with respect to whom the contact order was made, subsections (6) and (7) of section 11J have effect in relation to the application as they have effect in relation to an application for an enforcement order.

(7) An application to the court to exercise its powers under sub-paragraph (2) may only be made while the first order is in force.

(8) The court may not exercise its powers under sub-paragraph (2) in respect of a failure by the person to comply with the unpaid work requirement imposed by the first order unless it is satisfied that before the failure occurred the person had been given (in accordance with rules of court) a copy of, or otherwise informed of the terms of, a notice under section 11N relating to the first order.

(9) In dealing with the person under sub-paragraph (2)(a), the court may –

(a) increase the number of hours specified in the first order (but not above the maximum specified in section 199(2)(b) of the Criminal Justice Act 2003, as substituted by paragraph 3);

(b) in relation to the order, extend the period of twelve months specified in section 200(2) of the Criminal Justice Act 2003 (as substituted by paragraph 3).

(10) In exercising its powers under sub-paragraph (2), the court must be satisfied that, taking into account the extent to which the person has complied with the unpaid work requirement imposed by the first order, the effect on the person of the proposed exercise of those powers –

(a) is no more than is required to secure his compliance with the contact order or any contact order that has effect in its place, and

(b) is no more than is proportionate to the seriousness of his failures to comply with the contact order and the first order.

(11) Where the court exercises its powers under sub-paragraph (2) by making an enforcement order in relation to a person who has failed to comply with another enforcement order –

(a) sections 11K(4), 11L(2) to (7), 11M and 11N have effect as regards the making of the order in relation to the person as they have effect as regards the making of an enforcement order in relation to a person who has failed to comply with a contact order;

(b) this Part of this Schedule has effect in relation to the order so made as if it were an enforcement order made in respect of the failure for which the other order was made.

(12) Sub-paragraph (2) is without prejudice to section 63(3) of the Magistrates' Courts Act 1980 as it applies in relation to enforcement orders.

Provision relating to amendment of enforcement orders

10 Sections 11L(2) to (7) and 11M have effect in relation to the making of an order under paragraph 6(2), 7(2) or 9(2)(a) amending an enforcement order as they have effect in relation to the making of an enforcement order; and references in sections 11L(2) to (7) and 11M to an enforcement order are to be read accordingly.'

SCHEDULE 2

Section 15

MINOR AND CONSEQUENTIAL AMENDMENTS

Domicile and Matrimonial Proceedings Act 1973 (c. 45)

1 (1) In Schedule 1 to the Domicile and Matrimonial Proceedings Act 1973 (c. 45) (staying of matrimonial proceedings: England and Wales), paragraph 11 (effect of staying matrimonial proceedings on court's power to make certain orders) is amended as follows.

(2) After sub-paragraph (4) insert –

'(4A) Sub-paragraph (4B) applies where –

(a) proceedings are stayed as described in sub-paragraph (1) or (4), and

(b) at the time when the stay is imposed, a contact order (within the meaning of the Children Act 1989) made in connection with the stayed proceedings is in force.

(4B) While the stay applies to the proceedings, the court may not –

(a) make an enforcement order (within the meaning of the Children Act 1989) in relation to the contact order, or

(b) as regards an enforcement order already made in relation to the contact order, exercise its powers under paragraph 9(2) of Schedule A1 to the Children Act 1989 in relation to the enforcement order.'

(3) In sub-paragraph (5) (certain powers of court not affected) at the beginning insert 'Except as provided in sub-paragraph (4B),'.

Family Law Act 1986 (c. 55)

2 The Family Law Act 1986 (c. 55) is amended as follows.

3 (1) Section 5 (power of court to refuse application or stay proceedings) is amended as follows.

(2) After subsection (2) (stay where more appropriate for matters to be determined in proceedings outside England and Wales) insert –

'(2A) If the proceedings on the application are proceedings in which a contact activity direction has been made under section 11A of the Children Act 1989 (or an enforcement order has been made under section 11J of that Act), the court may when granting a stay under or by virtue of subsection (2) also suspend the contact activity direction (or the enforcement order).'

(3) After subsection (3A) (removal of stay granted under Article 15) insert –

'(3B) If the stay removed under subsection (3) or (3A) is a stay in relation to which the court suspended a contact activity direction made under section 11A of the Children Act 1989 (or an enforcement order made under section 11J of that Act), the court may when removing the stay under subsection (3) or (3A) also bring the suspension to an end.'

4 In section 29 (enforcement), in subsection (1) after 'enforcing the order' insert '(including, where an order with respect to contact is registered in England and Wales, the powers under section 11O of the Children Act 1989)'.

5 In section 30 (staying or sisting of enforcement proceedings), after subsection (1) insert –

'(1A) No application may be made under subsection (1) for proceedings to be stayed or sisted if the proceedings are proceedings on an application for an order under section 11O(2) of the Children Act 1989.'

6 In section 31 (dismissal of enforcement proceedings), after subsection (1) insert –

'(1A) No application may be made under subsection (1) for proceedings to be dismissed if the proceedings are proceedings on an application for an order under section 11O(2) of the Children Act 1989.'

Children Act 1989 (c. 41)

7 The Children Act 1989 (c. 41) is amended as follows.

8 In section 14B (making of special guardianship orders), in subsection (1) –

(a) omit the 'and' at the end of paragraph (a), and

(b) after paragraph (b) insert –

'(c) where a contact order made with respect to the child is not discharged, any enforcement order relating to that contact order should be revoked, and

(d) where a contact activity direction has been made as regards contact with the child and is in force, that contact activity direction should be discharged.'

9 In section 91 (effect and duration of orders etc) after subsection (2) insert –

'(2A) Where a contact activity direction has been made as regards contact with a child, the making of a care order with respect to the child discharges the direction.'

10 In section 104 (regulations and orders) –

(a) in subsection (1) for 'or the Secretary of State' substitute ', the Secretary of State or the National Assembly for Wales';

(b) after subsection (2) insert –

'(2A) Subsection (2) does not apply to a statutory instrument made solely by the National Assembly for Wales.'

11 In section 105 (interpretation), in subsection (1) at the appropriate place insert-

''contact activity condition' has the meaning given by section 11C;';

''contact activity direction' has the meaning given by section 11A;';

''enforcement order' has the meaning given by section 11J;'.

Family Law Act 1996 (c. 27)

12 (1) Schedule 3 to the Family Law Act 1996 (c. 27) (stay of proceedings: amendments of Schedule 1 to the Domicile and Matrimonial Proceedings Act 1973 (c. 45)) is amended as follows.

(2) In paragraph 9 (amendments of paragraph 11 of Schedule 1) after sub-paragraph (6) insert-

'(6A) In sub-paragraph (4A)(a) for 'sub-paragraph (1) or (4)' substitute 'sub-paragraph (1)'.'

Adoption and Children Act 2002 (c. 38)

13 The Adoption and Children Act 2002 (c. 38) is amended as follows.

14 (1) Section 26 (effect on contact of placing a child for adoption) is amended as follows.

(2) In subsection (1), after 'have effect' insert 'and any contact activity direction relating to contact with the child is discharged'.

(3) In subsection (6), after 'In this section,' insert ''contact activity direction' has the meaning given by section 11A of the 1989 Act and'.

SCHEDULE 3

Section 15

REPEALS

Short title and chapter	Extent of repeal
Children Act 1989 (c. 41)	In section 14B(1), the word 'and' at the end of paragraph (a). Section 16(3)(a).

APPENDIX 2

Adaptation of the Code of Guidance for expert witnesses in family proceedings

The objective of this Code of Guidance is to provide the court with early information to enable it to determine whether it is necessary and/or practicable to ask an expert to assist the court:

- To identify, narrow and where possible agree the issues between the parties
- To provide an opinion about a question that is not within the skill and experience of the court
- To encourage the early identification of questions that need to be answered by an expert
- To encourage disclosure of full and frank information between the parties, the court and any expert instructed

	Action	Party and timing
1	**THE DUTIES OF EXPERTS**	
1.1	**Overriding duty**	
	An expert in family proceedings has an overriding duty to the court that takes precedence over any obligation to the person from whom he is paid	
1.2	**Particular duties**	
	Among any other duties an expert may have, an expert shall have regard to the following duties: • To assist the court in accordance with the overriding duty • To provide an opinion that is independent of the party • To confine an opinion to matters material to the issues between the parties and in relation only to questions that are within the expert's expertise (skill and experience). If a question is put which falls outside that expertise the expert must say so	

	Action	Party and timing
	• In expressing an opinion take into consideration all of the material facts including any relevant factors arising from diverse cultural or religious contexts at the time the opinion is expressed, indicating the facts, literature and any other material that the expert has relied upon in forming an opinion • To indicate whether the opinion is provisional (or qualified, as the case may be) and the reason for the qualification, identifying what further information is required to give an opinion without qualification • Inform those instructing the expert without delay of any change in the opinion and the reason for the change	
2	**PREPARATION FOR THE FHDRA/ DIRECTIONS HEARING**	
2.1	**Preliminary enquiries of the expert**	
	Not later than 10 days before the FHDRA/ Directions Hearing the solicitor for the party proposing to instruct the expert (or lead solicitor if the instruction proposed is joint) shall approach the expert with the following information (note that any discussions/ correspondence with a jointly instructed expert should be disclosed to the other party): • The nature of the proceedings and the issues likely to require determination by the court • The questions about which the expert is to be asked to give an opinion (including any diverse cultural or religious contexts) • When the court is to be asked to give permission for the instruction (if permission has already been given the date and details of that permission) • Whether permission is asked of the court for the instruction of another expert in the same or any related field (i.e. to give an opinion on the same or related questions) • The volume of reading which the expert will need to undertake	Solicitor instructing the expert 10 days before the FHDRA/Directions Hearing

	Action	Party and timing
	• Whether or not (in an appropriate case) permission has been applied for or given for the expert to examine the child • Whether or not (in an appropriate case) it will be necessary for the expert to conduct interviews (and if so with whom) • The likely timetable of legal and (any relevant) social work steps • When the expert's opinion is likely to be required • Whether and if so what date has been fixed by the court for any hearing at which the expert may be required to give evidence (in particular the Final Hearing)	
2.2	**Experts response**	
	Not later than 5 days before the FHDRA/ Directions Hearing the solicitor intending to instruct the expert (or lead solicitor if the instruction proposed is joint) shall obtain the following information from the expert (note that any discussions/correspondence with a jointly instructed expert should be disclosed to the other party): • That the work required is within the expert's expertise • That the expert is available to do the relevant work within the suggested timescale • When the expert is available to give evidence, the dates and/or times to avoid, and where a hearing date has not been fixed, the amount of notice the expert will require to make arrangements to come to court without undue disruption to their normal clinical routines • The cost, including hourly and global rates, and likely hours to be spent, of attending at experts/professionals meetings, attending court and writing the report (to include any examinations and interviews)	Solicitor instructing the expert 5 days before the FHDRA/Directions Hearing
2.3	**Information to be provided to the Court**	
	Any party who proposes to ask the court for permission to instruct an expert shall provide the court at the FHDRA/Directions Hearing with information setting out the proposal to instruct the expert in the following detail:	The party proposing to instruct the expert

	Action	Party and timing
	• The name, discipline, qualifications and expertise of the expert (by way of CV where possible) • The expert's availability to undertake the work • The relevance of the expert evidence sought to be adduced to the issues in the proceedings and the specific questions upon which it is proposed the expert should give an opinion (including the relevance of any diverse cultural or religious contexts) • The timetable for the report • The responsibility for instruction • Whether or not the expert evidence can properly be obtained by the joint instruction of the expert by two or more of the parties • Whether the expert evidence can properly be obtained by only one party (e.g. on behalf of the child) • Whether it is necessary for more than one expert in the same discipline to be instructed by more than one party • Why the expert evidence proposed cannot be given by CAFCASS or by any guardian appointed for the child in accordance with their different statutory duties • The likely cost of the report on both an hourly and global basis • The proposed apportionment of costs of jointly instructed experts as between the parties, which will generally be shared equally on a joint instruction.	
2.4	**Draft Order for the FHDRA/Directions Hearing**	
	The party proposing to instruct the expert (or lead solicitor if the instruction proposed is joint) shall in the draft order submitted at the FHDRA/Directions Hearing request the court to give directions (among any others) as to the following: • The party who is to be responsible for drafting the letter of instruction and providing the documents to the expert	Any party proposing to instruct an expert at the FHDRA/Directions Hearing

	Action	Party and timing
	• The issues identified by the court and the questions about which the expert is to give an opinion • The timetable within which the report is to be prepared, filed and served • The disclosure of the report to the parties and to any other expert • The conduct of any experts' discussion (in a case where more than one expert is instructed) • The preparation of a statement of agreement and disagreement by the experts following any experts' discussion (in a case where more than one expert is instructed) • The attendance of the expert at the Final Hearing unless agreement is reached about the opinions given by the expert	
3	**LETTER OF INSTRUCTION**	
3.1	The solicitor instructing the expert shall within 5 days of the FHDRA/Directions Hearing or as directed by the court prepare (and agree with the other parties as necessary) and serve a letter of instruction to the expert which shall: • Set out the context in which the expert's opinion is sought (including any diverse ethnic, cultural, religious or linguistic contexts) • Define carefully the specific questions the expert is required to answer ensuring: – That they are within the ambit of the expert's area of expertise – That they do not contain unnecessary or irrelevant detail – That the questions addressed to the expert are kept to a manageable number and are clear, focused and direct – That the questions reflect what the expert has been requested to do by the court • List the documentation provided or provide for the expert an indexed and paginated bundle which shall include:	Solicitor instructing the expert within 5 days of the FHDRA/Directions Hearing or as directed by the court

	Action	Party and timing
	– A copy of the order (or those parts of the order) which gives permission for the instruction of the expert immediately the order becomes available – An agreed list of essential reading – All new documentation when it is filed and regular updates to the list of documents provided or to the index to the paginated bundle • A copy of this code of guidance • Identify the relevant lay and professional people concerned with the proceedings (e.g. any treating clinicians) and inform the expert of his/her right to talk to the other professionals provided an accurate record is made of the discussion • Identify any other expert instructed in the proceedings and advise the expert of his/her right to talk to the other experts provided an accurate record is made of the discussion • Define the contractual basis upon which the expert is retained and in particular the funding mechanism including how much the expert will be paid (an hourly rate and overall estimate should already have been obtained), when the expert will be paid, and what limitation there might be on the amount the expert can charge for the work which he/she will have to do. There should also be a brief explanation of the 'detailed assessment process' where appropriate • In default of agreement the format of the Letter of Instruction shall be determined by the court, which may determine the issue upon written application with representations from each party	
4	**THE EXPERT'S REPORT**	
4.1	**Content of the report**	
	The expert's report shall be addressed to the court and shall: • Give details of the expert's qualifications and experience	The expert in accordance with the court's timetable

	Action	Party and timing
	• Contain a statement setting out the substance of all material instructions (whether written or oral) summarising the facts stated and instructions given to the expert which are material to the conclusions and opinion expressed in the report • Give details of any literature or other research material upon which the expert has relied in giving an opinion • State who carried out any test, examination or interview which the expert has used for the report and whether or not the test, examination or interview has been carried out under the expert's supervision • Give details of the qualifications of any person who carried out the test, examination or interview • Where there is a range of opinion on the question to be answered by the expert: – Summarise the range of opinion and – Give reasons for the opinion expressed • Contain a summary of the expert's conclusions and opinions • Contain a statement that the expert understands his duty to the court • Where appropriate be verified by a statement of truth	
4.2	**Supplementary questions**	
	Any party wishing to ask supplementary questions of an expert for the purpose of clarifying the expert's report must put those questions in writing to the parties not later than 5 days after receipt of the report. Only those questions that are agreed by the parties or in default of agreement approved by the court may be put to the expert. The court may determine the issue upon written application with representations from each party.	Any party within 5 days of the receipt of the report

	Action	Party and timing
5	**EXPERTS DISCUSSIONS (MEETING)**	
	This section of the Code relates more commonly to public law children proceedings where more than one expert is instructed. Reference should be made to the Code in Appendix C of the Protocol for Judicial Case Management in Public Law Children Cases where, less usually in private law children proceedings, more than one expert is instructed and the court directs an experts' meeting.	
6	**ARRANGING FOR THE EXPERT TO ATTEND COURT**	
6.1	**Preparation**	
	The party who is responsible for the instruction of an expert witness shall ensure: • That a date and time is fixed for the court to hear the expert's evidence that is, if possible, convenient to the expert and that the fixture is made substantially in advance of the Final Hearing and, in any event, no later than 2 weeks before the Final Hearing • That if the expert's oral evidence is not required the expert is notified as soon as possible • That any proposed witness timetable accurately indicates how long the expert is likely to be giving evidence, in order to avoid the inconvenience of the expert being delayed at court	Any party responsible for the instruction of an expert prior to the Final Hearing
6.2	All parties shall ensure: • That where an expert witness is to be called the advocates have identified the issues which the expert is to address • That wherever possible (and appropriate) a logical sequence to the evidence is arranged with experts of the same discipline giving evidence on the same day(s) • That in the exceptional case the court is informed of the need for a witness summons	All parties prior to the Final Hearing

	Action	Party and timing
7	**POST HEARING ACTION**	
	Within 10 days of the Final Hearing the solicitor instructing the expert should provide feedback to the expert by way of a letter informing the expert of the outcome of the case, and the use made by the court of the expert's opinion. Where the court directs that a copy of the transcript can be sent to the expert, the solicitor instructing the expert should obtain the transcript within 10 days of the Final Hearing.	Solicitor instructing the expert within 10 days of the Final Hearing

Notes

This adaptation of the Code of Guidance for Expert Witnesses in Family Proceedings (Appendix C to the Protocol for Judicial Case Management in Public Law Children Act Cases) is intended to assist practitioners with the instruction of an expert witness in private law children proceedings. It is likely that the instruction of an expert in such cases will be sought by one or both parties at the First Hearing Dispute Resolution Appointment (FHDRA), in the event that the proceedings are not resolved at that stage, or at a subsequent directions hearing.

Aspects of this adapted code remain of greater of relevance to public law proceedings or the less usual private law cases, for example in relation to the instruction of more than one expert. It is suggested that practitioners should use this adapted code as an example template and further adapt as appropriate to the circumstances of the particular case.

APPENDIX 3

Forms C1 and C1A

Application for an order

Children Act 1989

Form C1

The court	To be completed by the court
	Date issued
	Case number
The full name(s) of the child(ren)	Child(ren)'s number(s)

Important Note
You should only answer question 7 if you are asking the court to make one of the following orders: **a Contact Order, a Residence Order, a Prohibited Steps Order, a Specific Issue Order or a Parental Responsibility Order.**

1 About you (the person completing this form known as 'the applicant')

State:

- *your title, full name, address, telephone number, date of birth and relationship to each child above*
- *your solicitor's name, address, reference, telephone, FAX and DX numbers.*

2 The child(ren) and the order(s) you are applying for

For each child state:

- *the full name, date of birth and sex*
- *the type of order(s) you are applying for (for example, residence order, contact order, supervision order).*

3 Other cases which concern the child(ren)

If there have ever been, or there are pending, any court cases which concern:
- *a child whose name you have put in paragraph 2*
- *a full, half or step brother or sister of a child whose name you have put in paragraph 2*
- *a person in this case who is or has been, involved in caring for a child whose name you have put in paragraph 2*

attach a copy of the relevant order and give:
- *the name of the court*
- *the name and contact address (if known) of the children's guardian, if appointed*
- *the name and contact address (if known) of the children and family reporter, if appointed*
- *the name and contact address (if known) of the welfare officer, if appointed*
- *the name and contact address (if known) of the solicitor appointed for the child(ren).*

4 The respondent(s)

Appendix 3 Family Proceedings Rules 1991; Schedule 2 Family Proceedings Courts (Children Act 1989) Rules 1991

For each respondent state:
- *the title, full name and address*
- *the date of birth (if known) or the age*
- *the relationship to each child.*

C1

2

5 Others to whom notice is to be given

Appendix 3 Family Proceedings Rules 1991; Schedule 2 Family Proceedings Courts (Children Act 1989) Rules 1991

For each person state:

- *the title, full name and address*
- *the date of birth (if known) or the age*
- *the relationship to each child.*

6 The care of the child(ren)

For each child in paragraph 2 state:

- *the child's current address and how long the child has lived there*
- *whether it is the child's usual address and who cares for the child there*
- *the child's relationship to the other children (if any).*

7 Domestic abuse, violence or harm

Do you believe that the child(ren) named above have suffered or are at risk of suffering any harm from any of the following:

- *any form of domestic abuse*
- *violence within the household*
- *child abduction*
- *other conduct or behaviour*

by any person who is or has been involved in caring for the child(ren) or lives with, or has contact with, the child(ren)?

	Yes	No
Please tick the box which applies	☐	☐

If you tick the Yes box, **you must *also fill in Supplemental Information Form (form C1A).*** *You can obtain a copy of this from a court office if one has not been enclosed with the papers served on you.*

8 Social Services

For each child in paragraph 2 state:

- *whether the child is known to the Social Services. If so, give the name of the social worker and the address of the Social Services department.*
- *whether the child is, or has been, on the Child Protection Register. If so, give details of registration.*

9 The education and health of the child(ren)

For each child state:

- *the name of the school, college or place of training which the child attends*
- *whether the child is in good health. Give details of any serious disabilities or ill health.*
- *whether the child has any special needs.*

10 The parents of the child(ren)

For each child state:

- *the full name of the child's parents*
- *whether the parents are, or have been, married to each other or civil partners of each other*
- *whether the parents live together. If so, where.*
- *whether, to your knowledge, either of the parents have been involved in a court case concerning a child. If so, give the date and the name of the court.*

11 The family of the child(ren) (other children)

For any other child not already mentioned in the family (for example, a brother or half sister) state:

- *the full name and address*
- *the date of birth (if known) or age*
- *the relationship of the child to you.*

12 Other adults

State:

- *the full name of any other adults (for example, lodgers) who live at the same address as any child named in paragraph 2*
- *whether they live there all the time*
- *whether, to your knowledge, the adult has been involved in a court case concerning a child. If so, give the date and the name of the court.*

13 Your reason(s) for applying and any plans for the child(ren)

State briefly your reasons for applying and what you want the court to order.

- ***Do not** give a full statement if you are applying for an order under Section 8 of Children Act 1989. You may be asked to provide a full statement later.*
- ***Do not** complete this section if this form is accompanied by a supplementary form.*

14 Attending the court

State:

- *whether you will need an interpreter at court. If so, please indicate what language interpreter you will use. If you require an interpreter you must notify the court immediately so that one can be arranged.*
- *whether you have a disability for which you require special assistance or special facilities. If so, please say what your needs are. The court staff will get in touch with you about your requirements.*

15 Parenting Information – Arrangements after Separation

	Yes	No
Have you received a Parenting Plan booklet? (If No, you may obtain a copy from a court office, a citizen's advice bureau or other family advice service.)	☐	☐
Have you agreed to a Parenting Plan? (If Yes, please include a copy of the Plan when you send your application to the court)	☐	☐
If you did agree a Parenting Plan, has the Plan broken down?	☐	☐

If Yes, please explain briefly why the Plan broke down –

Signed (Applicant)

Date

C1

6

Supplemental Information Form

Form C1A

Children Act 1989

The court	To be completed by the court
	Date issued
	Case number
The full name(s) of the child(ren)	Child(ren)'s number(s)

Important Note
Please read the C1A Notes for Guidance before completing this form.

Section 1 About you (the person completing this form)

1 **Personal details**

Full Name (including any title):

Date of Birth:

Address*:

*Do not state your address if you have asked the court to withhold your address

Day time telephone number:

Your relationship to each child named above:

2 **Your solicitor's details**

Name:

Address:

Reference:

Telephone Number:

Fax Number:

DX Number:

C1A (01.05)

Designed by Publications Branch

1

Section 2 Respondent's comments on allegations made by the Applicant

About this section:

- **Go straight to Section 3 (Further information) if:**
  (a) you are the **Applicant**; or
  (b) you are the **Respondent** and the Applicant has not filed form C1A Supplemental Information Form with his or her application.

- This section of the form should only be completed **by the Respondent** where the Applicant has served a completed form C1A with his or her application for an order.

- **You do not have to complete this section unless you wish to comment on any of the information given by the Applicant in his or her form C1A.** This section should not be used to comment on any other information given by the Applicant in his or her application.

- **Please comment in summary form only.** You will have an opportunity to make a more detailed statement later in the proceedings.

Comments on allegations made by the Applicant:

Section 3 Further Information

1 **Involvement with outside authorities and organisations**

If as a result of any incidence of domestic abuse, other harm or risk of harm to you or the child(ren) there is, has been or there is pending any known involvement with the police, social services, mental health services or other support services in respect of:

- *any child(ren)whose name(s) is/are given at the top of this form*
- *a full, half or step brother or sister of a child(ren) whose name(s) is/are given at the top of this form, or*
- *a person who is or has been involved in caring for the child(ren) or is having or has had contact with the child(ren) whose name(s) is/are given at the top of this form*

please provide details and identify:

- *which agency or service has been involved*
- *the name of the person who has been the main contact in that agency or service*
- *the date or dates of any involvement*
- *whether there is any current or continuing involvement*
- *whether or not you have any documents, reports or correspondence relating to the agency or service's involvement.*

2 **Incidents of abuse, violence or harm**

For each alleged incidence of violence, domestic abuse or harm, please provide in summary form the following information:

Note: You shall have an opportunity later in the proceedings to provide a more substantial statement

- *the date(s) on which the incident occurred*
- *the nature and seriousness of the alleged abuse, violence or harm*
- *by whom and against whom it was directed*
- *how frequently the alleged abuse, harm or violence occurred and the date(s) of the most recent occurrence(s)*
- *whether any hospital or medical treatment has been sought by the child(ren) whose name(s) is/are given at the top of this form, the applicant or other person in respect of any injuries sustained, and*
- *whether you consider there is a likelihood of further harm, abuse or violence occurring.*

3 **Involvement of the child(ren)**

If the child(ren) whose name(s) is/are given at the top of this form have seen or heard any of the alleged incident(s) of abuse within the household or been aware of any alleged abuse and its impact on the family, please give details and in particular state how you believe the child(ren) have been affected by this experience:

4 **Witnesses**

Has anyone else seen, heard or had reported to them any alleged incidence of violence, domestic abuse or harm? If Yes, would that person be able to provide supporting evidence?

---

5 **Medical treatment or other assessment of the child(ren)**

If any child(ren) whose name(s) is/are given at the top of this form have been referred for treatment or psychiatric or psychological assessment, by any medical or health service relating to his/her emotional, social or behavioural development (or where any such treatment or referral is pending), please state:

- *when and to whom such a referral was made*
- *details of any treatment or assessment recommended*
- *whether there is any continuing involvement with the relevant service in relation to the referral, and*
- *whether you are aware of or have in your possession any reports or other correspondence in relation to any treatment or assessment recommended.*

---

6 **Abduction**

If you feel the child(ren) whose name(s) is/are given at the top of this form are at real risk of being abducted please give the following information:

- *your reason for believing that the child(ren) may be abducted*
- *whether the child(ren) have previously been the subject of a threatened abduction, an attempted abduction or have been abducted*
- *whether the police or any other organisation has been involved in any alleged previous incident identified above, and*
- *whether each child has their own passport and who has that passport at the moment?*

---

7 **Steps or orders required to protect you and the children**

Please indicate what steps or orders you believe the court should take or make in order to protect the safety of the child(ren) whose name(s) is/are given at the top of this form and/or yourself.

---

8 **Attending the Court**

Please also indicate whether the court needs to make any special arrangements for you to attend court (e.g. providing you with a separate waiting room from the respondent or other security provision). Do you consider the court should give consideration to any special measures for you or any witnesses to give evidence at the hearing (e.g. use of video link equipment where available)? If Yes, please explain why.

Signed
(Applicant/Respondent)

Date

C1A

6

APPENDIX 4

Bibliography

BOOKS AND PRICED PUBLICATIONS

Bainham, A (2005) *Children: The Modern Law* (3rd edn), Jordan Publishing

Butterworths Family Law Service (loose-leaf, online and CD subscription)

Cretney, S, Masson, J and Bailey-Harris, R (2002) *Principles of Family Law* (7th edn), Sweet & Maxwell

Fortin, J (2003) *Children's Rights and the Developing Law* (2nd edn), LexisNexis Butterworths

Goldthorpe, L and Monro, P (2005) *Child Law Handbook: Guide to Good Practice*, Law Society Publishing

Hamilton, C and Perry, A (eds.) (2002) *Family Law in Europe* (2nd edn), LexisNexis Butterworths

Herring, J (2004) *Family Law* (2nd edn), Pearson Higher Education

Hershman and McFarlane's Children Law and Practice, Jordan Publishing (loose-leaf, online and CD subscription)

Swindells, H, Neaves, A, Kushner, M and Skilbeck, R (1999) *Family Law and the Human Rights Act 1998*, Jordan Publishing

Department of Health (1989) *An introduction to the Children Act 1989: A New Framework For the Care and Upbringing of Children*, The Stationery Office

Department of Health (1990) *The Care of children Principles and Practice in Regulations and Guidance*, The Stationery Office

Department of Health (1991) *Children Act 1989 Guidance and Regulations, Vols 1-10*, The Stationery Office

Legal Services Commission, *LSC Manual*, The Stationery Office (loose-leaf, online and CD subscription)

Law Society (1999) *The Guide to the Professional Conduct of Solicitors 1999* (8th edn), Law Society Publishing

Law Society (2006) *Family Law Protocol* (2nd edn), Law Society Publishing

Law Society, with the Association of Lawyers for Children, the Child Care Law Joint Liaison Group and the SFLA (2004) *Good Practice in Child Care Cases*, Law Society Publishing

Wall, J. and Hamilton, I. (2000) *A Handbook for Expert Witnesses in Children Act Cases*, Jordan Publishing

Wilson, C. and Powell, M (2001) *A Guide to Interviewing Children*, Routledge

RESEARCH, GUIDANCE AND GOVERNMENT PUBLICATIONS

Making Contact Work – The Advisory Board on Family Law: Children Act Sub-Committee's Report to the Lord Chancellor on the facilitation of contact between

children and their non-residential parents and the enforcement of contact orders (February 2002) (www.dca.gov.uk/family/abfla/mcwrep.pdf)

Parental Separation: Children's Needs and Parents' Responsibilities (Cm 6273) (July 2005) (www.dfes.gov.uk/childrensneeds)

Parental Separation: Children's Needs and Parents' Responsibilities: Next Steps (Cm 6452) (January 2005) (www.dfes.gov.uk/childrensneeds)

Report from the Joint Committee on the Draft Children (contact) and Adoption Bill Session 2004-05 HL Papers 100-I/HC 400-1 (www.parliament.the-stationery-office.co.uk/pa/jt/jtchilcon.htm)

Government Reply to the Report from the Joint Committee on the Draft Children (Contact) and Adoption Bill (Cm 6583) (8 June 2005) (www.parliament.uk/documents(draftchildrencontact)govtresponse.pdf)

Association of Chief Police Officers and Department for Constitutional Affairs (2004) *ACPO Pilots: Disclosure of Information in Family Proceedings: Police/Family Disclosure Protocol*

Crown Prosecution Service (November 2001, revised February 2005) *Policy for Prosecuting Cases of Domestic Violence* (www.cps.gov.uk/publications/docs/domesticviolencepolicy.pdf)

Department for Constitutional Affairs (February 2003, revised November 2004) *Domestic Violence: A Guide to Civil Remedies and Criminal Sanctions* (www.dca.gov.uk/family/dvguide04.pdf)

Department for Education and Skills (2001) *Special Educational Needs Code of Practice* (DfES/581/2001)

Department for Education and Skills (2001) *SEN Toolkit* (www.teachernet.gov.uk/wholeshool/sen/teacherlearningassistant)

Department for Education and Skills (2004) *Get it sorted: Guidance – Providing Effective Advocacy Services for Children and Young People Making a Complaint under the Children Act 1989* (www.dfes.gov.uk/childrensadvocacy/docs/GetitSorted.pdf)

Department for Education and Skills (August 2005) *Statutory Guidance on the Role and Responsibilities of the Director of Children's Services and the Lead Member for children's Services*

Department for Education and skills (September 2005) *Every Child Matters: Change for Children – An Overview of Cross Government Guidance* (overview of recent guidance and signposting to individual documents at www.everychildmatters.gov.uk/strategy/guidance)

Department of Health and Welsh Office (November 2002) *National Standards for the Provision of Children's Advocacy Services*

Department of Health and Welsh Office (May 2003) *What to Do If You Are Worried A Child is Being Abused: Children's Services Guidance*

Department of Health and Welsh Office and DfES (October 2004, updated January 2005) *National Service Framework for Children, Young People and Maternity Services*

Immigration Law Practitioners' Association (November 2004) *Working with Children Subject to Immigration Control: Guidelines for Best Practice*

Law Society and CAFCASS (March 2004) *Guidance on Working Relationship between Children Panel Solicitors and Children's Guardians*

Law Society (June 2005) *Children Panel: Criteria and Guidance Notes* (www.lawsociety.org.uk/professional/accreditationpanels.law under Children Panel)

Lord Chancellor's Department (June 2003) *Protocol for Judicial Case Management in Public Law Children Act Cases* (at www.hmcourts-service.gov.uk/docs/protocol-complete.pdf)

Lord Chancellor's Advisory Committee (June 2003) *Statement of Good Practice in the Appointment of Solicitors Where it Falls to the Court to Do So in Specified Proceedings*

Resolution (2006) (formerly Solicitors' Family Law Association) *Guides to Good Practice for Solicitors Acting for Children* (6th edn), (issued free to members)

Save the Children/UNHCR (2004) *Separated Children in Europe Programme – Statement of Good Practice* (3rd Edn) (www.separated-children-europe-programme.org)

UNHCR (1972, revised 1992) *Handbook on Procedures and Criteria for Determining Refugee Status* (can be found at www.hrea.org/learn/tutorials/refugees/Handbook/hbtoc.htm)

Welsh Assembly (2002) Special *Educational Needs Code of Practice for Wales* (www.learning.wales.gov.uk)

Welsh Assembly (February 2003) *National Standards for the Provision of Children's Advocacy Services*

APPENDIX 5

Useful contacts and information sources

ASYLUM AND IMMIGRATION

Asylum Aid
Advice
Tel: 020 7247 8741
www.asylumaid.org.uk

Asylum and Immigration Tribunal
Tel: 0845 6000 877
Minicom: 0845 6060 766
Fax: 01509 221699
www.ait.gov.uk

Immigration Advisory Service
3rd Floor
County House
190 Great Dover Street
London SE1 4YB
Tel: 020 7967 1200
Fax: 020 7403 5875
www.iasuk.org

Immigration and Nationality Directorate
www.ind.homeoffice.gov.uk

CAFCASS AND CHILDREN'S GUARDIANS

Children and Family Court Advisory and Support Service (CAFCASS)
Tel: 020 7510 7000
www.cafcass.co.uk

National Association of Guardians ad Litem And Reporting Officers (NAGALRO)
Tel: 01372 818504
Email: nagalro@globalnet.co.uk

CHILDREN

National Youth Advocacy Service (NYAS)
General
Tel: 0151 649 8700
Young person's helpline (Mondays to Fridays 8am–8pm, Saturdays 10am–4pm)
Tel: 0800 616101
Email: main@nyas.net
www.nyas.net

Childline
Helpline for children and young people
Tel: 0800 1111
www.childline.org.uk

National Society for the Prevention of Cruelty to Children (NSPCC) Child protection helpline	Tel: 0808 100 2524 (Wales) Textphone: 0800 056 0566 (English only) **www.nspcc.org.uk**
Bullying Online	Email: help@bullying.co.uk **www.bullying.co.uk**
Barnardo's	**www.barnardos.org.uk**
Children in Wales	Tel: 029 2034 2534 **www.childreninwales.org.uk**
National Children's Bureau	Tel: 020 7843 6000 **www.ncb.org.uk**
4Nations Child Policy Network (Information on policy and legislation)	**www.childpolicy.org.uk**
Voice for the Children in Care (VCC)	Tel: 020 7833 5792 **www.vcc-uk.org**
National Children's Homes	**www.itsnotyourfault.org.uk**
Information and advice for 13–19 year olds	**www.connexions.gov.uk**

COMMISSIONERS AND OMBUDSMAN

Children's Commissioner for England	Tel: 020 7273 5559 Email: support@childrenscommissioner.org
Children's Commissioner for Wales	Tel: 01792 765600 Email: post@childcomwales.org.uk **www.childcom.org.uk**
Children's Rights Director (CSCI)	Tel: 0800 528 0731 (freephone) **www.rights4me.org.uk**
Commission for Social Care Inspection (CSCI)	Tel: 020 7909 2000 Helpline: 0845 015 0120 Email: enquiries@csci.gsi.gov.uk **www.csci.org.uk**
Commission for Racial Equality England Wales	Tel: 020 7393 0000 Tel: 02920 729 200 **www.cre.gov.uk**

CONTACT CENTRES

Coram Family Child Contact Service	Tel: 020 7520 0300 Fax: 020 7520 0301 **www.coram.org.uk**

National Association of Child Contact Centres	Tel: 0845 4500280 Email: contact@naccc.org.uk **www.naccc.org.uk**
Supervised Contact and Parenting Assessment Centre, London E7	**www.focicentre.co.uk**

DOMESTIC ABUSE AND SUPPORT

Refuge 24-hour helpline, run in partnership between Women's Aid and Refuge	Tel: 0808 2000 247 **www.refuge.org.uk**
Rights of Women Administration Advice line (open Tuesdays to Thursdays 2–4pm, Fridays 12–2pm)	 Tel: 020 7251 6575 Tel: 020 7251 6577
Victim Support National Office Administration Victim Support helpline	 Tel: 020 7735 9166 Tel: 0845 3030900 **www.victimsupport.org.uk**
Samaritans	Tel: 08457 909090 Email: jo@samaraitans.org.uk **www.samaritans.org.uk**

EMERGENCY POWERS

Family Division Lawyer President's Chambers Royal Courts of Justice Strand London WC2 2LL	Tel: 020 7947 7197 Fax: 020 7947 7274
Police National Ports Office: Heathrow Airport 24-hour advice line	Tel: 020 7230 4800

GOVERNMENT DEPARTMENTS

Office of the Official Solicitor	Tel: 020 7911 7127 Email: enquiries@offsol.gsi.gov.uk **www.offsol.demon.co.uk**
Department for Constitutional Affairs	**www.dca.gov.uk**
Department for Education and Skills	**www.dfes.gov.uk/childrenandfamilies/** **www.dfes.gov.uk/youngpeople/**
National Assembly for Wales	**www.wales.gov.uk**

GRANDPARENTS

Grandparents' Association (formerly Grandparents' Federation)
Office — Tel: 01279 428040
Helpline — Tel: 01279 444964
www.grandparents-federation.org.uk

LEGAL

The Law Society
113 Chancery Lane
London WC2A 1PL
DX 56 London/Chancery Lane
Tel: 020 7242 1222
www.lawsociety.org.uk

Professional Ethics
Tel: 0870 606 2577
www.guide-on-line.lawsociety.org.uk

Children Panel
Tel: 0870 606 2555
Email: panels@lawsociety.org.uk
www.panels.lawsociety.org.uk

Association of Lawyers for Children (ALC)
Tel: 020 8224 7071
Email: admin@alc.org.uk
www.alc.org.uk

Resolution (Solicitors' Family Law Association)
Tel: 01689 820272
Fax: 01689 896972
Email: info@resolution.org.uk
www.sfla.org.uk

Family Law Bar Association
Tel: 020 7242 1289
Fax: 020 7831 7144
www.flba.co.uk

Legal Aid Practitioners Group
Tel: 020 7960 6068
www.lapg.co.uk

Legal Services Commission
www.legalservices.gov.uk

Liberty (formerly National Council for Civil Liberties)
21 Tabard Street
London SE1 4LA
Tel: 020 7403 3888
Fax: 020 7407 5354
info@liberty-human-rights.org.uk
www.liberty-human-rights.org.uk

LEGAL RESEARCH AND REFERENCE

The Stationery Office
Tel: 020 7873 9090
www.tsoshop.co.uk

British and Irish Legal Information Institute (BAILII)
www.bailii.org

Casetrack (transcripts of judgments)
www.casetrack.com

DCA Human Rights Unit
www.humanrights.gov.uk

European Court of Human Rights portal (HUDOC)	**www.echr.coe.int/echr**
Family Law Journal	**www.familylaw.co.uk**
House of Lords judgments	**www.parliament.the-stationeryoffice.co.uk**
HM Courts Service	**www.hmcourts-service.gov.uk**
Lawtel	**www.lawtel.co.uk**
Legislation	**www.opsi.gov.uk/legislation/idex.htm**

MEDICAL

Royal College of General Practitioners	**www.rcgp.org.uk**
Royal College of Paediatrics and Child Health (RCPCH)	**www.rcph.ac.uk**
Royal College of Physicians	**www.rcplondon.ac.uk**
Royal College of Psychiatrists	**www.rcpsych.ac.uk**
Institute of Mental Health Act Practitioners	**www.markwalton.net**

PARENTS

Gingerbread Helpline Mondays to Fridays 10am-4pm	Tel: 0800 018 4318 **www.gingerbread.org.uk**
Parentline Plus Helpline	Tel: 020 7284 5500 Tel: 0900 800 2222 Textphone: 0800 783 6783
Advicenow Information on rights and legal issues.	**www.advicenow.org.uk**
Community Legal Service Direct Referrals to local specialist legal adviser/solicitor	Tel: 0845 345 4345 **www.clsdirect.org.uk**
National Association of Citizen's Advice Bureaux Nearest CAB CAB information online	**www.nacab.org.uk** **www.adviceguide.org.uk**
Family Rights Group Advice and support for families whose children are involved with social services	Tel: 0800 731 1696 **www.frg.org.uk**
International Child Abduction Centre	**www.reunite.org**

Index